T0290529

An American Association for State and Local History Guide to Making Public History

ABOUT THE SERIES

The American Association for State and Local History Book Series addresses issues critical to the field of state and local history through interpretive, intellectual, scholarly, and educational texts. To submit a proposal or manuscript to the series, please request proposal guidelines from AASLH headquarters: AASLH Editorial Board, 2021 21st Ave. South, Suite 320, Nashville, Tennessee 37212. Telephone: (615) 320-3203. Website: www.aaslh.org.

ABOUT THE ORGANIZATION

The American Association for State and Local History (AASLH) is a national history membership association headquartered in Nashville, Tennessee. AASLH provides leadership and support for its members who preserve and interpret state and local history in order to make the past more meaningful to all Americans. AASLH members are leaders in preserving, researching, and interpreting traces of the American past to connect the people, thoughts, and events of yesterday with the creative memories and abiding concerns of people, communities, and our nation today. In addition to sponsorship of this book series, AASLH publishes *History News* magazine, a newsletter, technical leaflets and reports, and other materials; confers prizes and awards in recognition of outstanding achievement in the field; and supports a broad education program and other activities designed to help members work more effectively; and advocates on behalf of the discipline of history. To join AASLH, go to www.aaslh.org or contact Membership Services, AASLH, 2021 21st Ave. South, Suite 320, Nashville, TN 37212.

An American Association for State and Local History Guide to Making Public History

Edited by Bob Beatty

ROWMAN & LITTLEFIELD
Lanham • Boulder • New York • London

Published by Rowman & Littlefield
A wholly owned subsidiary of The Rowman & Littlefield Publishing Group, Inc.
4501 Forbes Boulevard, Suite 200, Lanham, Maryland 20706
www.rowman.com

Unit A, Whitacre Mews, 26-34 Stannary Street, London SE11 4AB

British Library Cataloguing in Publication Information Available

Library of Congress Cataloging-in-Publication Data
Names: Beatty, Bob, editor.
Title: An American Association for State and Local History Guide to Making
    Public History / edited by Bob Beatty.
Description: Lanham: Rowman & Littlefield, 2017. | Series: American
    Association for State and Local History book series | Includes index.
Identifiers: LCCN 2017024665 (print) | LCCN 2017027265 (ebook) |
    ISBN 9781442264151 (electronic) | ISBN 9781442264137 (cloth: alk. paper) |
    ISBN 9781442264144 (pbk.: alk. paper)
Subjects: LCSH: Public history.
Classification: LCC D16.163 (ebook) | LCC D16.163. A46 2017 (print) |
    DDC 900—dc23
LC record available at https://lccn.loc.gov/2017024665

Printed in the United States of America

To Candy, Ryan, and Tyler, I love you all very much.

Contents

Foreword

Over the past several years, I've found myself in many meeting rooms, on conference panels, and in social media chats talking about history's relevance and resonance. How do we connect with the public while serving the public?

We do this by demonstrating the history field's imperative to preserve our memories and the artifacts that provide evidence of our love, work, and family. Our differences, our humanity, and our legacy as individuals, as a nation, as community. Is preservation enough?

Talented history professionals respond to this imperative and refine it upward. They hear it call to them and it kindles their passion for this work. When they level up, their organizations deliver meaningful exhibits, programs, and initiatives that tap into the hearts and minds of their audiences and affect social change.

An AASLH Guide to Making Public History gives us a road map to critical thinking about what our audiences need and expect of us. The chapters herein harness the words, thoughts, and passions of some of the most exciting history practitioners of the twenty-first century.

Their experiences, sentiments, and wisdom are skillfully stitched together by one of my favorite people on the planet, Bob Beatty. Bob has worked every angle of public history—in the museum, in the classroom, and on behalf of us all at the association level. He knows the inspired face of the girl who makes the connection between learning about Rosie the Riveter in class and remembering her family's stories of her grandmother working in the Oakland, California, shipyards during World War II. He knows the stricken face of the adult museum-goer when he finally understands that the Civil War was not about states' rights but about slavery and that the legacy of this is evident today.

The chapter authors offer a set of new lenses for us to use as we make public history. We always need to take the wider view of our field, try some fresh thinking, and reapply ourselves to do the good work of public history.

Hopefully after reading the *Guide* you'll imagine the next best idea for your organization or research. I'll give you an idea of mine about how big and bold we need to think.

I'm convinced that we can ignite in our audiences a deeper connection to history by infiltrating pop culture (you're laughing now, I can hear it, it's ok). I've been thinking about the intersection of social media, Hollywood, networking, and history. The general populace, in my opinion, will become passionate about history and fight to protect it only when its practical applications are felt on a regular basis. This is, in part, when people will understand that history is "necessary to have" and no longer just "nice to have." Maybe we need to help them imagine a world without history.

Movies, books, and comics about alternate history are good examples to look at, but they focus on one or two pivotal events, not the whole absence of history. Young Adult (YA) fiction is obsessed with postapocalyptic scenarios, and adult fiction has been mining it to great depths for many years. All of these, at their core, focus on something that's missing in society that creates an alternate future that is usually quite uncomfortable and often tragic.[1] To demonstrate a world without history, we need to get creative and go viral with it. We need to show our communities what they are missing in the short and long run when we don't fund and support history.

There are a few ways we can illustrate this absence. I say we start by collectively mapping all of our degrees of separation from Hollywood influencers and begin networking and holding discussions about what we lose without history recorded and stewarded. So many of us working in the history field have these connections, and we're not leveraging them in a way that benefits the entire history field. We need to find A-list Hollywood champions with a freak flag waving for history who will work closely with history practitioners to change how history is taught and understood in the United States. Some of the products we can create together are short films, social media tactics, and curriculum that create a picture of what without history looks like.

In the end, people will know that history is under fire and decide they won't stand for it. People will be whipped into a frenzy for history! Advocacy efforts will start to burst at the seams, and the history field will move away from scarcity and toward abundance.

Big ideas like this and the ones introduced in this book will help us attract the resources the history field so richly deserves. More importantly, the study of history and the preservation and interpretation of it will be a priority for our communities.

A couple of years ago I asked my then-fourteen-year-old son what a world without history would look like. He said it would be really bland. We wouldn't know who we are and where we came from and a world like that is very uninteresting. Love that kid.

Cinnamon Catlin-Legutko
President/CEO
Abbe Museum

NOTE

1. Full disclosure: I'm completely obsessed with YA books (and some of the movies) and have been working my way through the genre for several years now. I've always been a student of pop culture, and I tend to dive headlong into entertainment trends. This one seems to be sticking around for a while. I can give you a list of must-read YA books if you want. You know you want it.

Acknowledgments

First, thank you to each of the program chairs and the authors of these theme documents. The thoughtful consideration of the former really helped me shape my own views of the discipline and public history. And without the latter, this book would be half as thick and much less interesting. Thank you also to the authors who commented on the chapter that led into their own.

They are (in chronological order):

2008 Program Chair Kent Whitworth, theme article author Candace Tangorra Metalic
2009 Program Chair D. Stephen Elliott, theme article author John W. Durel
2010 Program Chair Cinnamon Catlin-Legutko, theme article author Barbara Franco and Laura Roberts
2011 Program Chair Julia Rose, theme article author Edward Tabor Linenthal
2012 Program Chair Scott Muir Stroh III, theme article author David Donath
2013 Program Chair Katherine Kane, theme article author Max A. van Balgooy
2014 Program Chair and theme article author Erin Carlson Mast
2015 Program Chair Kyle McKoy, theme article authors Kent Whitworth and Scott Alvey
2016 Program Chair and theme article author David A. Janssen
2017 Program Chair and theme article author Dina A. Bailey

I am very grateful to Charles Harmon at Rowman & Littlefield for his patience with me as I finished up the manuscript. I have a much better understanding of the Editorial Board's work, having completed this task. Thank you to Russell Lewis of the Chicago History Museum, who was series editor when I wrote the proposal and whose thoughtful review reshaped the book considerably.

I appreciate my dissertation committee—Carroll Van West, C. Brenden Martin, Kristine M. McCusker, and John Dougan—for encouraging me to add more to the book than I had originally planned. While there were several times I cursed you through this process, the book and my own scholarship benefited from it. And extra thanks to Dr. West for reviewing and commenting on the manuscript.

A shout-out to my colleagues at AASLH who, throughout my time with the organization, have been as dedicated to the cause as anyone I'd hope to work with and for. I would be remiss if I didn't mention Gerri Findley, who is not only the graphic designer for *History News* but also a friend.

And for those I have met and grown close to through my association with AASLH (you know who you are), a BIG, HUGE THANK YOU. You are an inspiration to me as I learn from each of you how to navigate the world of public history and harness my passion for this work.

Most important, thank you to Candy, Ryan Anne, and Tyler Ashlyn Beatty, my wonderful family, who have been so supportive of all of my endeavors and who put up with "go places vacations" so Daddy can get his history fix. It is ultimately for each of you that I do this work.

Introduction

"The best laid schemes o' mice an' men/Gang aft a-gley," wrote Scottish poet Robert Burns in his 1785 poem "To a Mouse." We're all more familiar with the modern translation, "The best-laid plans of mice and men often go awry." Such is the case with this book project.

In 2014, I proposed to the American Association for State and Local History Editorial Board a book of essays I had previously featured as editor of *History News*, AASLH's quarterly magazine. The essays would be what we called internally the "theme articles" for each AASLH conference—3,000-word essays that amplify that year's annual meeting theme. This book contains these articles from 2008 through 2017.

I originally conceived of this book as a relatively simple way to share the conversation AASLH's constituents were having about the field. It became instead a capstone project of sorts for my PhD program in public history at Middle Tennessee State University (hence the Burns quote earlier). In reviewing my proposal for this venture, my dissertation committee of Carroll van West, C. Brenden Martin, Kristine M. McCusker, and John Dougan asked that I add more breadth and depth to the book. So a book of ten chapters has evolved into a book of twenty, with me writing ten lead chapters, one for each article that appeared in *History News*.

As the only national organization dedicated to the field of state and local history, AASLH has a unique vantage point from which to examine the public history profession. Each year, efforts culminate in an annual gathering of nearly 1,000 history professionals from across the nation. A multitude of professional development activities—panel sessions, discussion forums, workshops, labs, general sessions, keynote addresses, and the like—comprises the conference. It is the one time each year this particular segment of the field assembles in one place.

To gather with peers and discuss ideas, reflect, and refresh is a crucial part of the history profession. Reflecting on her experience at the conference, noted local historian and *History News* columnist Carol Kammen wrote about its importance.

> I was struck by the importance of 'being there'—of going off to sessions, program in hand; sitting with coffee, talking; and walking to and fro among colleagues. I liked overhearing the chatter, listening to others discuss a small point or large one, of being among people who love doing local history. There is no substitute for being amidst one's own people. . . . Walking among them felt comfortable. I knew that I resonated with their interests and that I shared with them certain knowledge and problems. It was good to be in the company of my peers.[1]

The meeting has always been one of the highlights of the year for me and for AASLH. But there was one major problem with it: its reach was often limited to those who attended in person, and attendance was costly. Since it is the largest annual gathering of state and local history practitioners, the conference has exponential significance and potential influence. When I arrived at AASLH in 2007, we began discussions on how to expand the reach of the conference. This book is the result of one of those efforts.

I initiated this concept in 2007 while working on my first annual meeting with 2008 program committee chair, Kentucky Historical Society director Kent Whitworth.[2] Kent has one of the field's most creative, fertile minds and working with him on the meeting remains an inspiration today. Kent and I conceived of a new way to not only develop annual meeting themes but also to highlight the theme throughout the year. We would transform the meeting itself by changing our own processes. One of those steps was these theme articles. That our theme in 2008 was "Developing the Power of Transformation" only resonated more deeply.

The theme itself is the responsibility of the annual meeting program chair. Appointed by the AASLH Council Chair, each program chair serves a three-year term: two years as a regular committee member, and a single year as program chair. Since 2008, we have drafted annual meeting themes that connect the past (or present) of our conference location to current issues facing the field. The development process of these theme documents (typically three to five paragraphs) includes the program chair, the host committee chair, and me. But the theme is ultimately the bailiwick of the program chair.

From there, we choose an author for the theme article, which appears in the spring issue of *History News*. We have used many people across the spectrum of the field: leaders and directors of history organizations, consultants, academic and public historians. Several program chairs themselves took on the task of writing the theme essay.

As I reflected on the years I have been working with this material, I began to realize how important these articles were in providing insight into some of the most pressing issues of the day for the field. They provide in-depth, real-world examples of the work of history organizations. They focus on the challenges and opportunities important to any nonprofit or small business— entrepreneurship, change, transformation, possibility/opportunity, partnerships— but also those unique to history organizations: leveraging the discipline to explore place, to commemorate the past, to demonstrate how everyday people make history (and not just the rich and famous), and to discern how to use the past to chart the future. Together, these chapters provide a road map of the national discussions the field of history museums and organizations has had (and is having) regarding its present and the future.

Several major issues emerge. First, the issue of financial and institutional sustainability is of paramount importance. This extends, of course, from community engagement to funders to advocacy. Second, the need to change/ transform our modus operandi, and strategies for doing so, permeates. The Internet has led to challenges of interpretive authority while we navigate the complex waters of deeper community engagement. Third, collections remain a blessing and a curse, simultaneously our biggest competitive advantage and one of our biggest burdens—with storage areas packed with millions of items (some of dubious worth) needing constant care.

Two additional motifs emerge; they are closely related. The first is diversity and inclusion. The field must address, and address quickly, the homogeneous nature of our audiences and our staffs as it relates to the multiculturalism of our communities and our audiences. The second is both a subset of that discussion and a behemoth in its own right: the relevance of our discipline. Throughout this book, you will see references to the History Relevance Campaign. This began as a grassroots effort by folks like you and me, public historians who sought to answer one simple question: "If there's an environmental movement and a STEM movement and an arts movement, why is there no movement for history?" Their work has resulted in some organizing precepts, most notably in a series of Value of History statements. I have used these statements throughout the book because I find them to be cogent arguments for the importance of our work.

I have not organized the material in the book chronologically. I have instead grouped chapters according to content. Chapters 1 through 6 address financial sustainability. Chapter 8 references it as well, and pivots toward the work of history organizations within communities, ideas covered in chapters 10 and 12. Chapters 14, 16, and 18 discuss the practice of history in history organizations. The book concludes with chapters on diversity and inclusion and an epilogue from AASLH president and CEO John Dichtl.

I have utilized in this book a myriad of material from AASLH publications, mainly *History News* articles and books published in our imprint with

Rowman & Littlefield. There is a wealth of other sources I have not mined, as I have chosen to focus on the resources AASLH has provided in the past decade. (It is *An AASLH Guide to Making Public History*, after all.)

And that brings me to my last point: What is public history? I was completely unaware of the term when I began my history career. I pursued a master's degree in American history at the University of Central Florida (UCF) while simultaneously working at a history institution. While there, UCF initiated its public history graduate program. I worked closely with some of the faculty as they launched it. But at that time, I honestly never thought of public history as anything other than history for a public, rather than an academic (or learned), audience. There are differences, however. The National Council on Public History (NCPH) offers the best definition of distinctions between public and academic history. "In terms of intellectual approach," NCPH notes, "the theory and methodology of public history remain firmly in the discipline of history, and all good public history rests on sound scholarship." But, as NCPH proffers, public historians "engage in collaborative work, with community members, stakeholders, and professional colleagues, and some contend that collaboration is a fundamental and defining characteristic of what public historians do."[3] This book focuses on the practice of history through history organizations: historic sites, museums, historic houses, historical societies, and the like. These are places where collaboration is a key component of the work that is carried on by staff and volunteers, some of whom have professional training in public history while others do not.

Ultimately, we are all striving toward the same belief as articulated by the History Relevance Campaign, "that history—both knowledge of the past and the practice of researching and making sense of what happened in the past—is crucially important to the wellbeing of individuals, communities, and the future of our nation." And sharing a sense of why history is important can help change the common perception that history is somehow a mere luxury rather than an essential.[4]

This is why we do the work we do, is it not?

Bob Beatty
Franklin, Tennessee
February 2017

NOTES

1. Carol Kammen, "In the Company of Our Peers," *History News* 63, no. 3 (Winter 2008): 3.
2. Kent coauthored the theme article that appears as chapter 10 in this book.

3. National Council on Public History, "How Is Public History Different from 'Regular' History?" http://ncph.org/what-is-public-history/about-the-field/, accessed February 10, 2017.

4. History Relevance Campaign, "The Value of History Statement," https://www. historyrelevance.com/value-history-statement/, accessed March 29, 2017.

Chapter 1

The Only Thing That Is Constant Is Change

Bob Beatty

In 2010, AASLH held its annual meeting in Oklahoma City in partnership with the Oklahoma Museums Association (OMA). As we began planning the conference in earnest in early 2009, program chair Cinnamon Catlin-Legutko of the Abbe Museum in Bar Harbor, Maine; Brenda Granger of OMA; host chair Dan Provo of the Oklahoma History Center, and I all understood there was no way we'd be able to ignore the proverbial elephant in the room. The U.S. economy was in the midst of its longest, and by many measures, worst economic downturn since the Great Depression.[1]

Though signs began appearing earlier in the year, most mark December 2008 as the beginning of the Great Recession. While many date its end as June 2009, the Bureau of Labor Statistics reported in 2012 that "many of the statistics that describe the U.S. economy [had] yet to return to their pre-recession values." The report cited measures such as unemployment, business openings and closings, job openings, consumer spending, productivity, and wages.[2] These numbers reflected a greatly troubled American economy, and they hit history organizations particularly hard.

Between October 2007 and March 2009, the Standard & Poor's 500 lost nearly 50 percent of its value and the Dow Jones Industrial Average 54 percent. In April 2012, the U.S. Treasury Department calculated that American households lost a cumulative $19.2 trillion. The nonprofit watchdog Better Markets calculated the number higher, about $21.4 trillion. Better Markets also attempted to measure the collapse's human cost. "It's hard to put a dollar value on [human suffering]," PBS's *Frontline* reported, "but the [Better Markets] report found plenty of grim data to offer some insight: The Census Bureau's 2010 estimate of 46.2 million people in poverty is the 'largest number in the 52 years for which poverty estimates have been published.' "[3]

The economic crisis cost Americans considerably and caught many in the history field unawares. As might be expected, giving dropped precipitously and many organizations that relied on public funding found monies directed elsewhere—often to address what funders believed were more pressing social needs. The Great Recession didn't only affect giving, the lifeblood of any nonprofit organization, but it also affected the financial stability of the organizations themselves. Declining endowment values of 50+ percent cost history organizations dearly.

In a 2011 survey of its membership, fewer than 25 percent of AASLH members reported being "not affected at all" or "only slightly affected" by the economic downturn. More than one-third of institutions made staffing changes: reduced staff hours, froze wages, furloughed employees, delayed hiring and/or left positions unfilled, encouraged retirements, cut staff, and lowered salaries.[4] Against this backdrop, we began planning for the conference in Oklahoma City.

What comes to mind first when one thinks of the Sooner State? For many it's the lyrics from the Rogers and Hammerstein musical *Oklahoma*: "Oklahoma, where the wind comes sweepin' down the plain." The state's infamous winds aren't just a catchy phrase for a show tune. They are, indeed, a part of Oklahoma's culture. Catlin-Legutko, Granger, Provo, and I seized on this ideal, for it also directly related to the disturbing winds blowing throughout the field.

"Much as Oklahoma's infamous tornadoes and storms generate both gentle and severe winds impacting the state, so too have the winds of opportunity impacted the nation's cultural landscape," Catlin-Legutko, Granger, and Provo wrote.[5] Many in the field had already begun quoting Rahm Emmanuel, now Chicago mayor but then serving on president-elect Barack Obama's transition team: "You never want a serious crisis to go to waste. And what I mean by that is an opportunity to do things that you think you could not do before."[6] Our use of the phrase "Winds of Opportunity" was intentional. We chose to focus attention on the possibilities rather than lament the hand that we'd been collectively dealt.

"Winds, while possibly destructive," the theme document continued, "also can usher in new perspectives, opportunities, and critical self examination that may lead to strengthening organizations and the development of previously unforeseen goals."[7] In the following pages, noted history and museum leaders Laura Roberts and Barbara Franco offer some examples of this principle in action.

The Great Recession was certainly not the first recession in history. Economists cite twelve sustained declines of the American economy since 1945 (including the 2007–2009 recession), so most of us have endured several in our lifetimes. What made this particular event stand out was its length

Image 1.1.　Abbe Museum president and CEO Cinnamon Catlin-Legutko served as program chair of the 2010 AASLH Annual Meeting. *Source*: Abbe Museum

(eighteen months) and its severity—not just in the United States but worldwide as well.

What Roberts and Franco pointed out, though, were some systemic challenges the field had failed to address over the years that made this event much more damaging. They raised the ever-present question of the volume of history organizations in the United States and the need to consider a "history system," an idea floated by Boston's Technical Development Corporation, Inc. (TDC) in 2009. Their piece discussed relevance and value, changing American demographics, and collaborations. These items were top-of-mind to many history professionals before 2010 and remain there today.

TDC's ideas seemed to offer some groundbreaking possibilities. In its 2009 white paper, *Building a Sustainable Future for History Institutions: A Systemic Approach: An Introduction to the History System Project*, TDC's Elizabeth Cabral Curtis and Susan Nelson advocated for a national approach to issues of public value and relevance. "We hypothesize," they wrote, "that by raising the level of conversation from the institution (and the individual leader) to the system as a whole, we could reframe the problem to enable the system to more effectively tell the American story and care for their collections. By looking at themselves in a larger context, institutions may be better able to understand their unique value in this context and determine which of their activities contribute to this value and which do not."[8]

The organization's plans included a study of more than 150 respondents in three national regions and "conceiving, articulating, and evaluating potentially sustainable solutions based on a systemic framework" for the history enterprise.[9] Roberts and Franco saw great promise in TDC's proposed plans, as did AASLH. Unfortunately, the idea never gained traction or funding to carry its work forward.

But while a national solution never came to fruition, a group of history professionals in the Phoenix metropolitan area (the East Valley) put the idea into practice. Lisa A. Anderson of the Mesa Historical Museum and Jody A. Crago of the Chandler Museum had each dealt firsthand with the effects of the economic downturn. Anderson's museum had lost all of its funding from the City of Mesa; budget shortfalls resulted in a 50 percent reduction in professional staff for Crago's. Peer institutions in the region experienced similar trends.[10]

Together with Peter Welsh, then of the Arizona Historical Society Museum at Papago Park, Anderson and Crago conceived of a new model: a history system for the region. In a 2011 article in *History News* they wrote, "It became clear to us that history museums, as a whole, and we in particular, need to find new models—interpretive as well as business—and new collaborations. . . . In seeking solutions, we were attracted to the idea of collaboration because many of our institutions have strengths in specific areas and weaknesses in others. We were curious to find a way for each institution to share strengths and mitigate weaknesses with strengths from other institutions."[11]

Anderson, Crago, and Welsh's conclusions reflected not only present economic conditions but also community needs. Phoenix underwent a massive swelling of its population and the expanding region engulfed once-isolated communities into a larger whole. What remained, however, were a bevy of history institutions. "Each [community] has its own historical society, museum, or both. In the Phoenix metropolitan area there are over thirty museums with a historical focus, and many tell essentially the same story of the community's founding, early agriculture, population rise during the late twentieth century, and boom economy of the 1980s and 1990s. . . . [D]esert farming was essentially the same in Mesa, Phoenix, Scottsdale, Chandler, and Tempe."[12]

The leaders' solution was to implement a history system in the East Valley, one that played on the strengths of each institution. Recognizing that the Chandler Museum had an outdoor learning environment focused on farming in the desert, the private Mesa Historical Museum transferred its agricultural equipment collection to the City of Chandler's museum. This allowed both organizations to better focus on their respective strengths. Most notably, the Chandler Museum could expand and tell a more complete story of agricultural development, and the Mesa Museum could focus on *Play Ball: The*

Cactus League Experience, an exhibit on spring training baseball. Later steps included the *East Valley Tribune* newspaper project wherein partners jointly managed the 100-year-old archives of the newspaper at a single physical repository.

Subsequent to these initial forays into collaboration, the group officially formed the East Valley Museum Coalition. Anderson documented the early stages of the coalition. She found its institutions to be philosophically oriented toward what she dubbed a "Society Model." This more traditional approach to history museums, she claimed, "Is based on the idea that when people share common territory, interactions, and culture, they create stories

Image 1.2.   Lisa Anderson and her colleagues founded the East Valley Museum Coalition to encourage a more sustainable history museum community in the Phoenix region. *Source*: Lisa Anderson

and materials that are worthy of engagement and representation within a museum." Anderson elaborated further. The model, she argued, often assumes that "there exists a deeply shared local history that transcends community change." These local museums hyper-focus on building their museum collections, leading to a glut of collections overlap. "One can never have too many wagon wheels!" Anderson wrote. (The collections of many museums often reflect this through spinning wheels.[13])

Fundamentally, phase two of this alliance focused beyond its initial collaborations to those of not only each individual institution's sustainability but also a more sustainable history community in the region. Not only were the stories similar, the players, and the artifacts they left behind, were as well. "The things that people brought . . . are common items many people carried with them in their migration west. Mass-produced items stacked within our museums by the dozens are rarely unique to individuals or to community development."[14]

Collections remain the biggest competitive advantage of our institutions, but they can also serve as some of our biggest anchors. How to care for and best utilize the vast material we are entrusted with—notwithstanding how to solve issues of holding collections unrelated to mission—are important aspects of the wider sustainability discussion. While the East Valley Museum Coalition's work extends well beyond collections, it is in this critical area that the group has offered some of its most progressive ideas.

The Active Collections Project is another endeavor that harnesses the winds of opportunity. It in some ways mirrors the activities happening in Phoenix. The Active Collections Project is an outgrowth of a session that independent museum professional Rainey Tisdale, Trevor Jones (now of the Nebraska Historical Society), and museum consultant Linda B. Norris hosted at the 2012 AASLH Annual Meeting in Salt Lake City, "Do History Museums Still Need Objects?" Tisdale's *History News* article of the same name presaged the session.

Tisdale's piece responded to a request I made for her to review Steven Conn's 2010 book *Do Museums Still Need Objects?* While she found Conn's book interesting and informative, its theoretical emphasis and focus on art, ethnographic, and science museums were insufficient for history institutions. Nevertheless, Tisdale answered Conn's question for the history field. History museums definitely still need objects, she argued, but the reason why was much more complex. She offered seven guiding statements that explored the sophisticated nature of the discussion:

1. We need objects now more than ever. "In the digital age," she noted, "Americans long for authenticity. . . . Objects are a mark of authenticity."

2. We don't need objects unless we do something great with them. "We need to develop object-centered historical experiences for visitors that are not only educational but also unique, memorable, moving, provocative. We talk about this a lot but we aren't doing it enough."

3. We may not need the ones we've collected. "Our collections aren't diverse enough to help us connect with the broad audience we want to, indeed we must, attract."

4. We don't all need the same ones. "How many spinning wheels, in what condition, do we need to expend resources preserving? Does every institution need two or three, or could we share?"

5. We need to restore the links between objects and places. "So much of history is place-based. . . . Geo-tagging and other digital tools allow us to restore these links."

6. We need a different model for access. "Are we meeting the access needs of our visitors any better today than we did in 1911? Members of the public have more tools for understanding the objects in museum collections, but more objects are held behind glass, velvet ropes, or closed doors."

7. Do history museums still need curators? "Today's curator is a subject expert who facilitates the process of creating a collective history by convening the conversation, asking interesting questions, suggesting trusted sources and methods for exploration, gently guiding the discussion, and checking for factual errors. But curators no longer provide the actual answers."

Tisdale hoped her piece would spur conversation. "Some of what I put forward may be controversial," she wrote. "You are unlikely to agree with all of it. But that's kind of the point. These are complicated issues that we need to continue to discuss in the months to come, both online and at water coolers throughout the country."[15]

In 2014, together with Jones and Elee Wood, director of the Museum Studies Program in the School of Liberal Arts at Indiana University-Purdue University Indianapolis, Tisdale launched the Active Collections Project "to generate discussion and action across the history museum field to develop a new approach to collections, one that is more effective and sustainable."[16]

As a first step, the group drafted *A Manifesto for Active History Museum Collections*. The *Manifesto* is well worth a full read. It reflects both Tisdale's thinking in her original 2011 piece and how the conversation has evolved with the inclusion of other voices. They wrote:

• There's little point in preserving collections if they don't actively support the mission. We believe collections must either advance the mission or they must go.

Image 1.3. The Greensboro, North Carolina–based Elsewhere is a museum and artist residency in a former thrift store where visitors can touch everything. Its exhibitions are an example of Rainey Tisdale's second finding about collections: "We don't need objects unless we do something great with them." *Source*: Rainey Tisdale

- Professional standards, funding models, and museum training programs still primarily support the idea that all collections are equally important, and that owning collections is as important as effectively using them. We believe a new model for thinking about collections is needed.
- Museums are uniquely positioned to use things to tell meaningful stories—but to do so they need to collect the right artifacts and make good use of them. We believe that artifacts can be powerful tools—touchstones filled with meaning and connection—but only when used effectively.
- We believe some objects support the mission better than others—not based on monetary value or rarity, but based on the stories they tell and the ideas they illuminate. The ones that provide the most public value should get the largest share of our time and resources.
- Museum professionals must change the conversation with boards, donors, and stakeholders about why and how artifacts help the institution meet its goals. . . . We believe we need to change the conversation from caring for artifacts to caring about people.
- Museums are fond of telling donors about the size of the collection, equating size with quality. We leave them with the idea that by simply getting

more stuff, that makes us more relevant. We believe we need to stop touting the size of museum collections and start talking about impact.[17]

Tisdale, Jones, and Wood did not stop with these mission statements, but offered also "A Path toward Change." These steps range from one that mirrors what Anderson and her colleagues are doing in Arizona—sharing artifacts in an interlibrary loan-type arrangement—to making collections an institution-wide concern, and from seeking to change the conversation about collections from a "collect and preserve at all costs" mentality to a process that better reflects present institutional realities.

In 2008 longtime history museum leader James M. Vaughan dubbed the latter "The Rembrandt Rule" and defined it as the ideal to "treat every object as if it were a Rembrandt." Vaughan asked, "Should we develop a tiered approach to collections and their care?"[18] The Active Collections Project *Manifesto* answered with an emphatic yes. "Create a tiered system for your collections," wrote its principles. "Go ahead and rank your collections! What pieces best support the mission? What are the ones that are just ok? What really has NOTHING to do with what you're trying to accomplish? Establish a triage system for your artifacts and spend your time, effort and money on the compelling ones."[19]

While few disagree that the collecting policies of history organizations cause tremendous stress on institutions nationwide, many may disagree with the progressive (some might say heretical) positions of the Active Collections Project. However, the group is by no means prescriptive in their solutions and continues to carry the discussion forward. In 2015, it held a "Future of Museum Collections" roundtable in Indianapolis, Indiana, and it maintains an active online presence.

Whether the ideas of the Active Collections Project are *the* solution to the challenges of caring for the 4.8 billion artifacts American museums care for, or just *a* solution is immaterial. The Winds of Opportunity are howling for the 59 percent of institutions that lack space to accommodate their collections safely and appropriately.[20] Inattention is simply no longer an option.

These are but two examples of how history organizations adapted to the winds of opportunity that sweep across the profession. Systemic change is needed, but it's not a simple endeavor. As the history enterprise enters the third decade of the twenty-first century, sustainability must be addressed in a multitude of areas: institutional overlap and collections included.

NOTES

1. Center on Budget and Policy Priorities, "Chart Book: The Legacy of the Great Recession," updated August 10, 2016, accessed August 22, 2016, www.cbpp.org/research/economy/chart-book-the-legacy-of-the-great-recession.

2. Bureau of Labor Statistics, "The Recession of 2007–2009," February 2012, accessed August 22, 2016, www.bls.gov/spotlight/2012/recession/pdf/recession_bls_spotlight.pdf.

3. Sarah Childress, "How Much Did the Financial Crisis Cost?" *Money, Power, and Wall Street* (Frontline), May 31, 2012, accessed August 22, 2016, www.pbs.org/wgbh/frontline/article/how-much-did-the-financial-crisis-cost/.

4. American Association for State and Local History 2011 Membership Survey.

5. Cinnamon Catlin-Legutko, Brenda Granger, and Dan Provo, "The Winds of Opportunity," 2010 American Association for State and Local History and Oklahoma Museums Association Annual Meeting theme.

6. Rahm Emmanuel *Wall Street Journal* CEO Council, Washington, DC, November 19, 2008, accessed August 22, 2016, go.aaslh.org/RahmEmmanuel2008.

7. Catlin-Legutko et al.

8. Elizabeth Cabral Curtis and Susan Nelson, *Building a Sustainable Future for History Institutions: A Systemic Approach: An Introduction to the History System Project* (Boston: Technical Development Corporation, Inc., 2009).

9. Ibid.

10. For example, the Phoenix Museum of History nearly closed; instead, the Arizona Science Center subsumed it.

11. Lisa A. Anderson, Jody A. Crago, and Peter H. Welsh, "A New Day for Local History: No Longer an Island," *History News* 66, no. 4 (Autumn 2011): 21–22.

12. Ibid., 22.

13. Lisa A. Anderson, "A New Day for Local History: Building a Museum Coalition," unpublished manuscript, 2015.

14. Ibid.

15. Rainey Tisdale, "Do History Museums Still Need Objects?" *History News* 66, no. 3 (Summer 2011): 19–24.

16. Active Collections Project, "About," accessed August 26, 2016, www.active-collections.org/.

17. Ibid.

18. James M. Vaughan, "Rethinking the Rembrandt Rule," *Museum* (March–April 2008): 33.

19. Rainey Tisdale, Trevor Jones, and Megan Wood, *Manifesto*, Active Collections Project, accessed August 26, 2016, www.activecollections.org/manifesto/.

20. Heritage Preservation, Inc., *A Public Trust at Risk: The Heritage Health Index Report on the State of America's Collections* (Washington, DC: Heritage Preservation, Inc., 2005), 1–2.

Chapter 2

The Winds of Opportunity

Barbara Franco and Laura B. Roberts

"You don't need a weatherman to know which way the wind blows," Bob Dylan sang in 1965 in "Subterranean Homesick Blues." While the counter-culture of the 1960s has become immortalized in the collections and exhibitions of history museums and archives, the winds of change keep blowing. In fact, the rate of change affecting our organizations continues to increase and many organizations find it hard to respond. While many history organizations have been buffeted by the changes and storms that are disrupting almost every sector of the economy, times of turmoil always present opportunities.

TODAY'S WEATHER

For many history institutions the 2008 recession felt as though a tornado had touched down and left a swath of ruin in its wake. Like a tornado's path, some organizations were left standing while others were devastated by deep cuts in budgets and staff. A mid-recession survey of state history organizations showed a range of cuts from 5 to 40 percent. Ohio and Pennsylvania saw their state-funded history programs nearly dismantled, while private nonprofits tightened their belts in the face of declining earned revenues, contributions, and endowment returns.

Regardless of how well a particular organization weathered the economic downturn, there is increasing acceptance that the typical business model can no longer be sustained. Despite best efforts to achieve professional standards and staffing, history organizations find sustainability an elusive goal. The steady decline in attendance has impacted museums dependent on ticket revenue, while we struggle to explain why it is happening and what can be done to reverse the trend.

A number of important studies identified long-term shifts affecting history organizations and other public sector institutions. *A Public Trust at Risk: The Heritage Health Index Report on the State of America's Collections* focused attention on the dire need for collections funding. *The Future of Museums and Libraries: A Discussion Guide* provides structure for ongoing dialogue about the future of museums and libraries organized around nine major themes: changing definitions and roles; shifts in power and authority; "third place" gathering spaces; technology; twenty-first-century learning and skills; new models for collaboration; sustainability grounded in relevance and economic reality; evaluating impact; and twenty-first-century workplace planning.[1]

History organizations have an enormous responsibility as collecting institutions to preserve heritage and culture for future generations. The country's sheer number of libraries, archives, museums, and historical societies complicates this. *Building a Sustainable Future for History Institutions: A Systemic Approach,* a study conducted by Technical Development Corporation (TDC) of Boston, called for a new history system to build a sustainable future and suggested that limited resources make it difficult for an individual organization to fulfill the needs and expectations of both stewardship and public access on its own.

In *Mastering Civic Engagement*, Robert Archibald, former director of the Missouri Historical Society, suggests that this new role "depends upon the creation of new and really collaborative relationships, where we do not presume to know what audiences need. In these new relationships we will regard ourselves as reservoirs of information and expertise and will relinquish our traditional authoritarian roles in favor of new responsibilities as both resources and facilitators of dialogue about things that matter most to people."[2]

As a field, we continue to struggle to understand exactly what is relevant to our constituents and our communities. Cary Carson and John and Anita Durel have published thoughtful essays that argue that the future success of history organizations depends on creating new relationships among audience, institutions, collections, and the process of history.

These studies identify major issues that can no longer be ignored including: demographic shifts that are redefining participation, technological advances, new ways of collaboration, and renewed interest in relevancy through civic engagement and volunteerism. The historic houses and collections that once held meaning for a community's longtime residents may have little or no relevance to current citizens who represent diverse nationalities and cultures. What meaning will be found in these organizations and their history if we don't update collections and interpretations? The field is also experiencing a major workforce transition as the large number of baby boomers who entered the field in the 1970s is replaced by a new generation of professionals, including many public historians trained in specialized academic programs and who bring new skills and perspectives to their work.

The vocabulary of audience may no longer be appropriate in an environment in which our constituents consider themselves co-creators of content along with our curators and educators. With history playing a decreasing role in formal education, informal history education through museum visits, personal and family research, books, media, and the Internet is now the major vehicle for Americans' civic education. The Web has become the primary way institutions communicate with the public, as well as how visitors make travel plans to visit them. Social media has replaced traditional media as a way to share news and information. At the same time, electronic communication presents serious issues about how we record and document history and the long-term storage and accessibility of historical records.

These burgeoning responsibilities of expanding collections, educating the next generation, and staying current with technological tools have all made the need to stay connected and to collaborate with each other more essential than ever.

FORECASTING OPPORTUNITIES

For history organizations this environment represents opportunities for change that can ultimately lead to new successes and strengthen our institutions.

Collaboration

More than ever, history museums have to think beyond the walls of their buildings and individual organizations. TDC's 2009 project argued for a system that combines complementary and diverse strengths of many institutions rather than expecting each to deliver all of the services needed. This systems approach, they argued, would strengthen institutions, each having a unique and viable strategic position while working within a broader infrastructure. This approach would provide greater efficiency through coordination of collections and information sharing, creating greater impact and richer context for each institution's stories. Consider the parallels with healthcare. A range of providers, from the walk-in clinic to a major teaching hospital, each provides care appropriate for a variety of ailments and patient needs. The success of each sharply focused provider depends on having the rest of the system offering complementary services. Could history institutions—both large and small—support each other's efforts in a similar way?

Indeed, there are many barriers to transforming the field's thinking from individual organizations to a coordinated system. Organizations are often fiercely protective of their turf, fearing that a narrower focus may mean they will lose members, funders, and audience. Being part of a coordinated system would require trusting that every component of the system will do its part reliably and professionally.

One way to shift from being keepers of the past to being useable community assets is to open our doors to real partnerships. It is often easier to build collaboration around programs and to establish trust among organizations by working together on specific, focused, and common goals. As collaborators understand more clearly the potential of working together and feel more comfortable, they are more likely to want to work together. Short-term efforts can become pilots for sustained relationships. The benefits of collaboration may go well beyond functional efficiencies and allow history organizations to expand interpretation, linking local stories to larger regional or national themes with greater relevancy for audiences. But history organizations should also look outside of the history system for partners. Often the real power of collaboration comes from diverse partner organizations with different audiences, expertise, or perspectives. Collaboration allows partners to accomplish something they could not attempt unaccompanied.

Greater collaboration is also needed within organizations to eliminate departmental silos. Many organizations, large and small, are reorganizing around staffing structures that support greater internal and external collaboration. Cross-training is more important than ever in an environment of change and innovation. It is key to strengthening organizational capacity and developing leadership.

New Audiences: Making History Personal

Changing community demographics present new opportunities as well as challenges. If organizations are not providing what people want to see and do, no amount of promotion will solve the attendance problem. Understanding audiences, especially non-traditional ones, is more important than ever. Many institutions are changing the way they plan by looking first at the wants and needs of audiences, developing products to address them, and measuring how well they meet them.

As Marilyn Hood found in her 1980 study of museum visitors and non-visitors in Toledo, Ohio, people who choose to spend their leisure time in pursuits other than visiting museums have a different set of values and priorities (social interaction, active participation, and feeling comfortable) than habitual museum visitors (doing something worthwhile, having new experiences, and learning). Excellent programs like Visitors Count! notwithstanding, historical organizations have made little progress in developing a deeper understanding of visitor interests and motivations.

People have come to expect the ability to personalize their experience. Even the content of history has changed to place greater emphasis on personal stories and connections rather than objects alone. The enormous popularity of StoryCorps, which has recorded stories from more than 100,000 people, is evidence of this. Increasingly, collections are viewed as tools for engagement rather than a sacred trust. Co- and self-production are becoming the norm, from tracing one's family history using online resources, documenting daily life in a scrapbook or social media, or posting videos on Instagram and YouTube. New technologies will undoubtedly continue to shape the way people think about and use museums in the future as partners rather than as consumers.

The Center for the Future of Museums identified the expectation that people *experience* narrative, rather than just *see or hear* it. They cite Conner Prairie's *Follow the North Star*, in which participants play the role of fugitive slaves on the Underground Railroad, as an experience in which the visitor becomes protagonist, rather than passive viewer. On Scholastic's online platform *The Stacks*, young readers can play games based on books, interact with other readers, and create new experiences around book characters. As these young readers grow up, this experience will undoubtedly shape their expectations about books and stories as well as museum exhibits.

Image 2.1.   Conner Prairie's *Follow the North Star* is a participatory museum theater experience in which attendees travel back to 1836 and assume the role of fugitive slaves seeking freedom on the Underground Railroad through Indiana. *Source*: Conner Prairie

Relevance and Impact

History organizations are being challenged to justify their value and relevance to society. Some are redefining themselves in terms of their community impact. Some are attempting to address real social problems of literacy, informal learning, after school care, and so on. Others are looking at how to build civic engagement, as a convener in a neutral and safe third place, bringing people together to help them understand historical information that relates to current issues and contemporary decisions. Nevertheless, the impact of history organizations remains diffuse and difficult to document.

It is intriguing to compare historical organizations with children's museums and zoos and aquariums. The Association for Children's Museums has embraced the challenge of childhood obesity and created *Good to Grow!* "to support children's museums in providing healthy choices and activities for children and families in their communities." The Association of Zoos and Aquariums actively promotes the message of conservation, including it in their accreditation standards; providing members with educational information, planning tools, databases, funding sources, and awards; and sponsoring volunteer efforts, reintroduction programs, and specialized conservation projects. By focusing on a particular issue or message of critical importance, these colleague institutions develop, test, and disseminate successful strategies; create clear public policy messages; and focus on specific, measurable outcomes. Is there a comparable significant, relevant message historical organizations can unite around?

A town may have a series of conversations about race, select a historical book for a reading initiative, or debate the wisdom of sprawl in planning board meetings. Members of the local history organization often participate in discussions, but the organization itself remains silent. We, as historically minded citizens, may walk out of a community meeting shaking our heads at the lack of historical context in contemporary debate, but at the same time our organizations often remain mute. Is it any surprise that we are not seen as relevant?

Technology

Each year we think technology has transformed our lives and our work, only to witness more dramatic transformations the following year. As the 2000s came to a close, many observers included Google as a verb among the most significant developments of the decade. Observers of the 2008 presidential campaign recognized that initiatives begun by Howard Dean's campaign in 2004 were just the beginning of a revolution in mass communication, political organizing, and fundraising. Pew Research Center's 2014 report on social media use noted that 71 percent of all adults who use the Internet and 56 percent of online adults sixty-five years and older are on Facebook. Overall, Facebook use has leveled off but no other platform is the clear next fad. Younger adults are on Instagram, women are on Pinterest, and 52 percent of adults use two or more social media sites.[3]

Technology has the capacity to share collections more widely and create new ways for the public to interact with history. The Maine Historical Society's *Maine Memory Network* provides access to more than 45,000 items from several hundred organizations from across Maine, as well as over 200 online exhibitions. *Maine Memory Network* is also the home to the *Maine Community History Project*, designed to foster collaborations between historical societies, public libraries, and schools. Community teams digitize local historical collections and exhibit them with supporting text on custom-designed local history websites. The site also has a "My Album" tool, which enables individual users to create, edit, and share their albums of images.

The Commons on Flickr, begun as a pilot project with 3,500 Library of Congress photographs, now includes images from 100 libraries and archives worldwide. Using crowdsourcing to tap the experience of many individuals, the public is invited to tag these photographs, with each viewer adding his or her perspective and additional information.

To assemble a collection for the National September 11 Museum and Memorial, museum planners created an interactive website where users uploaded photographs, videos, and personal stories: contributions that became a key part of the museum, which opened September 11, 2011.

While many institutions have Facebook pages (a search on "historical society" yields over 97,000 results), fewer have embraced other social media. Most use it to promote programs, note recent press, and occasionally share collections information. The Massachusetts Historical Society (MHS) went further and tweeted John Q. Adams's daily diary entries, beginning 200 years to the day he left Boston for Russia. The posts linked to maps pinpointing his progress across the ocean as well as to the longer entries of other Adams diaries (found on MHS's website). Similarly, the New London (CT) Historical Society posted a regular blog by Joshua Hempstead based on the diary he kept from 1711 to 1758.

Technology has already sharply redefined the challenge of collecting. A Stanford University study showed that only one-half of 1 percent of information produced worldwide finds its way to printed form. The vast majority of information, from daily correspondence and personal journals to public documents and records, is electronic. In an effort to be more environmentally sensitive, we are urged to think twice before printing electronic communication. Doctoral theses, professional conference proceedings, journals, and monographs are increasingly available in electronic-only versions. The era of Senator Edward Kennedy writing his autobiography based on a lifetime of daily journals is fading. Virtually all governors, senators, and representatives use Twitter, sharing the thoughts that prior officeholders might have recorded in journals or daybooks. Newspapers may be an endangered species. The *Detroit Free Press* prints only three hard copy editions a week; the *Christian Science Monitor* prints just a weekly edition. How shall we document history when the sources are all ephemeral? How shall those who come after us write it?

WEATHERING THE STORM

How organizations respond to these challenges and opportunities may well determine our field's future. Institutions must face the challenge of managing change. It is not easy, and it is particularly difficult to effect deep, enduring change. John Kotter, from Harvard Business School and one of the most cogent theorists of change management, has said that any successful change effort must begin with a sense of urgency. Some organizations will understand the urgency in these winds of opportunity, put up their sails to catch the breeze, and move toward substantive, lasting change. Other may decide to put up storm shutters, retrench, and wait for the winds to subside.

Regardless of how individual organizations respond, the field must respond in a proactive, creative way. The third of Kotter's eight steps in organization transformation is creating a shared vision. A shared vision of change for our field is beginning to take form but will depend on stakeholders willing to act on that vision, develop support for change, and institutionalize new approaches. The new paradigm is a shift in focus from the museum and archival collections and historic buildings to the customer. Access to information will be as important as access to places and things. We will need to be about stories and ideas, not merely objects.

Jay Rounds observes that in times of change, adaptive, innovative thinking should replace well-established and proven habits of mind. To weather these winds of opportunity, history organizations need to explore new ways of operating rather than exploiting old solutions. We must create a climate of entrepreneurship that welcomes new, fresh ideas and accepts some risk-taking. We need to give up control and instead adopt a new model of stewardship that shares authority and power with audiences and volunteers. We must expand networks and look for new partnerships within and beyond the public history system. We need to find our voice in the marketplace of ideas, bringing the insights and perspectives of history to the issues that confront our democracy. The winds of change are winds of opportunity that shouldn't be squandered.

NOTES

1. Curtis and Nelson, *Building a Sustainable Future for History Institutions*; Erica Pastore, *The Future of Museums and Libraries: A Discussion Guide* (Washington, DC: Institute of Museum and Library Services, 2009).

2. Robert R. Archibald, *Mastering Civic Engagement: A Challenge to Museums* (Washington, DC: American Association of Museums, 2002), 3.

3. See Maeve Duggan, Nicole B. Ellison, Cliff Lampe, Amanda Lenhart, and Mary Madden, "Social Media Update 2014," Pew Research Center, accessed December 14, 2016, www.pewinternet.org/2015/01/09/social-media-update-2014/.

Chapter 3

Discovering the Power
of Transformation

Bob Beatty

Two years before we created the *Winds of Opportunity* theme, AASLH met in Rochester, New York. Our host, The Strong National Museum of Play (now The Strong), was one of the preeminent history organizations in Rochester and had just completed a significant transformation into a community-focused museum that saw museum attendance explode from 130,000 in 1992 to more than 342,000 in 2002, and 551,000 in 2016.

Transformation is at the heart of the study of history and of the history enterprise as well. History is the study of change over time and sometimes, in the long view, the results show truly revolutionary change. As applied to the world of history organizations, transformation is more than just a buzzword; it's a necessity.

Gone are the days when museums could exhibit artifacts on their intrinsic merit alone (if that ever existed in the first place). As is true for the historical discipline writ large, history organizations must be able to answer the "why" question(s): Why does this artifact matter? or Why is this site or historic house important? and/or Why did something particular happen? In many cases, shifting institutional focus from the "what" of history to the "why" requires a systematic reimagining of the organization itself—often this reimagining results in complete institutional transformation.

What follows are descriptions of three different history organizations that have experienced transformation: a museum, a historic house, and a historical society. The first, The Strong, is a museum that opened in 1982 and experienced a well-documented transformation in the 1990s–2000s. The second example is the Harriet Beecher Stowe Center, founded in 1941 and opened to the public in 1968 as the Stowe Beecher Hooker Seymour Day Memorial Library and Foundation. The Stowe Center has already undergone

one transformation and is in the midst of a second. The final case is the Connecticut Historical Society, one of the oldest historical societies in the United States. It is still in the early stages of its transformational journey.

These examples are all from the same area of the country but represent three different institution types as well as different stages in transformation. Taken together, they reflect Matelic's transformational model. Each diligently sought the core of what made the institution unique, that which reflected the organization's raison d'être and then adapted work and activities toward that end. In the case of The Strong, it was the museum's benefactor's love of play. For the Stowe Center, it was to answer the question, "Why does Harriet Beecher Stowe matter?" (answer: the impact of Stowe's words on the world). And for the Connecticut Historical Society, it is the role historical societies can play in improving the public good through the study and understanding of history.

Each carefully considered the question: "Why does this organization matter?" The answer provided both internal and external focus for these three institutions. There are countless other examples of history organizations and museums doing likewise. I'm sure you've already thought of additional instances. As you read on, I hope you will find inspiration for your own work and at your own institution.

THE STRONG

Rochester, New York, where The Strong is located, was long a hotbed of transformation. Rochester became the fastest-growing city in America after the opening of the Erie Canal in 1825. Throughout the nineteenth century, the city and its region developed a reputation for supporting transformative social causes. Women's suffragist Susan B. Anthony lived and worked in Rochester. In Seneca Falls, sixty miles to the southeast, her longtime collaborators Elizabeth Cady Stanton and Lucretia Mott held the first Women's Rights Convention in 1848. Frederick Douglass called Rochester home and from there published his abolitionist newspaper *The North Star*. The city of Palmyra, thirty miles from Rochester, is the birthplace of the Latter-day Saint movement. Commonly called the Mormon church, it has nearly fifteen million members today.[1]

The twentieth century saw Rochester develop into a pioneering business hub. The city was home to several revolutionary companies, including Eastman Kodak, Bausch & Lomb, and Western Union. The Eastman Kodak connection is where The Strong's story begins. In 1969, Margaret Woodbury Strong, the company's largest individual shareholder, died without heirs. She left an estate of $80 million and a collection of nearly half a million objects she had acquired over the years. This included "furniture and appliances, paintings and drawings, clothing, coins and stamps, Asian art, handicrafts, and knickknacks by the tens of thousands."[2]

Strong's will instructed trustees to either build a museum or distribute the money among nineteen other entities in Rochester, including other museums. Although Strong never specified what type of museum she had in mind, she had obtained a charter from New York state for a "Museum of Fascinations" in 1968.[3] Thus began a decades-long quest to create a museum based on Strong's wishes.

Initial planning for the museum, under the direction of Holman J. Swinney, included national museum leaders from Colonial Williamsburg, the Smithsonian, Winterthur, Old Sturbridge Village, and the New York Historical Association. The strength of Strong's collection was its toys and dolls, which was, vice president for Play Studies Scott Eberle wrote in 2008, "believed to be the largest and most comprehensive privately held collection in the world."[4] Yet these experts overlooked these collections out of a prejudice against these objects, judging them unworthy of study. One wrote of "an instinctive . . . mental, cultural, and perhaps even a 'moral' block against . . . dolls . . . paintings . . . tin toys," a bias that was "difficult to combat." Swinney agreed. "Most of what has been written about dolls," he opined, "is characterized by what might be courteously called a complete lack of scholarship."[5]

Swinney and his staff eschewed and quickly dismissed the interpretive themes the consultants identified—children, play, imagination, fun—in favor of an institution focused on "products and the means of producing them during America's industrializing period between 1820 and 1940." Exhibits focused on the transition from rural life to the modern economy, with exhibits on flow-blue china, collecting, gardening, eating, rustic furniture, and other elements of domestic life.[6]

Despite overlooking the strength of the collection, the initial Margaret Woodbury Strong Museum was a pioneering effort for the museum field. When it opened in 1982, its focus on everyday life reflected the impact of the New Social History on the history field. The museum presented its collections in open storage, with tens of thousands of artifacts—dubbed "study collections"—displayed by type following a format Robert G. Chenhall developed for classifying manmade objects. This format for display led many in the field to see the Strong Museum as "the museum person's museum."[7] Yet, despite this innovation, the community rapidly lost interest in the museum; attendance plummeted from 150,000 to less than 70,000 by 1986.[8]

The museum's transformation into the National Museum of Play began with the 1987 hiring of G. Rollie Adams as CEO. Initially, Adams and his team broadened the institution's mission to include life after the Industrial Revolution. From there, they mounted a series of exhibits on contemporary social issues: alcohol and drugs, prejudice, bereavement, family, and health-care. While these activities resulted in spikes in attendance, visitation soon leveled out to around 130,000 annually.

On the surface, hosting a quarter-million visitors a year in a city the size of Rochester is a rousing success. One might question the need for *any* change after nearly doubling attendance in Adams's tenure. As Candace Matelic wrote,

> They didn't *have* to do anything—they had (relatively speaking) all the money in the world, and their attendance was just slowly declining. And the museum field loved them, with all of the new social history exhibits and publications. They transformed because IT WAS THE RIGHT THING TO DO. They listed to the feedback from the community when they told them that the community really needed a place for children and families.[9]

To discover more about the needs of the community, Adams and his team engaged in something relatively new for the field: market research. This provided the impetus for other significant changes. Two studies reported that 70 percent of the museum's audience were families with young children and noted that focus on this audience should double attendance in three to five years. As a result, staff and leadership created more interactive exhibits, and began an exhibit partnership with *Sesame Street*. The Strong also established a department of visitor services, provided hospitality and service training for all staff, and empowered staff to do whatever was necessary to make every visitor's day extraordinary. A conscious focus on visitor experience extended beyond museum interpretation: from amenities such as turning its diner into a restaurant to moving its entry doors closer to the parking lot to activating its historic merry-go-round. Attendance soon increased to more than 300,000—exceeding the five-year projected number of 280,000.[10]

A board—staff team commissioned by the institution's executive committee in 2003 recommended the museum become the only collections-based museum in the world devoted to the concept of play. By 2004, The Strong's board adopted its new mission: to explore play "in order to encourage learning, creativity, and discovery."[11]

Compared to museums across the country, the results have been astounding, and not only in a tenfold increase in attendance. The focus on play created a museum that connects to a fundamental part of human interaction. Play uses the strength of the institution's collections and, most significantly, also best reflects Margaret Woodbury Strong's collection and lifelong passions. While Strong did not leave specific written instructions for a Museum of Fascinations, the historical record was not blank. Staff found oral histories from her contemporaries and newspaper articles noting that what she most

Image 3.1. In 1997, The Strong opened *Can You Tell Me How to Get to Sesame Street?*, a permanent exhibition developed in partnership with producers of the popular PBS television series. Courtesy of The Strong, Rochester, New York

cared about was dolls, toys, and children. And Strong had devoted most of her life to pursuits of play: traveling; sports such as archery, golf, and bowling; gardening; and collecting.[12] In answering "why," The Strong provided for itself and its constituents a focus on the concept of play, one of the most basic elements of life and learning. And it built on its institution's core collections, which its benefactor Strong bequeathed.

From this, the institution has grown to include the International Center for the History of Electronic Games to collect, study, and interpret video games and the ways electronic games change how people play, learn, and connect with each other; the Brian Sutton-Smith Library and Archives of Play devoted to the history of play; the National Toy Hall of Fame; World Video

Image 3.2.   G. Rollie Adams led The Strong from 1987 until 2016, transforming the museum into the only collections-based institution in the world devoted to play. Courtesy of The Strong, Rochester, New York

Game Hall of Fame; the interdisciplinary publication, *American Journal of Play*; and the Woodbury School for children from three to five years old.[13]

Were you to ask Adams or his staff about this transformation, no one would say it was easy. Candace Matelic found, "Organizational change and transformation are inherently complex and difficult." (She later named this Key Understanding One.) Yet she also found stakeholders believed the transformation worth the effort because of how it helped the organization serve its public. This is certainly true at The Strong.

THE STOWE CENTER

The Harriet Beecher Stowe Center in Hartford, Connecticut, offers another example of institutional transformation, moving from an under-known resource presenting a static historic house tour to a community and national leader in social justice. Like The Strong, the Stowe Center focuses on a core interpretive precept. For the former, it was its patron's love of play; at the Stowe Center it is author Harriet Beecher Stowe's impact and example.[14] "Harriet Beecher Stowe inspires us to believe in our own ability to effect change," its website reads. "Her life demonstrates one person's ability to make a difference. Stowe changed public perception of a young nation's divisive issue, slavery, using her words to change the world. Her example is as important today as it was in her time."[15] Stowe became world-renowned for her best-selling antislavery novel *Uncle Tom's Cabin* (1852). *Uncle Tom's Cabin* molded public opinion and, Frederick Douglass said, won over those indifferent to abolition, yet its title character became a racial slur routinely used today. "Her words changed the world, and you can too," Executive Director Katherine Kane often says.

Kane arrived at the Stowe Center in 1998. The institution's board had given serious thought to the Center's future, and hiring Kane reflected the desire to better incorporate into its interpretation Harriet Beecher Stowe's life and legacy and the complicated American history it reflects. "Stowe's story is local history," Kane wrote. "It's also international history because of the impact of her work."[16] It's the latter that is so important to the transformation of the institution. Kane and her team seized on themes of social justice and positive change connected with *Uncle Tom's Cabin*, Stowe's most famous work. Stowe's life and work provide powerful examples for today and for the future. In reinventing the organization into a dynamic program center that addresses contemporary issues, they vigorously demonstrate relevance and value. This answers the "Why."

Founded in Hartford by a Beecher descendent in 1941, the Stowe Beecher Hooker Seymour Day Memorial and Foundation opened the Stowe House to

Image 3.3. Katherine D. Kane is executive director of the Harriet Beecher Stowe Center. Under her leadership, the museum focuses on how the author's career as a writer and social change agent connects with today's social issues. *Source*: **Global Arts Photography**

the public in 1968 as one of the first Victorian house museums in the country and one of the first focusing on a woman. Now it is a museum, research library and program center, and an international tourist attraction—a scholarly resource and a neighborhood anchor. In 1994, the board changed the name to the Harriet Beecher Stowe Center to reflect that it is more than a historic house, but a dynamic community entity.

Upon her arrival, Kane found an institution that reflected historic houses across the nation. Like its peers nationwide, the Stowe Center focused on the house's architecture and material culture. Together with the board, Stowe created a more innovative institution, using strategic thinking and planning to envision a future and built toward it. These plans guided and provoked thinking. And staff seized opportunities for capacity building. For example, a year of programming commemorating the 150th anniversary of *Uncle Tom's Cabin* addressed the book's complicated history head on and resulted in key blocks in building the trust necessary for the institution to reach a diverse audience. A multifaceted, multiyear collections preservation project renovating storage and public spaces grew community and legislative relationships and fundraising capacity. And public programs focused on contemporary issues that tie to Stowe's work have built engagement, visibility, and revenue.

Today, the Stowe Center preserves and interprets Stowe's home and its collections, creates a forum for vibrant discussion of her life and work, and inspires commitment to social justice and positive change. This mission expresses the belief that Stowe's life and work are powerful examples for today. The institution uses issues of race, gender, and class in programs that align and connect to the site, its stories, and its extensive collections. Guided by this mission over the past two decades, the institution has transformed from a quiet house museum to an innovative community catalyst, presenting programs that promote civic engagement, social justice, and positive change. Award-winning programs reflect the interests of the Center's diverse community, attracting a multicultural local and national audience.

Reflecting on her tenure as Stowe Center director, Kane shared insights in the context of Matelic's rubric on the following pages:[17]

Key Understanding Two: Deep organizational change requires human reflection and interaction at the level of heart and soul. "Nonprofits carry the meaning in our world. We must each find the meaning in this work—and build the meaning into the programs," concurs Kane. What Matelic dubs heart and soul, Kane calls emotion. "Emotion is key to how our stories connect with visitors, program participants, board members, and colleagues. Facts are fleshed out with emotion—emotion can build empathy and understanding, it can build bridges." Kane believes this is an important part of her role as a transformational leader. "Absolutely, part of my job as change agent was to use emotion to get everyone going the same direction—and to know why it's the right direction."

A visual provided inspiration for Kane and the Stowe Center staff and board. The organization debuted a new logo in 2006, a flaming pen. This was a transformation in itself; its previous logo was an adaptation of a nineteenth-century book plate. "Then we had to come to work every day and live up to the new logo," she reported, "one that was aspirational." The board provided leadership and pushed Kane and her team to stay true to the institution's mission. An early decision was to put *Uncle Tom's Cabin* front and center. As Kane notes, "[This] changed everything. We had to talk about racial stereotyping, Stowe's human imperfections, slavery and its legacy, social imitations on women, and the like."

Key Understanding Four: Leadership matters a lot during change, and transformational leadership is a particularly effective strategy and approach. Kane agrees that leadership is critical. And while "charisma is not the most important thing," she recollects, "you need enough charisma to set the tone, to inspire everyone, to describe what you're trying to do in a way that gets people excited." But Kane differs somewhat from her peers on whose job it is to set the final vision. "The leader doesn't have to develop the vision. I like it to come from the group—the board, the staff, the public. I like it to be revealed with effort." In the case of Kane and the Stowe Center, leadership is a shared responsibility during times of transformation. This is the classic approach of a transformational leader in terms of building a shared vision that emerges from the collective input of stakeholders.

Key Understanding Five: The quality of stakeholder participation in change and transformation processes affects the outcome. This played a key role in transformation at the Stowe Center. "Building trust with diverse audiences changed everything," she wrote. "I thought of it as changing the 'folklore'—what people said about us. We purposely programmed to attract people. We asked them what they thought. We participated in grassroots organizations. We built connections. We responded." Also important is that the institution's volunteer leadership reflects these principles. At Stowe Center, Kane notes, "The board membership reflects these goals. Every board member is invested in the mission—they are not recruited first for their resources."

The Stowe Center represents a model of institutional transformation, one that many can emulate. Find your core and build on it. For the Stowe Center, it was Harriet Beecher Stowe's words and impact. "Her words changed the world." The institution seeks to as well.

CONNECTICUT HISTORICAL SOCIETY

The Connecticut Historical Society (CHS) is the Nutmeg State's official historical society, and one of the nation's oldest such institutions, housing a collection of more than four million pieces. This wealth of material provides the institution countless opportunities to engage citizens with the state's past. In 2013, Jody Blankenship became the organization's ninth director (and fifth paid one) since its founding in 1825, meaning his predecessors served an average of more than twenty years each. This type of stability can be both a blessing and a curse. And often, a change in leadership offers opportunity for transformation.

Upon taking the job, Blankenship immediately sought to expand the society's existing work, a transformational strategy that follows the mantra, "A rising tide lifts all boats." He wrote, "CHS will endeavor to find creative, mutually beneficial ways to collaborate with and promote the numerous historical organizations across the state. . . . CHS will continue to create opportunities where history can be applied for the advancement of the public good, turning the creativity, passion and courage of Connecticans toward developing strategies for acting on the critical challenges of our time."[18]

Much of the institutional transformation is reflected in the organization's formal strategic plan, instituted two years into Blankenship's tenure. It not only reflects his view on the role of history organizations but in many ways provides insight into how other history leaders are transforming the field. "We built the plan upon two beliefs," he wrote. "The first . . . is that our history defines us as individuals and communities. History provides context for our present. It allows us to examine and comprehend how we have come to be, and it provides examples of our past decisions and the consequences that followed. As we face ever-more complicated situations we can look to this body of evidence for caution, comfort, and inspiration."[19]

"The second belief," he continued, "is that the content and skills that historical societies can teach act as both scaffolding and a toolbox for understanding and thriving in a constantly changing world." This is important. "These skills," Blankenship argued, "allow us to think deeply about those things that matter most and to examine events through the lenses of others. By thinking this way we can strengthen our sense of tolerance and empathy,

Image 3.4. Through a renewed focus on collections, Connecticut Historical Society CEO Jody Blankenship (pictured here with Callie Prince and Melissa Traub) and his team have created new engagement through affinity groups and a crowdsourced exhibit, *Connecticut: 50 Objects/50 Stories. Source:* Jody Blankenship

open our minds to new perspectives, and, ultimately, expand our understanding of the world around us."[20]

Asking stakeholders what they want from a history organization is an important first step toward understanding how an institution can best serve its community.[21] CHS followed this model and spoke to constituents statewide, seeking to understand how residents defined history and its value, and preferences for participating in the history endeavor. It is not surprising that this process found "relevance in history when it revolved around personal and local content. Personal and local history helped [people] define themselves by explaining their sense of loyalty and identity, unusual quirks, and strongly held values."[22]

Through launching new collections-based affinity groups and a crowd-sourced exhibit, *Connecticut: 50 Objects/50 Stories*, CHS is transforming itself into an organization that helps people discover and share their own stories. Thus, Blankenship reported, "We are able to construct a wonderfully diverse, complex, and rich history that, rather than explaining where we came from, begins a discussion about where we wish to go."[23]

In many ways, this represents a transformation in interpretation as well, moving it beyond simply sharing information, and adding an element of self-discovery as well. This mirrors trends historian Rick Beard documented in "Is It Time for Another Revolution?" "The next great revolution in interpretation has already begun," Beard wrote, "as museums, in partnership with their audiences, move to craft transformative experiences that engage visitors of all ages. Success will rely upon the history community's ability to fuse the new technology and social media with its greatest assets—real objects, places, stories, lives, and ideas."[24] This is the transformation occurring at the Connecticut Historical Society and should be the future of historical interpretation for the field as a whole.

The transformation at the Connecticut Historical Society reflects well four of the key understandings Matelic notes in the following pages:[25]

Key Understanding One: Organizational change and transformation are inherently complex and difficult. As Blankenship reported, "It is most difficult when the change comes as a result of a change in leadership and without something that causes immediate urgency. It is even harder when the organization has resources and is stable.[26] Most staff and board members are focused on immediate and local needs and therefore are not looking years down the road or paying attention to industry or community trends that have the potential to disrupt the current operating model. Leaders have to highlight the upcoming concerns with regularity and show how they have the potential to hurt the organization's ability to carry out its mission."

Key Understanding Three: Change agents in history organizations play important roles in change and transformation processes. "Change agents come from all ranks in the organization," Blankenship shares. "It is most helpful to identify these people, bring them into the process, spend extra time nurturing their understanding of the needed change, and let them help lead the change. At the CHS I put a change agent in charge of each of the five goals in the strategic plan. They had the authority to call meetings and set agendas. I worked closely with each goal leader in a one-on-one manner so I could keep their work within the larger framework of the plan while demonstrating to the wider staff that they were in charge of the team's work. This worked to varying degrees. After the plan was complete, these people became champions for their goal acting as a cheerleader and pushing the work forward."

Key Understanding Five: The quality of stakeholder participation in change and transformation processes affects the outcome. Blankenship's experience at the helm of CHS reflects some inherent difficulties with transformation in general. "Many people pushed back on transformational leadership saying it was 'pie in the sky' thinking, neglected industry standards, or wasn't necessary and overly complicated. Most of these people just wanted to do their job. Often their job was also their hobby. They didn't see the mission as a 'higher calling.' I found it most effective to remove these people from their positions, when possible." The latter is rarely easy in the immediate term, but may be required in order to fully implement the desired transformation.

Key Understanding Six: Organizational learning is a generative strategy and process that helps to build organizational capacity. "I believe that this is true," he reports. "But one must be deliberate and make this a priority, otherwise our daily work gets in the way. I've found this comes mostly from hiring people who want to continuously learn, people who are professionally curious." Transformation is never easy, it is a process that involves not only leadership but the people implementing it.

We know history is vital to us as individuals, to our communities, and to our future. What is important is how effectively we transform our organizations to reach their full potential in meeting the ways history is essential, in nurturing personal identity, teaching critical thinking, providing vitality to our communities, stimulating economic development, fostering engaged citizens, inspiring leadership, and providing a legacy.[27] The Strong, Stowe Center, Connecticut Historical Society, and perhaps your own institution reflect ways we can meet this charge.

In the chapter that follows, Candace Matelic provides the framework history organizations can use in their own transformation. Stasis is not an option. It is up to us to put these precepts into action.

NOTES

1. Independent Television Service, "The City," *July '64*, accessed September 6, 2016, www.pbs.org/independentlens/july64/city.html.
2. Scott G. Eberle, "How a Museum Discovered the Transforming Power of Play," *Journal of Museum Education* 33, no. 3 (Fall 2008): 265–66; G. Rollie Adams, "Ready, Set, Go! *Finally*, a Museum of Play," *History News* 61, no. 3 (Summer 2006): 7.
3. New York is the only state in the United States that issues museum charters.
4. Eberle, 266.
5. Eberle, 266; Adams 8. Whether these comments reflect a predisposition against the material culture of adolescence or are more a response to gender dynamics is an area worthy of further study.
6. Eberle, 267.
7. Today, Chenhall's system is the standard cataloging tool for thousands of museums across the United States and Canada. Quote from a conversation author had with Paul G. Bourcier, editor of the revisions of Chenhall's lexicon *Nomenclature 3.0* (2010) and *Nomenclature 4.0* (2015).
8. Adams, 8.
9. Candace Matelic, email message to author, January 8, 2017.
10. Ibid., 9. In an email correspondence on December 15, 2016, Matelic wrote, "I remember arriving one morning to do dissertation interviews. A family came in and the baby promptly spit up all over the father. Without as much as a blink of the eye, a staff member escorted the father to the gift shop and offered him a new T-shirt, free of charge. She took his soiled shirt, cleaned it up, and put it in a bag for them. She didn't have to go up the chain of command, ask permission, call a manager, etc. It was amazing to watch. . . . I asked staff about it and they spoke of this as just a part of the commitment to become a visitor-centered institution."
11. Eberle, 270.
12. Adams, 9.
13. See www.museumofplay.org for details on all of these programs and activities.
14. Though Kane notes that she sometimes has to remind people who Harriet Beecher Stowe was in the first place.
15. Harriet Beecher Stowe Center, "About Us," accessed September 6, 2016, www.harrietbeecherstowecenter.org/about/.
16. Katherine Kane, "It's All about the Leadership," *History News* 69, no. 1 (Winter 2014): 24.
17. All quotes from email correspondence with Katherine Kane in September/October 2016. Author's personal collection.
18. Connecticut Historical Society, "Connecticut Historical Society Announces New Executive Director," August 15, 2013, accessed October 3, 2016, chs.org/press-release/connecticut-historical-society-announces-new-executive-director/.
19. Jody Blankenship, "CHS's Strategic Plan in Action," June 13, 2015, accessed October 3, 2016, chs.org/2015/06/chss-strategic-plan-in-action/.

20. Ibid.

21. Chapter 10 offers another example of this in action.

22. Jody Blankenship, "The Self-Directed Nature of Interpretation," *History News* 70, no. 2 (Spring 2015): 24.

23. Ibid., 25.

24. Rick Beard, "Is It Time for Another Revolution?" *History News* 70, no. 2 (Spring 2015): 26.

25. All quotes from Jody Blankenship, email to author, September 22, 2016.

26. This echoes Matelic's findings, "Facilitating and Inhibiting Conditions for Organizational Change in History Organizations," later in this chapter.

27. Adapted from History Relevance Campaign, "The Value of History: Seven Ways It Is Essential," accessed October 3, 2016, www.historyrelevance.com/history-is-essential.

Chapter 4

Understanding Change and Transformation in History Organizations[1]

Candace Tangorra Matelic

Increasing numbers of history organizations—ranging from all-volunteer staff to million-dollar operations—are undergoing major change and transformation. The reasons range from economic survival to a fundamental redefinition in purpose, based on the belief that our field is embarking on an era in which the traditional activities of collecting, preserving, researching, and exhibiting are simply no longer adequate. Museums and history organizations worldwide have been challenged to justify their existence by the public value, and positive contribution they make to their communities. Many history organizations are going beyond audience development to engage their communities to discover what they care about, redefine their missions and visions, and evolve into places that facilitate important civic conversations. They are utilizing interpretation as a transformative process to establish deep and personal connections with new audiences, neighbors, and stakeholders, and embracing innovative public programming as an organizational priority rather than a departmental function. Partnering with diverse community organizations, they are discovering shared goals, visions, plans, and outcomes, and pursuing more activist agendas to improve their communities.[2]

It is important for history organizations to understand the changes that are occurring. The processes of civic engagement and partnerships require that history organizations fundamentally transform the way they do business. History organizations are learning that organizational development is more than increased funding or new facilities—it includes developing the capacity of people and transforming organizational identity. Many history organizations are using teams to redefine work processes, involving stakeholders in making important decisions, and incorporating organizational development into their strategic planning and implementation. Boards are becoming more active and effective as they work with staff and community groups to build

43

capacity, strategize for long-term sustainability, undertake partnerships and collaborations, develop new streams of mission-related enterprise, and plan for leadership succession.

While the terms *change* and *transformation* are often used interchangeably, researchers have attempted to distinguish between organizational change that is episodic or infrequent, and that which is constant and evolving. Transformation is described as frame-breaking, large-scale, major, and revolutionary—the type of change that challenges strategy, culture, assumptions, values, and current operating premises of organizations and their members. For organizational transformation to be meaningful, it must be deep change, major in scope, discontinuous with the past, and generally irreversible. Transformation is a big step, with potentially big rewards, and for some history organizations, it may be necessary in order to survive. But regardless of scope, the process starts on a personal level by examining and perhaps altering fundamental assumptions, values, and knowledge, and then developing new theories about ourselves, our relationships, and our organizations. This rate of change will speed up as we move through this century, as organizational survival often depends on it.[3]

I have based the following chapter on my three decades of research and practice focused on organizational change and transformation. Rather than a series of case studies, my research looked for patterns, idiosyncrasies, similarities, and differences *across* organizations, and compared the experiences and perspectives of multiple stakeholders, including directors, trustees, staff, volunteers, community representatives, and former directors. My research approach gathered richly descriptive and thoughtful, albeit sometimes very painful, accounts of organizational change processes. The change experiences of these museums are representative of many history organizations, and are relevant for many other types of museums. They faced budget deficits and downsizing, built new facilities, developed external-focused missions, reprioritized activities, reorganized and diversified boards and staff, and integrated new technologies into programs, exhibits, and operations. Some smaller organizations are more flexible and less bureaucratic, with fewer entrenched behavior norms and expectations and may find it less daunting to start the transformation process if the board is community based.

This chapter offers a few tips (or ground rules) for learning about organizational change, and seven key understandings that incorporate findings from my research and experience with change in history organizations.[4] In a number of places I offer additional models and findings from organizational scientists to support the key understandings—these emerged as useful tools from teaching about change and transformation in museums since 2007.

THREE GROUND RULES FOR LEARNING ABOUT CHANGE AND TRANSFORMATION

1. Go Outside the Field for Relevant Research and Theory. There has been very little empirical research on organizational change in museums and history organizations. Broader organizational research provides models, theories, metaphors, and concepts used in describing, predicting, and analyzing change processes and leadership. The majority of academic models conceptualize change as processes of initiating, articulating, and implementing change, as well as solidifying the results in the culture of an organization, although newer theorists conceptualize change as a continuous process.[5]

2. Context and History Are Important. Studying organizational change requires taking a long view rather than an episodic slice of life. Change cannot be understood through studying just a few case studies, or through looking at a single change effort at a given time period. Like the discipline of history, we must understand an organization's past and the external context in which change occurs. Even if an organization undertakes change with an entirely new board and staff, there exists an institutional history and memory, and these things can become a powerful force of resistance when trying to establish momentum to propel change. Table 4.1 provides an overview of the facilitating and inhibiting conditions for organizational change in history organizations.

Table 4.1. Facilitating and Inhibiting Conditions for Organizational Change in History Organizations

OPPORTUNITIES CONDITIONS FACILITATING CHANGE	CONSTRAINTS CONDITIONS INHIBITING CHANGE
Relatively unstable environment, crisis	Relatively stable environment
Dramatic shifts and/or decline in attendance, financial support	Gradual increase in attendance, financial support
Support for new and/or experimental programs, exhibits, events, with focus on visitor experiences, external input	Modest changes and/or revisions in programs, exhibits, events, with focus on scholarship, internal expertise/input
Major expansion of collections and/or facilities	Slight growth in collections and/or facilities
Staff salaries/benefits stable/declining, but human resources (HR) viewed as important organizational investment	Small but steady increases in staff/benefits, but HR viewed as significant organizational cost

(Continued)

Table 4.1.   (Continued)

OPPORTUNITIES CONDITIONS FACILITATING CHANGE	CONSTRAINTS CONDITIONS INHIBITING CHANGE
Strong support for new direction/ initiatives, for example, new grants, new legislation, community engagement initiatives	Strong resistance to change from internal stakeholders, for example, board members, professional staff, volunteers w/ long tenure
Director/CEO: new, with mandate and support for change and transformation	Director/CEO: long tenure, support for status quo, established control systems
Support for risk and shared power— decentralized structures	Fear of risk, loss of power and control— centralized structures
Changing community, new expectations, lack of awareness or support for organization	Relatively stable community support, traditional expectations and awareness of the organization
Support for new professional initiatives, trends, and mandates	Insulation from professional initiatives, trends, and mandates
Culture of learning, new mindset of museums as community-driven organizations (continually transforming themselves)	Culture of preserving tradition and norms, conservative mindset ("museums don't change")
Effectiveness paradigm: long-term outcomes, value placed on qualitative measures, for example, learning, systems thinking, group processes, new partnerships	Efficiency paradigm: short-term focus, value placed on quantitative measures, for example, attendance figures, bottom line, balancing budget, productivity from tasks

Field-wide mandates, initiatives, and trends also impact organizations. During the past quarter century, there have been numerous calls for change from the museum field, for example, to increase diversity, to reach out to under-served audiences, and to engage communities. Influential trends, initiatives, and movements have also served as catalysts for change. These trends or forces included new content scholarship; growing research on audiences and learning; focus on interpretation and the public dimension; embracing new technologies; changing roles for curators, educators, and directors; understanding museums as organizations; and improving governance. History organizations have responded to these calls and trends by looking both inward and outward, reexamining their mission, institutional history, resources, and practices and learning more about their communities. However, there is a long way to go toward relevance and sustainability, and the museum field is just beginning to learn about community engagement (not the same thing as audience development!) and moving toward social entrepreneurship.

3. Look at Multiple Perspectives, Advocacies, and Roles. To comprehend the nature of change, we need to understand how various stakeholders perceive and respond to organizational change. It is not enough to hear only what directors have to say. It is important to pay attention to what people hold allegiance to, and deeply care about, during change processes. This is more significant than functional position. For example, a director has responsibility for an overall organization but may care most about collections and research. On the other hand, a curator may be deeply concerned about visitors and learning. Therefore, functional titles or positions can be deceiving. The comparison of different advocacy groups, such as the overall organization, community, research/collections, and audiences/programs, can provide insight into how people feel about and respond to change.

Organizational researchers Rosabeth Moss Kanter, Barry A. Stein, and Todd D. Jick offered a "Big Three Model of Change." This model is useful for capturing the dynamics of change processes, and for articulating three change roles for stakeholders: (1) strategists, (2) implementers, or (3) recipients. It is not unusual for individuals to take on more than one role; for example, one could strategize change, and then be responsible for implementing it. These connections between stakeholders' advocacy and their change roles can help us understand important dimensions of change and transformation and illustrate who serves to initiate and guide change.[6] A summary of the Kanter, Stein, and Jick model is shown in table 4.2.

Table 4.2. Summary of the Big Three Model of Change

MOVEMENT	FORM OR TYPE	ROLES
Macroevolutionary: Motion of the organization as a whole as it relates to its environment— related to its field or industry.	**Identity:** The relationship between the organization as an entity and its environment, for example, its business products and services.	**Strategists:** Concern for the connection between the organization and its environment, and for the organization's overall direction— conception of change.
Microevolutionary: Motion of the parts of the organization in relation to one another— developmental, related to size, shape, throughout its lifecycle.	**Coordination:** Related to the problems of shape, structure and effectiveness as an organization ages.	**Implementers:** Concern for the microdynamics of the change effort— structure, coordination, management, and execution.

(Continued)

Table 4.2.   (Continued)

MOVEMENT	FORM OR TYPE	ROLES
Revolutionary: Focusing on the political dimensions, the jockeying for power and struggle for control among organizational stakeholders.	**Control:** Related to who is in the dominant coalition, or the predominant set of interests, who owns and governs the organization.	**Recipients:** Those who are strongly affected by the change and its implementation— their reactions reflect political and control dimensions of organizations.

Adapted from Rosabeth Moss Kanter, Barry A. Stein, and Todd D. Jick, *The Challenge of Organizational Change: How Companies Experience It and Leaders Guide It.*

KEY UNDERSTANDINGS ABOUT CHANGE IN HISTORY ORGANIZATIONS

Key Understanding One: Organizational change and transformation are inherently complex and difficult. Undertaking major organizational change is not for the faint of heart. It takes courage, perseverance, and passion. Change is very rewarding, but it is often a difficult, chaotic, and complex endeavor. Organizational researchers describe change through a number of metaphors, for example: navigating a ship through a storm, steering a white-water river ride, riding a wild roller coaster, and zombies in the night of the living dead. Change does not necessarily follow a linear sequence of planned steps and stages. It is usually a multifaceted unfolding of decisions, events, role changes, and redefinitions. Bolman and Deal (1991) argue in *Reframing Organizations: Artistry, Choice, and Leadership* that there are four important frames, or perspectives for understanding how change occurs in organizations: human resources, structure, politics, and organizational symbols. Leaders must address all frames to address inherent organizational complexity.[7] Particularly in naturally conservative and risk-aversive places like museums and history organizations, change processes are inherently traumatic because they challenge deeply embedded traditions and the status quo.

In my research, history museums bucked long-standing and inwardly focused traditions and professional standards as they transformed their organizations to focus outward, and serve communities in more meaningful ways. The new direction was inspirational and uplifting. However, they faced tough challenges along the way, sometimes at the level of brute survival. Changing functional roles was extremely difficult, especially if stakeholders did not understand their contribution in a new role, or felt the change threatened their existing power and/or stature and muffled their voice. A big challenge was helping stakeholders understand why history organizations should change at all, even when their organizations were in crisis. People anguished over change processes, particularly the toll that it took on many stakeholders. Even those who were the strongest champions of change expressed this sentiment. However, stakeholders reiterated that organizational change and transformation was worth the effort because it positioned history organizations to provide more meaningful service to their communities, with increased public accountability and value.

Key Understanding Two: Deep organizational change requires human reflection and interaction at the level of heart and soul. Recent research suggests that the classic approach to leading change—seeking first to implement goals, organization charts, structures, job descriptions, and control systems and dealing with "people problems" later—are doomed to failure. This inevitable failure is due to management's view that they are separate from the people and systems to be changed, that staff are a problem to be fixed. Instead, researchers suggest focusing on developing the affective and spiritual qualities that help every person become a change leader, or feel empowered to initiate change and take responsibility for its implementation. To change organizations, we must start by changing ourselves and our relationships, examining and perhaps altering fundamental assumptions, values, knowledge, and rules. We must listen to our inner voices, and learn to honor the uncertainties and interconnectivity of the workplace. The qualities that we associate with soul—meaning, memory, beauty, divinity, and union—are fundamental aids for navigating the future and understanding the underlying patterns of human behavior. Organizational change researchers John Kotter and Dan Cohen discovered that the successful implementation of change was dependent on how well leaders managed the emotions of stakeholders, as shown in table 4.3. This research, along with the growing body of knowledge about the importance of emotional intelligence, supports the salience

Table 4.3. Example of Heart and Soul

EMOTIONS THAT UNDERMINE CHANGE	EMOTIONS THAT FACILITATE CHANGE
anger	passion
false pride	reality-based pride
pessimism	optimism
arrogance	enthusiasm
cynicism	hope
anxiety	excitement
panic	urgency
exhaustion	trust
insecurity	faith

Adapted from John P. Kotter and Dan S. Cohen, *The Heart of Change: Real-Life Stories of How People Change their Organizations.*

of addressing heart and soul when leading or experiencing organizational change.[8]

Stakeholder experiences matched the research about heart and soul in organizations. People were passionate about pursuing a big vision and doing something that mattered in their communities. They commiserated about how "staff bore the brunt" of change, particularly during excessive reorganization. They tried to invest in people more than ideas, build trust, be honest, and recognize accomplishments along the way. Organizational change was very personal in these history museums—it affected individuals at all levels, often touching heart and soul. Their response to change ranged from individual transformation and growth to hardened cynicism and life-altering pain.

Key Understanding Three: Change agents in history organizations play important roles in change and transformation processes. Change agents are those individuals who champion organizational change, reinforce why it is important, and guide the process. Change agents in history museums consciously attempted to shift their organizations toward a more dominant external focus, often challenging the existing museum culture and standards (resistance to this shift did not come from communities or external stakeholders). They used visioning processes, articulating shared values, and established teams to serve as guiding coalitions. Visioning is an effective strategy to build excitement and momentum for change because it increases learning throughout the organization and creates buy-in from stakeholders. If a vision is inspirational, it creates energy, increases organizational commitment, and attracts resources like a powerful magnet. Teamwork changed roles, work patterns, decision making, power structures, and long-standing relationships—helping some people, while threatening others. Since change does not threaten teams as much as individuals left to fend for themselves, they are effective in guiding organizational transformations. Some change agents structurally reorganized their institutions to increase effectiveness and efficiency, but it is important to note that changing structure is not a quick fix—when leaders tried this approach to launch change, it inevitably failed because they did not understand the critical role of established relationships among co-workers. Stakeholders wanted change agents to guide them through change processes, listen and respond to their concerns, and treat them with respect and dignity.

The change agents in these history museums were primarily the strategists. They existed at all levels and in all functional areas, as well as in communities and external environments. The largest groups of strategists were those people who advocated for the overall organization, for community (including board members), and for audiences and programs. Many people took on multiple roles, serving as change agents, but then also working to implement the changes in organizational structure, policy, activities, and culture.

   Key Understanding Four: Leadership matters a lot during change, and transformational leadership is a particularly effective strategy and approach. Effective change leaders utilize visioning to mobilize energy and support for change, and demonstrate behaviors focused on people and tasks. Transformational leadership is effective in a variety of situations and engenders trust and respect for leaders from their followers. Rather than offering rewards (salaries or authority) to get performance from followers, transformational leaders appeal to followers' higher values to build commitment to an inspirational purpose for the organization. They empower others to share the leadership role; their actions are more serving and supporting than commanding and controlling. As stakeholders become engaged in a shared vision, their enthusiasm and motivation grows, and they transform themselves and the organization. This leadership approach takes integrity and the courage to do what is right for the organization, regardless of personal ambition. James Kouzes and Barry Posner present one of my favorite expressions of the transformational leadership approach, beginning with their 1995 book *The Leadership Challenge*. These researchers surveyed more than 60,000 leaders at all levels of a wide variety of public and private organizations, and discovered a recurring set of five leadership practices and behaviors, with ten commitments these practices embody. The essence of their leadership approach is summarized in table 4.4.[9]

Table 4.4.   Model of Transformational Leadership

FIVE PRACTICES OF EXEMPLARY LEADERSHIP	TEN COMMITMENTS (OR EFFECTIVE LEADERSHIP BEHAVIORS)
Model the way	Find your voice by clarifying personal values.
	Set the example by aligning actions with shared values.
Inspire a shared vision	Envision the future by imagining exciting and ennobling possibilities.
	Enlist others in a common vision by appealing to shared aspirations.
Challenge the process	Search for opportunities by seeking innovative ways to change, grow, and improve.
	Experiment and take risks by constantly generating small wins and learning from mistakes.
Enable others to act	Foster collaboration by promoting cooperative goals and building trust.
	Strengthen others by sharing power and discretion.
Encourage the heart	Recognize contributions by showing appreciation for individual excellence.
	Celebrate values and victories by creating a spirit of community.

Adapted from James M. Kouzes and Barry Z. Posner, *The Leadership Challenge: How to Get Extraordinary Things Done in Organizations.*

True transformational leaders are rare, but a few leaders demonstrated distinguishing characteristics of transformational leadership, including seeking inspirational organizational purposes even when facing survival concerns. This empowered leaders at all levels to build commitment, and demonstrate integrity and credibility. To make decisions, they relied on intuition as well as knowledge and experience, and encouraged innovation, experimentation, and learning. They used nontraditional approaches when faced with formidable challenges. Instead of cutting operational expenses to address a multimillion-dollar deficit, they spent money to invest in new programs and products. This approach led to increased major foundation support.

There were other important findings about change leadership. Leaders often struggled to balance internal and external focus. Persistence, patience, perseverance, and resilience, as well as being comfortable with uncertainty and ambiguity, were useful traits for leading change. Interestingly, charisma was not a dominant trait in effective change leaders, as the focus needs to be on the collective rather than on the individual leader. Boards needed to model the transformation they desired by becoming change agents, building support for change, building organizational capacity, and becoming more effective governing bodies. The traditional strict boundaries—board focusing on fundraising and setting policy while staff focus on operations and implementation—were not useful during the chaos of change. Instead, boards partnered with directors and staff to drive transformation forward. Leaders noted that without strong board support and involvement, it would have been very difficult to shift priorities toward providing more relevant community service.

Key Understanding Five: The quality of stakeholder participation in change and transformation processes affects the outcome. Meaningful participation helped stakeholders understand the reasons for change, build buy-in, and change attitudes and behaviors. The reverse was also true. History organizations used strategic planning processes and structural changes, particularly cross-functional teams, to facilitate and strengthen the quality of participation. Teamwork and project management changed stakeholder roles as well as decision making and work patterns. People relied on longstanding relationships with others to get work done, sometimes in spite of their administrators, and sometimes consciously bucking a newly established reorganization that they felt did not work. Leaders built external support for change through sharing authority and giving the community a meaningful (rather than token) voice in organizational planning.

Stakeholder reactions to change ranged from enthusiastic commitment through outward resistance. Change supporters expressed joy about coming to work, being involved in something important, and the positive responses from their communities. Alternatively, many resisted change because of deeply held beliefs and assumptions, and fear of losing control, power, competency, resources, or status. The research on organizational change mirrors this range of reactions. Stakeholders' most critical concern was whether people were treated well or poorly during change, and this determined whether they overtly or covertly supported or resisted new organizational policies and processes. They learned to take care of each other during change processes, especially when colleagues felt lost, not supported, or unappreciated. Their network of established relationships served as a safety net.

Leaders and change agents needed to spend significant time helping people understand the process of change and stakeholders needed more time to figure out how to implement change, particularly how it would affect existing roles, relationships, and responsibilities. Stakeholders recommended identifying the informal leaders at all levels of organizations, enlisting them as champions for change processes and empowering them to help others understand and cope with change.

In a very practical and useful book *Managing Transitions: Making the Most of Change*, William Bridges argues that organizational change will not work unless transition occurs. Bridges differentiates between change and transition, suggesting that *change* is an external situation with a focus on outcomes, for example, a new team role, new job, or new policy, while *transition* is the internal process that people experience that allows them to embrace the new and let go of the old. As shown in table 4.5, Bridges suggests that people go through three stages of transition, *endings*, a chaotic *neutral zone*, and then *new beginnings*. The neutral zone is particularly conducive to creativity and innovation as stakeholders discover and define new roles for themselves—this is a great opportunity for people to move out of restrictive job descriptions and utilize their full talents and skills. As we become aware of these important transitions, we can utilize a number of tools to help stakeholders navigate them with more ease. Bridges's research reinforces the central premise of this key understanding about organizational change—it is all about people work.

Table 4.5.   William Bridges's Three Stages of Transition and Action Tools

TRANSITION STAGE	ACTION TOOLS
Endings: letting go of something	Honor the past; acknowledge grief and losses.
Neutral Zone: chaotic time between the old, comfortable reality and the new uncomfortable beginning	Explain purpose of change, and the plan for getting there. Envision how change will look and feel. Articulate and support everyone's new role.
New Beginnings: new reality as change is implemented	Reinforce change purpose, plan, and support for new roles.

Adapted from William Bridges, *Managing Transitions: Making the Most of Change.*

Key Understanding Six: Organizational learning is a generative strategy and process that helps to build organizational capacity. Organizational learning goes beyond maintaining the status quo, and focuses on enhancing the capacity to create, grow, and evolve. Components include building capacity, valuing human resources, facilitating meaningful stakeholder participation in change, utilizing systems thinking, and embracing learning as a valued organizational outcome. The organization also values innovation, experimentation, flexibility, and initiative. Measures focus on organizational (rather than individual) outcomes—new behaviors or action patterns. The acquisition of new knowledge, tools, understandings, or values is not enough on its own. Organizational learning shifts focus away from short-term efficiency models and toward long-term effectiveness.

Peter Senge is credited with introducing the organizational learning concept to organizations, with his 1990 seminal book, *The Fifth Discipline: The Art and Practice of the Learning Organization.* Senge posited that organizations must continually expand their capacity to create their future—this is beyond surviving. "Survival or adaptive learning" is important and necessary. But in learning organizations, adaptive learning is joined by "generative learning" that enhances our capacity to create and innovate. To do this, organizations must simultaneously nurture and support five disciplines, individually and as integrated ensemble:

- **Personal mastery:** continually clarifying and deepening our personal vision, focusing our energies, developing patience, and seeing reality objectively.
- **Mental models:** the deeply engrained assumptions, generalizations, or images that influence how we understand the world and how we take action.
- **Shared vision:** developing shared pictures of the future that foster genuine commitment and enrollment rather than compliance.
- **Team learning:** the capacity of members of a team to suspend assumptions and enter into a genuine thinking together, recognizing patterns of interaction in teams that undermine learning, such as defensiveness.
- **Systems thinking:** the conceptual framework (knowledge and tools) that makes full patterns clearer to help us see how to change them effectively, contemplating the whole rather than only its parts, seeing patterns of change, seeing interrelationships rather than individual things.

These disciplines include practices (what we do), principles (guiding ideas or insight that guides actions), and essences (the state of being in those with high levels of mastery, and where the disciplines start to converge).[10]

History organizations built capacity by investing in staff and the board through cross-functional training (courses, workshops, and sessions), study travel, reading groups, teamwork, recognition, mentoring, and improved communication. History organizations changed the way that they set priorities and did business after learning from and about communities and audiences. Community members joined with board members and management to serve as strategists and change agents.

In terms of systems thinking, organizational transformations occurred as these organizations became aware of internal systems, sought external input, built partnerships, and saw themselves as part of larger community systems. Stakeholders accepted teamwork as a new work pattern, but struggled with the complexities of implementing teams within existing structures. Changing structure was easy, they argued, compared to altering the complex systems of working relationships and friendships. Implementing systemic change required relentless attention because, inevitably, the old systems fought back. Leaders had to work diligently to keep old patterns and habits from reappearing, and push to achieve real change. In extreme situations, entire organizations can retrench back to old patterns of authority and control (they actually retrench deeper) if there is a change in leadership, and shared and/or participatory management threatens the new leaders.

Key Understanding Seven: Organizational change and transformation are inherently paradoxical, as history organizations balance their uniqueness and connectedness. History organizations face some unique paradoxes in attempting to undertake and implement major change. Some examples include the following:

1. The *tyranny of tradition or conservative mindset paradox* posits that history organizations are traditionally conservative places that are not expected to change. This paradox relates to the collecting and preserving mandate that spills over to organizational norms and practices, entrenching the status quo as if it was part of the collection. This mindset constrains new thinking about organizational structures, processes, and outcomes.[11]
2. The *mission-driven survival paradox* suggests that history organizations seek higher purposes or altruistic goals and develop visionary plans while often struggling to survive.
3. The *organizational learning paradox* describes how history organizations focus on the learning of visitors but often do not value the learning of stakeholders and the organization.
4. The *paradox of effective governance* describes the challenges of developing productive governance partnerships, especially while overseeing organizational change.

These four paradoxes resonated, and each deserves a deeper explanation and discussion. The presence of the *tyranny of tradition* may contribute or

lead to survival challenges. Also, during change, history organizations struggle to balance their uniqueness with their connectedness to the larger field,
which promotes mandates for change and the underlying values of nonprofit
or public organizations.

CLOSING THOUGHTS

The best things in life, the things that really matter, whether in our personal
or work lives, are worth the trouble required to achieve them. Transforming
history organizations into places that address what people really care about is
a noble and worthy quest. History organizations often bemoaned the personal
hell people went through to achieve deep change. But more importantly, they
expressed a deep satisfaction about doing the right thing, as they redirected
resources and energy toward increasing public service and addressing the
enduring needs in their communities. They recounted the benefits of their
transformation journeys—strengthened governance, new facilities, increased
financial support, deeper connections with audiences, new community relationships and partnerships, deeper respect and caring for their colleagues, and
more relevant and vibrant organizations.

The ground rules and key understandings in this chapter provide insight
and perspective for people who are leading or experiencing organizational
change, as well as for those who study and teach about change and transformation processes. Think about the seven key understandings as a jump-start
to the journey of learning about organizational transformation. As we let go
of old-school models and approaches, honestly listen to community ideas,
and discover what really matters to people, we will realign our programs
and services in response. Most likely, the progression will be from audience development to community engagement, and then to facilitating social
change. My hope is that this chapter will touch hearts and souls, and help us
find the courage and faith to envision and undertake change and transformation to shape more effective and relevant history organizations.

NOTES

1. The 2008 article benefited from thoughtful comments and observations from
a number of colleagues, including Donna Braden, Alice Dommert, Barbara Franco,
George McDaniel, Laura Roberts, Barbara Silberman, and Kent Whitworth. This
chapter has been expanded to include a number of models and tools from organizational scientists—I have been using these (and many others) in teaching about organizational change in museums since 2007. Based on feedback and evaluations, students

and workshop participants have found the key understandings and the additional material to be useful.

2. See Harold K. Skramstad, "An Agenda for American Museums in the Twenty-First Century," *Daedalus*, 128, no. 3 (Summer 1999): 109–28; Stephen E. Weil, "From Being *about* Something to Being *for* Somebody" and "Transformed from a Cemetery of Bric-a-brac," in *Making Museums Matter* (Washington, DC: Smithsonian Institution Press, 2002), 28–52 and 81–90; Sam Carbone, "The Dialogic Museum" *Muse* 31, no. 1 (Winter 2003): 36–39; and Candace Tangorra Matelic, "New Roles for Small Museums," in *Small Museum Toolkit, Book 4: Reaching and Responding to the Audience*, eds. Cinnamon Catlin-Legutko and Stacy Klingler (Lanham, MD: AltaMira Press, 2012), 141–62.

3. See Robert E. Quinn, *Deep Change: Discovering the Leader Within* (San Francisco: Jossey-Bass, 1996).

4. This dissertation, *Organizational Change in History Museums*, was completed for a doctorate in organizational studies, School of Business, The University at Albany, SUNY, 2007. Data were collected through long interviews in fall 1999 and produced 1,700 pages of transcripts. The seven history museums in the study were Henry Ford Museum & Greenfield Village (now The Henry Ford), Dearborn, Michigan; Detroit Historical Museum, Detroit, Michigan; Minnesota Historical Society, St. Paul, Minnesota; Missouri Historical Society, St. Louis, Missouri; The Strong (formerly the Strong National Museum of Play), Rochester, New York; Historical Society of Washington, DC (now the City Museum of Washington, DC); and National Museum of American History, Smithsonian Institution, Washington, DC.

5. A notable exception is Sherene Suchy, *Leading with Passion: Change Management in the 21st-Century Museum* (Walnut Creek, CA: AltaMira Press, 2004). However, Suchy offers only the perspective of directors. It is also important to mention the groundbreaking work of Robert R. Janes and his study of the Glenbow Museum in Calgary, Alberta (the book is now in its third edition).

6. See Rosabeth Moss Kanter, Barry A. Stein, and Todd D. Jick, *The Challenge of Organizational Change: How Companies Experience It and Leaders Guide It* (New York: Free Press, 1992).

7. See Lee G. Bolman and Terrence E. Deal, *Reframing Organizations: Artistry, Choice, and Leadership*, fifth edition (San Francisco: Jossey-Bass, 2013).

8. See John P. Kotter and Dan S. Cohen, *The Heart of Change: Real-Life Stories of How People Change their Organizations* (Boston: Harvard Business School Press, 2002). To learn more about emotional intelligence, start with Daniel Goleman's work, *Emotional Intelligence: Why It Can Matter More Than IQ* (New York: Bantam Books, 2005). My favorite books about heart and soul include Alan Briskin, *The Stirring of Soul in the Workplace* (San Francisco: Jossey-Bass, 1996); John P. Kotter and Dan S. Cohen, *The Heart of Change: Real-Life Stories of How People Change Their Organizations* (Boston: Harvard Business School Press, 2002); and Richard L. Daft and Robert H. Lengel, *Fusion Leadership: Unlocking the Subtle Forces That Change People and Organizations* (San Francisco: Berrett-Koehler, 2000).

9. Gary Yukl, *Leadership in Organizations* (Upper Saddle River, NJ: Prentice-Hall, 1998); James M. Kouzes and Barry Z. Posner, *The Leadership Challenge: How*

to Get Extraordinary Things Done in Organizations (San Francisco: Jossey-Bass, 1995) provide good overviews of transformational leadership. Table 4.4 comes from Kouzes and Posner's *Leadership Challenge Workbook*, 2003. Yukl notes that charismatic leaders are often not transformational because their focus is on themselves rather than the entire organization. The seminal treatises, from the 1970s and 1980s, are by James M. Burns and Bernard M. Bass.

10. This literature is growing rapidly. Start with Peter M. Senge, *The Fifth Discipline: The Art and Practice of the Learning Organization* (New York: Doubleday, 1990) and Chris Argyris and Donald Schön, *Organizational Learning II: Theory, Method, and Practice* (Reading, MA: Addison-Wesley Publishers, 1996). Senge and colleagues have also published a number of workbooks.

11. See Robert R. Janes, *Museums and the Paradox of Change: A Study in Urgent Adaptation* (Calgary, Alberta, Canada: Glenbow Museum, 1995). The third edition of this book came out in 2013.

Chapter 5

Making History a Twenty-First-Century Enterprise

Bob Beatty

One of the most salient issues in the profession is the issue of financial sustainability. Formally, sustainability is "the long-term capacity of a stewardship organization to ensure adequate audiences and financial support to preserve and maintain its buildings and landscapes," according to the American Association for State and Local History.[1] Yet "sustainability" is a term so often wielded in discussion that it is in danger of becoming devoid of meaning, part of the jargon of the history profession. But it is far more important than that and needs regular reconsideration and reflection.

That sustainability has entered (and remained) in the lexicon is an outgrowth of any number of things: declining attendance at larger historic sites, a malaise regarding the discipline of history (though not necessarily its practice), the sheer proliferation of history organizations nationwide (more than 19,000 according to a recent count), and ever-present funding challenges.[2] The latter is, perhaps, the biggest issue facing the field and is, in many ways the sum of these parts. While funding is by no means a new concern, the past several decades have really brought the subject to the fore.

History museums, as a whole, were ill prepared to weather drastic cuts in federal monies since the U.S. Bicentennial. The Bicentennial also spurred a tremendous proliferation of history organizations, intensifying the impact of the funding decreases. National Endowment for the Humanities funding dropped from $403 million in inflation-adjusted dollars in 1979 to less than $150 million today.[3] In addition, American foundations shifted funding strategies to programmatic grants rather than providing general operating support, and later began restricting funding to ever-smaller percentages of overhead or staff costs. This helped move many nonprofit organizations (not just history organizations) to a more business-focused approach, but it also created an almost infinite loop of grant application writing, new projects to implement with little additional resources, reporting back to the funder, and the end of the project when funding ended—often because it was unsustainable financially in the first place.

The latter topic was discussed in depth at the 2007 *Sustainability of Historic Sites* summit hosted by the National Trust for Historic Preservation at its Kykuit site in Sleepy Hollow, New York. It included more than thirty leaders of historic sites, funders, and representatives of national organizations and focused on standards/best practices, innovation, alternative uses for historic sites, and institution and funder expectations. These leaders concluded that this cycle of program-focused funding "can reduce long-term sustainability by shifting focus away from operating and endowment needs and by encouraging the growth of non-mission-related programs."[4]

Two of the group's recommendations dealt directly with this finding:

• Foundations and granting agencies should refocus their philanthropy away from short-term program support to grants that assist sites in building their capacity to sustain themselves for the long term, including GOS (General Operating Support) and endowment.

Image 5.1. The 2007 *Sustainability of Historic Sites* summit at Kykuit in Sleepy Hollow, New York, focused on standards and best practices, innovation, alternative uses for historic sites, and institution and funder expectations. *Source*: Adobe Stock

- Foundations should be supported in their efforts to terminate repeated "drip support" to historic sites to focus their support on sites taking positive steps to achieve long-term sustainability.[5]

The economic collapse of the global economy in 2008, sometimes called the Great Recession, followed closely on the heels of Kykuit. Just as history organizations were beginning national discussions on sustainability, they had the rug pulled out under them.

While some museums did close as a result of the declining economy (most notably, the City of Manassas Museum system), it didn't result in a wholesale winnowing of history museums nationwide. Instead it resulted in even more belt-tightening at institutions already running at very tight margins. The billions of dollars in lost wealth surely cost the nonprofit sector dearly, and the history museum community was not immune to its impacts.

Against this backdrop came the following chapter by John W. Durel. He has had a long, distinguished career in the field of state and local history, first at Strawbery Banke in Portsmouth, New Hampshire, and most recently as a respected consultant in the field of leadership and organizational development.

Durel's chapter addresses the concept of history and individual institutions as cultural enterprise, the theme of the 2009 AASLH/Association of Indiana Museums Annual Meeting in Indianapolis. This idea built on the progress Indianapolis had made in creating and nurturing its creative economy. Inherent within this was the city's embrace of the importance of its past as it charted a course for the future.

The chapter also highlights entrepreneurial ways institutions can leverage one of their greatest strengths: the perception that history organizations are overwhelmingly recognized as authentic, as non-biased keepers of historical truth. It is a powerful position we find ourselves in and with it comes both tremendous opportunity and responsibility. However, the chapter highlights a tension between our role as keepers of historical truth and the entrepreneurial requirement to respond to what audiences value. The field continues to grapple with that tension.

It may seem odd to think of history professionals as entrepreneurs. We're certainly not entrepreneurs in the classic sense, the kind you see on the cover of magazines or on the television show *Shark Tank*. This is because our product is rarely tangible. Often it's experiential, a feeling engendered through a connection with the past.

Yet history organizations do not exist in a vacuum. The tired model of "come and appreciate us because we've got old stuff" doesn't work. Institutions must compete for audience. To do so often requires an entrepreneurial spirit, something that can sometimes be found lacking in a profession that often begins from a position of scarcity. Entrepreneurship requires risk and embrace of change and possibility—two factors antithetical to the bureaucracies and silos that develop in many organizations.

The Harvard Business School (HBS) utilizes Howard Stevenson's definition of entrepreneurship: "Entrepreneurship is the pursuit of opportunity beyond resources controlled." Thomas R. Eisenmann of HBS further defines the term: "'Pursuit' implies a singular, relentless focus. . . . 'Opportunity' implies an offering that is novel. . . . 'Beyond resources controlled' implies resource constraints."[6] These elements are all part of the entrepreneurial strategies Durel highlights in his chapter.

In 2008, as our nation grappled with the beginnings of its worst financial crisis since the Great Depression, program chair D. Stephen Elliott (now of the Minnesota Historical Society), host chair John Herbst (Indiana Historical Society), and Garet Livermore (now of The Sagamore Institute of the Adirondacks) drafted the following:

> Our products should be developed, delivered, and marketed with a level of passion and knowledge that makes it meaningful and valuable to visitors, donors, and stakeholders. Cultural entrepreneurship does not end with the fiscal bottom line. It inspires meaningful interaction among visitors, multiple constituencies, and staff; it connects personal history to the larger history of our nation and our world; and it promotes positive social change.[7]

Ultimately, this results in public value, the key to the entire equation. As James Heaton of the Tronvig Group (a marketing and branding firm that serves museums and nonprofit organizations) notes, "No one buys what you sell." He goes on to say, "They buy what is of value to them." While Heaton presents this in a marketing context, it is easily applied to the service(s) we offer as well. The cultural entrepreneur knows to identify audiences and what they value and develops strategies to discern how his or her organization meets or can be made to meet *their* needs.[8]

Eight years after AASLH first published Durel's essay, history organizations are still adjusting to the "New Normal" as the country continues to grapple with the short- and long-term effects of the economic collapse of almost a decade ago. And while Wall Street's numbers have rebounded (and exceeded) the highs of the pre–Great Recession era, the need for bigger thinking at history organizations has not waned.

Our use of the term "enterprise" was intentional, and it remains so. It is the business of history through institutions—historical societies; museums; historic houses; statewide historical agencies; archives and special collections; historic sites; genealogists—and through the work of academic, public, and avocational historians. Historian Bruce W. Dearstyne argues that the "historical enterprise" conveys "the notion of a big, bold, important, some-times challenging undertaking requiring energy, initiative, and imagination."[9]

The history enterprise requires innovative entrepreneurs who, according to Dearstyne, "Constantly ask questions that challenge common wisdom and spend a good deal of time thinking about how to change things. . . . They encourage and support experimenting." These entrepreneurs, he writes, "constantly seek new knowledge and have the ability of associating—connecting seemingly unrelated questions, problems or ideas from different fields."[10]

I often co-mingle leadership with entrepreneurship. Perhaps it's just that the latter is a very effective tool of the former. Either way, it's extremely difficult to be entrepreneurial if you don't feel empowered to take the risks to pursue opportunities beyond resources controlled. Business professor and leadership guru Stewart Friedman maintains that leaders "never stop search-ing for new ways to contribute their talent and energy to causes they believe in. They inspire others to focus energy on the collective good."[11] This is the very definition of the cultural entrepreneur.

It is imperative to consider leadership as *everyone's* role. Entrepreneurial discussions should not be reserved for those at the highest levels: the CEO, senior leadership, or board. Leadership occurs at all levels. Museum lead-ers Julie I. Johnson and Randy C. Roberts observe, "We often think of the words *leader* and *director* in the same breath, but this way of thinking sets up a situation where staff members across the institution treat the identified leader with such deference that they abdicate their own power to make a difference in achieving organizational outcomes."[12] And leaders serve at all levels of an organization, argue Anne W. Ackerson and Joan H. Baldwin, coauthors of *Leadership Matters* (2014). "Leadership is about individuals *and* institutions. . . . [E]ach of us has the power to make choices about personal leadership. . . . [I]t is this intentional practice of leadership that will change the field."[13] The Ohio History Connection's Jackie Barton put it more succinctly, "Lead from where you are."

No matter the lens through which you view the subject of cultural entre-preneurship—an entire community, an institution, or personally—you play a crucial role in making history a twenty-first-century enterprise.

NOTES

1. American Association for State and Local History Historic House Affinity Group Committee, "How Sustainable Is Your Historic House Museum?" Technical Leaflet #244, *History News* 63, no. 4 (Autumn 2008): 2.

2. Institute of Museum and Library Services, "Government Doubles Official Estimate: There Are 35,000 Active Museums in the U.S.," May 19, 2014, accessed

July 25, 2016, www.imls.gov/news-events/news-releases/government-doubles-offi
cial-estimate-there-are-35000-active-museums-us.

3. American Academy of Arts and Sciences, *Humanities Indicators*, "National
Endowment for the Humanities (NEH) Funding Levels," accessed July 25, 2016,
www.humanitiesindicators.org/content/indicatordoc.aspx?i=75.

4. Jay D. Vogt, "The Kykuit II Summit: The Sustainability of Historic Sites,"
History News 62, no. 4 (Autumn 2007): 17.

5. Ibid., 21.

6. Thomas R. Eisenmann, "Entrepreneurship: A Working Definition," *Harvard Business Review*, January 10, 2013, accessed July 25, 2016, hbr.org/2013/01/
what-is-entrepreneurship.

7. D. Stephen Elliott, John Herbst, and Garet Livermore, "Making History a 21st-
Century Enterprise," 2009 American Association for State and Local History and
Association of Indiana Museums Annual Meeting theme.

8. James Heaton, "What Is Marketing Discovery?" accessed August 5, 2016,
www.tronviggroup.com/marketing-discovery/.

9. Bruce W. Dearstyne, *Leading the Historical Enterprise: Strategic Creativity,
Planning, and Advocacy for the Digital Age* (Lanham, MD: Rowman & Littlefield,
2015), 1.

10. Dearstyne, 50.

11. Stewart Friedman, *Total Leadership: Be a Better Leader, Have a Richer Life*
(Watertown, MA: Harvard Business School Press, 2008), quoted in Anne W. Ackerson and Joan H. Baldwin, *Leadership Matters* (Lanham, MD: Rowman & Littlefield,
2014), 4.

12. Julie I. Johnson and Randy C. Roberts, "The Practice of Leadership in a Changing Environment," *Dimensions*, November–December 2009, accessed August 5, 2016,
www.astc.org/astc-dimensions/the-practice-of-leadership-in-a-changing-environment.

13. Ackerson and Baldwin, 1.

Chapter 6

Entrepreneurship in History Organizations

John W. Durel

In 2016, John W. Durel wrote the following preface to his 2009 article: When this article appeared in spring 2009, history organizations had begun to feel the impact of the 2008 global recession, and the future was uncertain. In the years immediately following, most experienced declines in revenue, resulting in layoffs in some instances as steep as 50 percent, and had to curtail services and operations. Many organizations responded with an entrepreneurial spirit, finding opportunities in the change that they were facing. They discovered more efficient ways to serve their constituents and developed new sources of revenue as the economy slowly recovered.

If the notion of entrepreneurial history organizations seemed somewhat preposterous in early 2009, that is the case no longer. Experimentation and entrepreneurship have become increasingly common as individuals have embraced change and ventured into new territory. Here are a few notable examples.

NEW REVENUE SOURCES

- In response to trends in American culinary tastes, especially interest in locally produced food, David Donath and his colleagues at Billings Farm & Museum are making and selling artisan cheese. This added source of revenue enhances the Billings brand as the gateway to Vermont's rural heritage.
- The demand is high for downtown office space in Portsmouth, New Hampshire. Seizing this opportunity, Larry Yerdon at Strawbery Banke has had notable success in preserving and renovating historic buildings that have long stood vacant. Donors have liked the idea of giving to revenue-generating

projects, and the annual rental income is now approaching $500,000. Offices are on the second floor of buildings and the first floors are used for exhibitions and other visitor experiences.

SCIENCE, TECHNOLOGY, ENGINEERING, AND MATH (STEM)

The surge of interest in STEM (science, technology, engineering, and math) education has led to several innovative approaches by history organizations.

- Conner Prairie in Indiana received a multimillion-dollar grant from the National Science Foundation to experiment with teaching STEM through history. Former director Ellen Rosenthal and her staff have worked with the Minnesota Science Center to develop and evaluate prototypes, such as teaching concepts of electricity in the context of the rural electrification movement of the 1930s. The plan is to build a STEM/history museum at Conner Prairie, so that they can attract visitors year-round.
- Ellen Spear and her staff at Heritage Museums and Gardens on Cape Cod have started a STEM preschool, responding to growing demand for early childhood education. Working with state and local educators, the program turns the museum's campus into a classroom for the study of history and nature.

NEW AUDIENCES

As the traditional history audience ages, it has become evident to many that something needs to be done to attract younger people. At the moment a lot of attention is being paid to millennials.

- Museum Hack has emerged as a leader in developing new ways to engage this cohort using tour techniques that combine collections and historical content with a bit of humor and irreverence. For example, working with the Heart of the Civil War organization in Frederick, Maryland, they interpreted the strategic movements of a battle through a simple dance—move to the right, advance, fall back, and so on—and had the participants learn the dance. Reactions are mixed and not unlike reactions to ghost tours in 2009.
- The Historic House Trust (HHT) in New York City, formerly led by Franklin Vagnone, has become a thought leader in finding ways to make historic houses more relevant and appealing to new audiences, again with an emphasis on fun and a bit of irreverence. From bike tours to the *Anarchis'st Guide*

to Historic House Museums, HHT continues to experiment and challenge notions of why history organizations exist and what they should be doing.

LONG-TERM EFFICIENCIES

Entrepreneurship entails not only attracting new audiences and increasing revenue but also finding ways to curtail expenses. While many organizations have experienced reductions in staffing and other costs, one effort stands out as having potential long-term impact.

In 2009 a sacred notion still held sway: that history organizations are required by their missions to save everything in perpetuity, and to maintain collections to the highest possible standards of care. This placed an inordinate burden on history organizations as they grappled with declining revenue. Should limited resources be spent on collections, or to increase staffing, or to support educational and community programming, or to invest in fund development in order to raise more money? No easy answers.

Around 2011, Trevor Jones, Rainey Tisdale, and Elee Wood began to challenge our thinking about collections, urging others to redefine collections in terms of impact, rather than just in terms of size and condition. Their "Active Collections" website includes thought pieces, case studies, resources, and crazy ideas. This fresh thinking promises to lead to more sustainable collections, as well as more sustainable financial models for our institutions.[1]

HISTORY RELEVANCE

Morris Vogel, director of the Lower East Side Tenement Museum, once told one of my students in an interview, "When you do something that matters, the money will come." This is the essence of entrepreneurship. Do something that is highly valued, that really makes a difference, and people will either pay for it or give you money to do it. The History Relevance Campaign seeks to capture this idea for the entire field of history organizations. By urging history practitioners to define and describe their work in terms of relevance and impact, the campaign leaders hope not only to heighten the value of history but also to strengthen history organizations financially.[2]

It seems almost preposterous to describe historical and cultural institutions as entrepreneurial. The popular view of an entrepreneur in America can be seen any month on the cover of *Inc.* Young, smart, ambitious, hard driving, probably living in California, with a bright idea or new product that will make millions. These are not typically the kinds of people one usually finds working in archives or at historic sites.

Equally absurd, it would seem, is a discussion of entrepreneurial museums at a time when our country is experiencing the worst economy since the Great Depression. Isn't it entrepreneurship, with its unbridled risk-taking and greed, that got us into this mess? Don't we need to get back to basics, avoid new and unproven programs, and stick to what we know?

These popular, but flawed, views belie the true nature of entrepreneurship, which has nothing to do with greed or even getting rich. The term signifies an approach to work that can be applied to any endeavor, including achievement of a nonprofit's mission. Indeed, an entrepreneurial approach may be critical to success, especially in a time of rapid cultural, technological, and economic change What follows are my original thoughts from 2009.

WHAT IS ENTREPRENEURSHIP?

Entrepreneurship is the practice of finding opportunity in change. Entrepreneurs see change as normal and healthy. They routinely analyze how things are changing and shift organizational resources to take advantage of new circumstances. Entrepreneurship is the function that enables an organization to remain effective and relevant as the world around it changes.

If things did not change, doing more of the same, over and over, would maximize the value an organization brings to the public and generate the resources it needs to carry on the work. But of course, things do change. To cite just a few examples, over the past two decades we have seen changes in the ethnic composition of our communities, the ways in which people spend leisure time, the technologies used to communicate, and most recently in the amount of money people have to spend. Every organization has to deal with such changes. Entrepreneurial organizations seek ways to exploit them, turning the changes into new opportunities for building capacity and achieving missions.

In general, leaders in successful entrepreneurial organizations follow these practices:

- **Strategic Thinking**—Leaders regularly think about and discuss how the world external to the organization is changing, and how those changes may offer new opportunities to deliver the mission and build capacity. They see the big picture and the long view. They find ways to match their organizational strengths and assets to external trends in a way that produces something of value to others.
- **Business Thinking**—Although making money is not the goal, they are mindful of the need to generate financial resources to fund the work. They

select opportunities that promise to generate revenue and become financially sustainable.

- **Discipline**—They make decisions based on research and data (not just a hunch), establish specific goals and targets for each undertaking, and track results.
- **Experimental**—They are willing to try new things to see if they will work, with the discipline to learn from both failures and successes.
- **Letting Go**—They are able to abandon efforts and activities that are not producing results, no matter how "sacred."
- **Nimble**—They are able to respond quickly to opportunities, not hampered by internal resistance or bureaucratic decision making.

PERSONAL CHARACTERISTICS OF ENTREPRENEURS

It is a common misperception that entrepreneurs are like gamblers betting on a game of chance. A more apt metaphor would be an adept player competing in a game of skill. They like the uncertainty of a new endeavor and thrive on testing themselves with new challenges. They push themselves into new situations to see if they can make things work. They are constant learners. It is not uncommon to hear an entrepreneur say, "I haven't got this figured out yet, but I will."

Successful entrepreneurs see themselves as making educated decisions, informed by their own knowledge and experience, by their observations, and by what they learn through research. They may follow their gut, but it is an educated gut. This requires discipline. To succeed not only must one gather information and analyze data at the front end, one must also keep a close eye on measurable indicators to know whether or not the endeavor is succeeding. With experience, an entrepreneur becomes adept at reading the external environment for opportunities that others do not see.

Entrepreneurs prefer a flexible rather than a highly structured work environment. They gravitate to the big idea and long-term thinking, and may have difficulty with details. They tend to process information quickly and often are ready to make a decision before others are. This can be frustrating both for the entrepreneur who gets impatient and for others in the organization who need more time to sort through the details and get comfortable with the new idea.

Entrepreneurs are risk-takers. The most successful take the time to assess the risk and make sure that failure of an endeavor does not jeopardize the entire organization. They know to start small and build on success, and are not afraid to cut loose if things are not going well.

This chapter features six entrepreneurial leaders of historical and cultural organizations. Each possesses many of the characteristics just described. In addition, they all share a commitment to preservation, education, scholarship, and interpretation of the past. They are not outsiders brought in to introduce business practices to nonprofit organizations. Rather, they are nonprofit leaders who are by nature entrepreneurial.

BUILDING ENTREPRENEURIAL ORGANIZATIONS

The St. Augustine Lighthouse and Museum in Florida and the Mid-Atlantic Center for the Arts (MAC) in Cape May, New Jersey, are prime examples of entrepreneurial cultural organizations. Each is led by an entrepreneur and each earns approximately 80 percent of annual operating revenue through fees, sales, and other earned income activities. Each exists in a seaside city where tourism is the main economic activity.

In Florida, Kathy Fleming has built an organization with a mission to "discover, preserve, present, and keep alive the story of the nation's oldest port, as symbolized by the working St. Augustine lighthouse." By maximizing the money generated by the lighthouse, including a very profitable gift shop, her organization has been able to support a marine archaeology program, conservation of artifacts, and educational programs.

Fleming embraces the label of entrepreneur. Her organization maximizes revenue so that it can maximize mission. She has seized opportunities to earn revenue, not for the purpose of making a profit, but to build organizational capacity to achieve the mission. She has built a staff that understands the relationship between mission and profit, so that they regularly design programs and services that accomplish both.

Michael Zuckerman in Cape May considers himself an entrepreneurial manager instead of an entrepreneur. In contrast to the business entrepreneurs on his board, who risk their own money on ventures, Zuckerman sees himself as risk-averse. He would not put his own resources on the line, and is very careful about the organization's funds. Still, he is very comfortable with his board's expectation that earnings account for the vast majority of income.

MAC was barely a year old when the board decided to purchase the franchise for the local tourist trolley. They saw this as an opportunity to make money. Zuckerman saw it as an opportunity to create a museum without walls, effectively turning the entire city into a place to present history. From a single open-air trolley three decades ago, MAC now operates five enclosed trolleys that take visitors around the city, including to its own historic properties, the Physick Estate (a nineteenth-century historic house), and the Cape May lighthouse. MAC interpreters ride the trolleys, giving visitors an

Image 6.1.   The St. Augustine Lighthouse and Museum in Florida and the Mid-Atlantic Center for the Arts in Cape May, New Jersey (pictured above), are examples of entrepreneurial organizations. Each is located in a coastal town in which tourism drives the local economy, and each garners nearly 80 percent of its revenue from fees, sales, and other earned income activities. *Source*: Maciej Nabrdalik

engaging and accurate interpretation of the city's history. In addition to the trolleys and historic properties, MAC generates revenue through a host of arts and community events and retail shops. MAC has grown to be one of the largest employers in Cape May.

In their respective organizations, Fleming and Zuckerman have built financial models that generate earned revenue in order to achieve educational missions. Had they been different types of leaders, the outcomes would have been different. Had Zuckerman been averse to entrepreneurship, he would not have survived in his job, given the nature of his board. Had Fleming been just an entrepreneur without a commitment to preservation and education, the St. Augustine Lighthouse would simply be a tourist attraction. Both leaders understand that entrepreneurship in a cultural organization is a means to a greater end.

BRINGING ENTREPRENEURSHIP TO EXISTING ORGANIZATIONS

An organization need not be new, small, or in a tourist environment to be entrepreneurial. Some leaders in large, traditional historical organizations have taken an entrepreneurial approach to bring about change. They have met resistance and persisted, knowing that there was greater risk in doing nothing.

Norman Burns arrived at Maymont in Richmond, Virginia, intent on making change. After only five months of assessing the situation, he surprised his senior managers with an announcement that everyone was fired. He then went on to say: "If the gates of Maymont were closed today and tomorrow morning a new leadership team walked in, would they run Maymont with all its current assets the same way we do?" To a person, every manager answered "No," and then they launched a process to "Remake Maymont."

Maymont is a 100-acre park open free to the public, funded primarily through government and foundation grants and other fundraising activities. The park includes natural habitats for Virginia wildlife, a nature center, gardens, and a historic house. For years these varied components had been treated as distinct entities, mirrored by silos in the staff where one department had little to do with another. In remaking the organization, Burns moved to break down the silos and integrate the visitor experience. Some managers have not survived the transformation. Those remaining have shifted from being a management group to a leadership team, where members take responsibility for the whole, rather than just their respective parts.

Burns challenged the team to increase earnings from food concessions, souvenir shops, and facility rentals. Slowly staff learned how to think with a business sense. The institution implemented a strategy to increase visitor stay time through better integration and linking of the different experiences. Strategic placement of food concessions and retail shops led to increased revenue. A breakthrough came recently when two of the leaders, not Burns, came up with an idea to close an unprofitable shop in order to free space for a more profitable facility rental program.

Challenging the staff in a bureaucracy can be especially difficult. Bureaucrats are primarily concerned with following policies and rules and are wary of change. The staff usually responds to a new idea with a discussion of the reasons why it won't work. If they cannot quash the idea immediately, they will study it for an extended period of time until the idea fades away. They feel justified in these responses because the way they have always done things is the only correct way. In a deep bureaucracy, people are entrenched in a culture that prevents them from seeing and being comfortable with anything new.

Anita Walker was in such a situation as director of the Iowa Department of Cultural Affairs, which includes the State Historical Society. Her direct reports, the bureau chiefs (their titles hint at the nature of the organization) had been with the historical society for many years, some more than twenty. In both her personality and ideas for the future she stood in sharp contrast to the others.

Walker understood that the society had to change. Public participation and appreciation for the organization's work was low, as was morale. For years budget reductions had resulted in a significantly reduced number of staff. The remaining staff felt they had inadequate resources to do their basic jobs, let alone anything new.

When she received a directive to make yet more cuts, Walker gathered the staff and asked them to look around the room at their colleagues. Another half-dozen of them would lose their jobs unless they did something different. They needed to find ways to earn revenue. Not wanting to face more cuts, the staff went along, some reluctantly, others with enthusiasm. They found ways to provide services for a fee to other historical organizations around the state. They increased rentals of the building for events and functions, including weddings. They boosted programming to attract more people to the museum and store. This was not a sea change. The society did not suddenly become an entrepreneurial organization. However, Walker was able to break through resistance and create an opening for staff to initiate innovative programs.

Walker, who now directs the Massachusetts Cultural Council, says, "I think the big learning from my Iowa experience was to recognize the value the non-entrepreneur brings to the table and harness that in a way that everyone can enjoy success. In other words, there are no enemies here, just people who will get there on a different path and a different pace."

PRACTICE MAKES BETTER

One way to foster entrepreneurship is to develop a **3-Month Innovation Cycle** in your organization. Every three months the staff tries something new in order to reach a targeted constituency and achieve organizational objectives. You will need to have an "innovation fund" in your budget, large enough to support the initiatives, but not so large that you risk losing too much money if an initiative fails. In the following example, $1,000 is used for each initiative.

The innovation cycle has three phases. These three phases should take no more than three months. This is to ensure that you are practicing being nimble and quick.

1. Idea Phase

- $1,000 to support an innovative initiative (program, product, or service).
- Initiative must be designed to reach a target constituency and achieve an organizational objective.
- Give funds to an individual (who must create a team and pull others into the process to make it happen).
- Engage people who are creative, entrepreneurial, and comfortable with risks.
- Promote unstructured, out-of-the-box generation of ideas.
- Go outside of the organization to get new ideas.
- Bring outsiders in to spark imagination.
- Come up with something that just might work, but might not.
- Be clear about what you hope will happen, what objectives you hope to meet, and what constituency you hope to serve.

2. Testing Phase

- Develop a detailed, structured implementation plan, with measurable objectives and benchmarks.
- Get advice from people who are really well organized and who know how to get things done.
- Ensure that resources are adequate and used efficiently.
- Set a timetable and stick to it.
- Communicate with all who will be affected by the initiative, so that they know what to expect and can help when needed.
- Include a plan for monitoring progress and evaluating both the output (activities) and the outcome (impact).

3. **Learning Phase**

- Evaluate the initiative against the hoped-for objectives.
- Use dialogue to get a number of perspectives on what worked well and what did not.
- Do not indulge in blaming; the purpose is to learn.
- Assess not only what happened when the initiative was executed but also the process that was used to create the program.
- Come up with ways to do things better next time.

At the end of the Learning Phase you can decide that:

1. **The project is not worth continuing**. Begin a new innovation cycle with a new project.
2. **The project worked fairly well** and you want to run it through the cycle again with improvements.
3. **The project was very successful** and it should become part of your regular services and operations.

CHALLENGING OUR ASSUMPTIONS ABOUT HISTORY ORGANIZATIONS

In bringing change to their organizations, some entrepreneurial leaders have challenged our assumptions about what history organizations do. At the heart of entrepreneurship is the ability to see an organization from the outside in. In Steven Weil's words, it requires a shift in perspective from being *about something* to being *for someone*. An entrepreneur first seeks to understand the needs, interests, and aspirations of others, and then finds ways to realign the organization so that it better serves the public.

In Pittsburgh, Andy Masich and his leadership team at the Senator John Heinz History Center have embraced popular approaches and uses of history. Rather than first deciding what history should be presented and then attempting to get people to visit, they have observed how people already engage with history and adapted their programs and exhibits accordingly.

It is generally accepted that in American society more people are interested in sports than in history. Instead of simply accepting this, the History Center folks found ways to use sports to build interest in history. In one innovative approach they connected Pittsburgh Steelers fans to the Lewis and Clark Expedition through the Rooney family, Pittsburgh natives and longtime owners of the franchise. In 2003, Dan Rooney and members of his extended family retraced the expedition, which began in Pittsburgh 200 years earlier and ended at the Pacific coast in Oregon. Fans were able to share the adventure on the website for the Steelers, in an exhibit at the museum, and in a publication.

Similarly, while some in our field have decried the TV program *Antiques Roadshow* because of its emphasis on the monetary value of historical objects, Masich saw an opportunity. The History Center partnered with a local station to produce *Pittsburgh's Hidden Treasures*. More than 2,000 people showed up at the History Center on a Saturday to have artifacts appraised, which resulted in a series of seven half-hour TV shows that drew 150,000 viewers and the highest Nielsen ratings in the region for the time slot. People learned not only the monetary value of an object but also how it fit into the context of the city's history.

Masich is deeply passionate about history. His entrepreneurial approach blends popular culture with sound historical scholarship. This is evident in the use of radio, television, and the Internet to reach new audiences. In ten years, public awareness has increased from 4 to 80 percent and attendance and revenue at the History Center have nearly doubled.

Another organization that has contested traditional notions of historical organizations is The Strong (nee, The Strong National Museum of Play) in Rochester, New York.[3] Change occurred there because its leaders were dissatisfied with the number of visitors they served. They could have continued to produce social history exhibits that attracted about 130,000 visitors a year, a respectable number for a history museum. Instead they surveyed the needs and interests of their community, responded with exhibits and programs for children and families, and now serve more than a half million visitors annually.

CEO G. Rollie Adams and his colleagues at The Strong took heat for their actions. Professional colleagues criticized them for abandoning the mission of preserving and interpreting the past. For several years the museum seemed to have two faces, a children's museum on the first floor and a history museum on the second. It took time to resolve this ambiguous situation. It wasn't fully settled until the leaders articulated a new mission that revolved around the cultural importance of play. This integrated the family audience with the greatest strengths of the historical collections: dolls, toys, and games.

As Adams's experience at The Strong reflects, entrepreneurship requires a degree of comfort with ambiguity. Things are not always perfectly clear in advance, but that's okay. Part of the challenge, and reward, is to put things in motion and see what happens.

RISK AND FAILURE

In the 1990s there were some high-profile entrepreneurial ventures in the history field that failed. That was a time when many thought that a dramatic expansion of facilities and programs would lead to greater visitation and revenue; if you built it, they would come.

I was personally involved in one such case, as deputy director and later as executive director of the Baltimore City Life Museums. We took a big risk in opening a new exhibition facility without having raised sufficient funds for programming and endowment. When visitation did not meet expectations, we began a downward spiral of cuts in staff and programs, which ultimately led to closing the institution.

The Baltimore case is an extreme example of a situation many historical organizations have faced. Decisions to expand programs and facilities have led to increased operating costs with no increase in revenue. Sometimes the organization carries a debt, placing a further drag on operations. In making such decisions, leaders have failed to fully grasp and manage the risk involved. To guard against excessive risk, successful entrepreneurs examine with great care the assumptions behind financial projections. Notably they take small steps to test ideas and track results, rather than putting the entire organization at risk.

Here is what Kathy Fleming in St. Augustine says, "Many actions fail. I can't put my finger on all the failures there are so many. If it doesn't work it isn't a tragedy, we just try something else. Our museum Super Bowl event [the year the game was played in nearby Jacksonville,] that was a big [letdown]. Products fail daily. So far using eBay has not worked really well for us."

Michael Zuckerman in Cape May describes the failure of a retail shop on the boardwalk in nearby Wildwood, a seaside town that has experienced a renaissance based on its heyday in the 1950s and 1960s. For several years MAC offered Doo Wop tours of Wildwood and opening a themed shop there appeared promising. As it turned out they lost $100,000 in two years. Zuckerman says, "It was painful, but not life threatening."

Entrepreneurial organizations learn from success as well as failure. Exceptional results can lead to more innovation. In a comment made in early 2009 about her organization's response to the economic downturn, Fleming says, "We noticed that specialty tours at a certain price point are doing very well, so we've created mini task forces of teams of employees to create new specialty tours and offerings."

These comments reveal typical entrepreneurial behavior with regard to risk: look for new opportunities, respond in a timely way, take small steps, track results, build on success, and drop anything that doesn't work before it becomes a major failure.

GHOST TOURS

"Over my dead body." This was Zuckerman's response when tour givers approached him in 2000 with a proposal to conduct ghost tours in Cape May. However, by 2003, MAC was facing falling visitation due to changes in the tourism market, as well as state budget cuts. So they began to offer ghost tours, Halloween programming, and lectures about the history of spiritualism in the nineteenth century. These activities now account for about 5 percent of revenue.

Similarly, Kathy Fleming's staff initially resisted ghost tours of the St. Augustine Lighthouse, in spite of growing demand spurred by the tower being featured on a popular television program about haunted places. Their response was to offer tours through a for-profit subsidiary that they had set up previously as a merchandizing and consulting venture. These profitable "Dark of the Moon" tours are helping the organization weather the economic recession. The tours focus on the facts of who really lived and died at the historic site, and not just the telling of ghost stories. They also allow time to quietly experience the site without spoken interpretation. The revenue from this program will top $200,000.

There is no question that growing interest in the supernatural and paranormal has been a trend in American culture over the past decade. This is the kind of observable fact that entrepreneurs ponder. Does this trend offer an opportunity to generate revenue in support of one's mission? Leaders with an entrepreneurial bent are more comfortable than others in entertaining, and even capitalizing on, this possibility.

Is this a compromise in values? Some may think so. However, just as museum leaders of The Strong lived with ambiguity as they realigned their mission, it may well be that in time the spiritual dimension of historic places will come to be viewed as a legitimate way to experience the past. Stay tuned.

HOW ENTREPRENEURIAL IS YOUR ORGANIZATION?

This assessment will reveal how entrepreneurial your organization is: the higher the score, the greater the degree of entrepreneurship.

In order to identify areas for improvement, ask staff to complete this questionnaire. Senior leaders should then analyze the results and determine a course of action to increase the practice of entrepreneurship.

	Strongly Disagree	Disagree	Not Sure	Agree	Strongly Agree	Total
Our work schedules are flexible and somewhat unpredictable, depending on what is needed at a given time.	1	2	3	4	5	
We like to experiment with new programs and new ways of doing things.	1	2	3	4	5	
We have high levels of energy and enthusiasm at work.	1	2	3	4	5	
We regularly talk about what is going on outside of our organization in our community and in the lives of the people we serve.	1	2	3	4	5	
We regularly go out, observe, question, and listen to our stakeholders (e.g., members, visitors, donors, community leaders).	1	2	3	4	5	
Before we implement a new idea we clearly define what we want to achieve and a way to track results.	1	2	3	4	5	
We have an inclusive, yet quick, decision-making process.	1	2	3	4	5	
We base our decisions on an analysis of data, and we act once we are about 60 percent sure of the best course of action.	1	2	3	4	5	
We are curious about why some activities work well for us, and some do not.	1	2	3	4	5	
We build on our successes by reallocating time and resources away from activities that are not as successful.	1	2	3	4	5	
We do not shy away from talking about our organization as a business.	1	2	3	4	5	
We do not hesitate to stop doing a program or activity that is not (or is no longer) producing the desired results.	1	2	3	4	5	
We are able to respond to opportunities quickly, not hampered by internal resistance or bureaucratic decision making.	1	2	3	4	5	

(Continued)

John W. Durel

(*Continued*)

	Strongly Disagree	Disagree	Not Sure	Agree	Strongly Agree	Total
We reward innovation—whether it succeeds or not.	1	2	3	4	5	
We treat mistakes and failures as opportunities to learn.	1	2	3	4	5	
We manage risks by taking small, incremental steps and tracking results.	1	2	3	4	5	
We have money held in reserve to try new programs and ways of doing things.	1	2	3	4	5	
We are comfortable with ambiguity and uncertainty.	1	2	3	4	5	
We expect things to change and look upon change as an opportunity to better achieve our mission.	1	2	3	4	5	
TOTAL						

NOTES

1. See chapter 1 and www.activecollections.org.

2. See chapter 10 for more details on the History Relevance Campaign or www.historyrelevance.com.

3. See chapters 3 and 6 for more details on The Strong.

Chapter 7

A Twenty-First-Century Renaissance

Bob Beatty

Despite the fact that many history institutions have proven their worth as community leaders, our audiences still do not reflect the changing demographics of American society. Public history must address the disconnect why audiences (and the field itself) are trending older and white. People in communities across the nation embrace heritage, identity, and place—elements history can empower. Demographics are an issue certainly, but our challenges extend beyond engaging diverse participation. The way we present history must change even for our current demographics as well.

It is simply not enough to preserve the oldest house in town or to display cases of artifacts. We must do as public historian Tim Grove documents in *A Grizzly in the Mail and Other Adventures in American History*. We must "show that history is not the boring subject of a childhood classroom but a rich and profound exploration of the tapestry of life."[1] History museums, historic sites, historical societies, historic house museums, and the like are the ideal places where this profound exploration occurs. These institutions are where connections happen.

In 2016, AASLH held its annual meeting in Detroit, Michigan, in partnership with the Michigan Museums Association. The city itself had gone through many profound changes throughout its history, as David A. Janssen, the 2016 program chair, writes here. As we worked together on a theme for the meeting that would reflect history's role in individual and corporate life, we found one that resonated with the field as well, *The Spirit of Rebirth*.

"Collectively and individually," Janssen wrote in the meeting theme document, "we are constantly evolving, embracing new opportunities, and reacting to forces beyond our control. Navigating these contemporary challenges, while facing an unpredictable future, requires periodically rethinking our direction." History organizations and history professionals are an essential part of this renaissance for communities. "We rely on the past for context, examples, and inspiration. The role of a public historian is especially critical during times of transition."[2]

Seizing the responsibilities and opportunities that role provides is critical to the public history profession. This requires a renewed commitment to staying abreast of challenges and opportunities writ large and small. "We must anticipate changes within our profession. The shifting demographics of our audiences and our offices; the increasing pressure on our finances and partnering organizations; and questions about the relevance of our work in a nation beset by discordant political dialogue all require self-reflection." Most importantly, he argued, "We need to review the assumptions that have served us to this point, question old processes, and ponder outdated interpretations."[3] This is the very definition of rebirth.

Janssen was an obvious choice to chair the Program Committee in Detroit. Not only had he spent a significant part of his career in the Motor City, he had also lived through and led efforts in rethinking the historical enterprise at Brucemore in Cedar Rapids, Iowa, and in stints in the Detroit area at the Edsel and Eleanor Ford House and at the Detroit Historical Society. Janssen was also one of thirty invited attendees to the 2007 Kykuit Summit.[4]

Although it occurred a little over a year before the beginning of the Great Recession, the subject matter of that 2007 gathering nonetheless reflected well the "New Normal" the recession wrought. Conferees deliberated on standards and best practices for the field and on Donna Ann Harris's *New Solutions for House Museums* (a book that explored in depth the concept of adaptive reuse of historic buildings versus the advisability of opening new museums).[5] The conversation also included funders and attendees grappling with the funder-issued challenge of institutions better defining their cultural value (or relevance).

Nearly a decade after the gathering, Kykuit's findings still resonate. They reflect questions and issues that in many ways define the profession's present and its future. Jay D. Vogt articulated the findings in the Autumn 2007 *History News*.

- Successful stewardship of the nation's historic sites requires financial sustainability.
- Sustainability begins with each historic site's engagement with its community and its willingness to change its structure, programs, and services in response to the changing needs of that community.
- The long-accepted tourism business model is not a sustainable business model for most historic sites.
- Serving the needs of the local community (not the tourist audience) is the most valuable and most sustainable goal for most historic sites.

- Attendance figures are not the most valid measure of the positive value and impact of the historic site experience.
- Many professional standards and practices in the historic site field were borrowed from the museum community and, in practice, often deter creativity and sustainability at historic sites.
- New standards of stewardship for historic sites should be modeled to reflect the distinct nature of these places.
- Responsible site stewardship achieves a sustainable balance between the needs of the buildings, landscapes, collections, and the visiting public.
- The buildings, landscapes, and collections are the means but not the ends of the work of historic sites.
- Innovation, experimentation, collaboration, and a broad sharing of the resulting information are essential to achieving historic site sustainability on a broad scale.
- Undefined collecting, coupled with professional standards and practices regarding deaccessioning, is an impediment to change and sustainability.
- Program, challenge, and matching grants can reduce long-term sustainability by shifting focus away from operating and endowment needs and by encouraging the growth of non–mission-related programs.
- Returning sites to private ownership with proper easements can be a positive means of ensuring long-term stewardship.[6]

These thirteen findings are included here whole cloth because they remain relevant to the world of history organizations. In many ways they reflect the "How" of the business model of our institutions. And since the "business" of public history can be a sometimes messy and somewhat unfulfilling slough of budget-balancing, preservation challenges, and fundraising, it is important to again revisit the "Why" of our work. History is critically important to ourselves in identity and critical thinking; to our communities as vital places to live and work and in economic development; and to the future in nurturing engaged citizens, inspiring leadership, and leaving a legacy for future generations.[7]

The findings warrant deeper examination. One sums up well the entire history enterprise, "Sustainability begins with each historic site's engagement with its community and its willingness to change its structure, programs, and services in response to the changing needs of that community."[8]

In preparation for the Kykuit meeting, John and Anita Nowrey Durel drafted "A Golden Age for Historic Properties," a white paper later reprinted in *History News*. In it, the Durels called for change in how the field thought about audience. "Stop thinking of 'visitors' and start thinking of 'members' . . . Stop thinking of 'them' and start thinking of 'us.'"[9]

The Durels' model encouraged history organizations' deep engagement with what all assumed would be the soon-to-be-retiring baby boomer

generation (the recession postponed the retirement plans of many). They proposed strategies for history organizations that capitalized on the opportunity
to provide a venue for like-minded people to pursue common interests. "Many
retirees will want to deepen their knowledge or perfect a skill," they wrote.
They saw our institutions as the perfect antidote. "Many sites have collections,
libraries, work spaces, equipment, and expertise to enable them to do so."[10]

They advocated the establishment of affinity communities of volunteers
serving institutions in capacities far beyond what volunteers are typically
allowed to do. History organizations become a place for these groups to
gather, and they plan programs and activities for their own affinity community under the aegis of the museum or site.

The affinity group model is one I have employed in a variety of ways in
my career. I was dubious the first time I saw it in action, but I am a full-
fledged believer and evangelist for the process. I've used the model at a
history museum, at AASLH, in a community advisory community, in service
on boards of directors, and other ways. It deeply involves volunteers in their
work for the cause, and it leads to increased connection to the institution
(often resulting in memberships and donations). It is an example of engagement with a community and a willingness to change structure, programs, and
services in response to changing community needs.

These connections highlight another of the Durels' arguments that as
history institutions we should move from a pure focus on intellectual and
social content and begin including spiritual content as well. "Historic sites
are physical spaces with strong spiritual qualities," they wrote. "Moving
beyond the materialism that has dominated American life for the past half-
century, more and more people are looking for meaning and purpose in
their lives. . . . The spiritual qualities of historic sites can serve as sources
of insight and inspiration for people who seek an experience that transcends
the mundane."[11] History organizations should cultivate these meaning-
inspired activities.

This requires a revolution in intellectual authority as well. "Stop thinking
of interpretation and start thinking of facilitation," they urged. It is a theme
that resonates. Tim Grove called the concept "Radical Trust." Historian
Benjamin Filene and Laura Koloski and Bill Adair of Pew's Heritage Philadelphia Program dubbed it "Letting Go." Robert P. Connolly and Elizabeth
Bollwerk use the term "Co-creation." Researchers Tom Satwicz and Kris
Morrisey label it "Public Curation." Others refer to it as "Shared Authority."[12]
Whatever the phrase, each term hearkens the change in authoritative voice
long held by museums and history organizations. While not new in the world
of history organizations, one factor has hastened its implementation—the
ubiquity of the Internet. This has created what Lee Rainie, director of the

Pew Internet and American Life project, dubs "the golden age of the flowering of amateur experts." Radical trust, Grove notes, "offers opportunities to reach and engage new audiences," but it is certainly challenging for history professionals.[13]

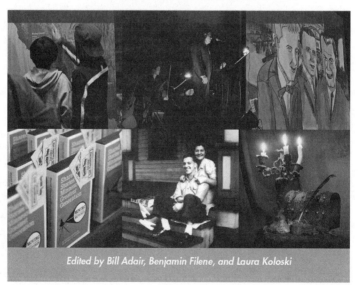

Image 7.1.   Books by Bill Adair, Laura Koloski, and Benjamin Filene (left) and Robert P. Connolly and Elizabeth Bollwerk (right) each address strategies history organizations can effectively employ in the era of shared authority. Source: Pew Center for Arts and Heritage and Rowman & Littlefield

POSITIONING YOUR MUSEUM AS A CRITICAL COMMUNITY ASSET

A PRACTICAL GUIDE

Edited by ROBERT P. CONNOLLY & ELIZABETH BOLLWERK

Rose Sherman of the Minnesota Historical Society sees many positives in the trend especially as it relates to community engagement. "If our institutions are to be centers for civic engagement," she acknowledged, "then we must embrace radical trust in our online programs as well as our onsite programs. We need to loosen the reins of control inherent to the authoritative voice." This helps achieve the ideal of deeper community immersion. "By empowering our publics to participate in the documentation of history," Sherman noted, "we acknowledge that we don't have all the information. We create passionate fans who feel that they've contributed to history."[14]

Some do not feel as sanguine about the principle. "I believe strongly that museums should share authority with the public," Jim Gardner of the National Archives expressed. But he also voiced concern "about the blurring of the line between knowledge and opinion." The former, Gardner maintained, "is at the heart of our brands as historical organizations . . . [and] we need to resist the current impulse to welcome (and thereby validate) any and all opinions." This issue greatly vexes the field. In a world of information overload, how do we negotiate a role that, as Gardner argues, "both builds on who we are and what our strengths are and also engages and challenges the public in new ways"?[15]

Gardner advocated for a more active role on behalf of history organizations in this endeavor. Kent Whitworth of the Kentucky Historical Society felt likewise: "If in fact a new, younger audience is engaging with history through organizations that trust them to do so, then I want us to participate and benefit. On the other hand, I certainly don't want to pursue a radical trust approach until we can properly resource it. . . . [T]his will require staff resources—and the right staff. So much for radical trust!"[16]

Whitworth's final comment reflects a struggle many public history professionals have with the concept: How can one engage in radical trust when she or he only hands over partial control to the public? Is this truly radical trust? Interestingly enough, institutional involvement in these activities is not mutually exclusive from radical trust. In fact, it enhances the experience, as Adair, Filene, and Koloski concluded in *Letting Go? Historical Authority in a User-Generated World* (2011). "'Letting go,'" Filene reported, "requires *more* involvement, not less, from museum professionals."[17] "Audiences express themselves more creatively and confidently," they discovered, "if operating within, not beyond, boundaries." It may seem counterintuitive, but they found that "constraints—word counts, canvas boundaries, time limits—[actually] encourage free-form work. The amount and quality of creative participation increases when visitors are guided by smart question prompts, stencils, or menus of choices."[18]

Adair, Filene, and Koloski found that "the public wants rich interpretations and fresh, accurate information."[19] And therefore interpretation remains important; it just should include the community's voice as well. Expertise is therefore "deployed in different forms and alloyed with the talents of others." This takes considerable skill. Staff don't simply open an institution's doors (literally or metaphorically) and leave participants to do what they wish. Instead, the authors wrote, "They lay the groundwork to enable visitors to participate successfully: they identify multiple pathways through the content; build bridges that visitors can cross between the stories from the past and their own experiences; and offer tools visitors can use to make new discoveries, cut new pathways, and build new bridges."[20]

This is where facilitation enters the equation. History professionals, they conclude, "supplement content knowledge with expertise at interpreting, facilitating, engaging, listening, and learning with their visitors." As Adair, Filene, and Koloski argue, "What the institution 'lets go' of is not expertise but the assumption that the museum has the last word on historical interpretation. . . . This scenario involves letting go of the notion (usually illusory in any case) that one can or should control all outcomes in the museum."[21] This is the very essence of the principles of radical trust and letting go.

While these concepts aren't new, the Internet has certainly made them much more easily attainable for history organizations and for our audiences. The latter expects this process of co-creation. They often demand the opportunity to curate their own experience. History organizations are seeking ways to provide this. "If we let visitors go in new directions," the authors of *Letting Go?* suggest, "they may take us to areas of fresh discovery, give our work more reach, and, along the way, forge stronger relationships with the museums that have enabled the journey."[22] Substitute the words "visitor" and "museum" with "stakeholder" and "historical society" or "guest" and "historic site," or any term that fits your unique circumstance. Either way, the principle remains the same: history organizations are much more successful and essential when they provide opportunities for deeper, more meaningful engagement.

This leads to another Kykuit finding. Most would agree that "attendance figures are not the most valid measure of the positive value and impact of the historic site experience." Done well—"making a place for magic," as Bill Tramposch wrote—the effect can be so much more. "We can measure attendance, fundraising efforts, revenues, size of collections," Tramposch continued, "but do we appreciate as much the immeasurable aspects of our work? Education by definition brings about change. Sometimes that change can be measured, but more often our *ultimate* influence upon our visitor eludes us."[23]

A better measure of success is this: "Does your audience love you?" The answer, Janssen believes, "Defines a level of support beyond volunteering, donating, and advocating. It suggests an identity for historic sites that is not based solely on pride in local history, but in an immediate, real, and regular contribution to the lives of neighbors."[24]

Thus far the only way our field has found to measure these contributions are either financial—do we operate in the black and not the red?—or attendance numbers. But this does not get to the figurative or literal heart of the work of public history: the impact of involvement with history organizations. We've articulated the value of history, but we have not measured it.

In their groundbreaking 1998 book, *The Presence of the Past: Popular Uses of History in American Life*, historians Roy Rosenzweig and David Thelen offered a finding that remains, nearly twenty years later, oft-cited in the circles of public historians and history professionals. Museums, Rosenzweig and Thelen found, were Americans' single most trustworthy source of information—more than relatives, eyewitnesses, history professors and teachers, books, and movies and television.[25]

Though their research is more than two decades old, it speaks to the tremendous opportunities ahead for historical agencies in impacting our communities, our states, and our nation.[26] But this is simply a starting point. Yes, it's great to know that history organizations are trusted, and that radical trust/letting go strategies are helping us to further fan the flames of that trust, but we do not know the true value we provide. And if we cannot verbalize it, how can we expect our stakeholders to do so on our behalf?

Despite years of evaluation in one way or another, we lack the mechanism for articulating our true value as history organizations. As I'm writing, AASLH is working with the History Relevance Campaign on a set of common metrics to articulate how history organizations meet the Value of History statement. Here's hoping that effort bears fruit. This is the existential question of our time.

NOTES

1. Tim Grove, *A Grizzly in the Mail and Other Adventures in American History* (Lincoln: University of Nebraska Press, 2014), xiii.

2. David A. Janssen, "The Spirit of Rebirth," 2016 American Association for State and Local History Annual Meeting theme.

3. Ibid.

4. While the meeting focused on historic sites, its conversations and lessons apply across the spectrum. See chapter 5 for more thoughts on the Kykuit summit.

5. Harris's book is a must-have on the bookshelf of any public historian. See Donna Ann Harris, *New Solutions for House Museums: Ensuring the Long-Term Preservation of America's Historic Houses* (Lanham, MD: AltaMira Press, 2007).

6. All of the information on the Kykuit meeting culled from Jay D. Vogt, "The Kykuit II Summit: The Sustainability of Historic Sites," *History News*, 62, no. 4 (Autumn 2007): 21.

7. History Relevance Campaign, "The Value of History: Seven Ways It Is Essential," 2014, http://www.historyrelevance.com/value-statement, accessed October 28, 2016.

8. Vogt, 21.

9. John Durel and Anita Nowrey Durel, "A Golden Age for Historic Properties," *History News* 62, no. 3 (Summer 2007): 7.

10. Ibid., 9.

11. Ibid., 7, 11–12.

12. Connolly and Bollwerk, *Positioning Your Museum as a Critical Community Asset*; Bill Adair, Benjamin Filene, and Laura Koloski, eds., *Letting Go? Sharing Historical Authority in a User-Generated World* (Philadelphia, PA: The Pew Center for Arts & Heritage, 2011), 196.

13. Tim Grove, "Grappling with the Concept of Radical Trust," *History News* 65, no. 2 (Spring 2010): 5. See also "What's Radical about Radical after Trust?" audio recording of 2010 AASLH/OMA Annual Meeting session, at http://resource.aaslh.org/view/whats-radical-about-radical-trust/ and online discussion at http://aaslhcommunity.org/historynews/radical-trust/.

14. Grove, "Grappling," 5.

15. Ibid.

16. Ibid.

17. Benjamin Filene, "Letting Go? Sharing Historical Authority in a User-Generated World," *History News* 66, no. 4 (Autumn 2011): 8.

18. Adair et al., 12.

19. Ibid.

20. Ibid., 13.

21. Ibid.

22. Ibid., 15.

23. Bill Tramposch, " 'That Would Be Good Both Going and Coming Back,'" *History News* 68, no. 1 (Winter 2013): 17.

24. David A. Janssen, "The Power and Predicament of Historic Sites," *History News* 65, no. 2 (Spring 2010): 9.

25. Roy Rosenzweig and David Thelen, *The Presence of the Past: Popular Uses of History in American Life* (New York: Columbia University Press, 1998), 21.

26. Recent research from Reach Advisors notes that this trustworthiness from the public remains. See chapter 21.

Chapter 8

The Spirit of Rebirth

David A. Janssen

Detroit, Michigan, has a long, proud, and remarkable history. Just as the Detroit River connects great lakes, the city has linked great societies. For more than three centuries, its promise of opportunity and its legacy of innovation drew countless traders and tradesmen, entrepreneurs, and entertainers; inventors and industrialists; laborers and leaders. Administered at various times by French, British, and American governments, Detroit remains one of the busiest international crossing points in the United States. Today, the rich heritage of the oldest city in the Midwest offers a timely setting to consider the relevance of our past in shaping our future.

While the backstory of the city is impressive, the contemporary challenges faced by Detroit's citizenry are daunting. In both practical and symbolic terms, there may be no other region in America in greater need of choosing a road forward. The ways in which experience and identity may inform those choices are pertinent to any discussion about the relevance of history. Public historians hoping to validate that connection may point Detroiters to their past for ideas, examples, and inspiration. However, gathering on the banks of the Detroit River is also a chance to turn that lens back on ourselves. As a field, we may also be at a bifurcation point. Competing with loosely vetted information streams, appealing to distracted audiences, in the midst of social shifts of both local and national proportions, we too need to define our path. In that endeavor, Detroit is a source of inspiration for us as well.

Detroit is a study in change and adaptation. Each century brought with it a new set of challenges and opportunities. Human occupation of the area dates back to 9000 BCE. By the time French traders pushed into the Great Lakes region of the continent's interior, there were already an estimated 10,000 native people—Potawatomi, Ottawa, Ojibwa/Chippewa, Miami, and Huron—living in what is now Michigan.[1]

The name Detroit (for both the city and the river) stems from the French reference to the "strait of Lake Erie," or *le Detroit du Lac Erie*. In 1701, with permission from the French government, Antoine Laumet de La Mothe, sieur de Cadillac, began laying the groundwork for Fort Pontchartrain du Detroit to secure an outpost between Lake Erie and Lake Huron. The settlement grew based on farming and trade with Native Americans, and by 1751 the village counted 483 residents, including 33 enslaved people.[2]

In the second half of the eighteenth century, warring factions vied for command of the strategic settlement. Great Britain took Fort Detroit during the French and Indian War, validated by the 1763 Treaty of Paris, and fought off subsequent attacks led by Ottawa Chief Pontiac. Although the United States formally won control of Detroit through the 1783 Treaty of Paris, the English lingered until the Jay Treaty in 1796 settled the matter.

Detroit's nineteenth century began inauspiciously when fire all but destroyed the village in 1805. The territorial government of Michigan secured Congress's permission to expand the town as part of its rebuilding plans. In 1806, the city incorporated, three decades before Michigan was formally admitted to the Union. By midcentury, Detroit grew to a city of 21,000, who secured a prominent role for the city in that generation's overriding issue: human bondage. Through the efforts of black and white residents like George de Baptiste, Seymour Finney, Dr. Nathan Thomas, and countless others, Detroit served as a terminus on the Underground Railroad for enslaved people fleeing the South. With the Fugitive Slave Act of 1850, Detroit's international border with Canada transformed it from safe haven to throughway for people no longer legally protected from being returned to slavery. The city thus served as the doorway to freedom for thousands of enslaved people.

By 1900, Detroit boasted a population of more than 285,000. In the next fifty years, that number doubled an astonishing six times, surpassing 1.84 million people by the end of World War II. At the heart of that expansion was the automobile. Led by Henry Ford's introduction of the Model T in 1908, Detroit transformed into an industrial juggernaut that turned an expensive novelty into a middle-class rite of passage. Ford Motor Company doubled its production every year between 1909 and 1919, when it produced over 535,000 cars. Across Detroit in 1910, 5,304 people were directly employed in automobile manufacturing. Ten years later, that number jumped to over 35,000, and by 1929, Detroit employed over 158,000 in automobile factories. In 1929, the region cranked out over 5.4 million cars.[3]

Those factories heralded the onslaught of industrial modernization and drew hundreds of thousands of people to the urban workforce. The automobile transformed American society in incalculable ways, and Detroit's combination of revolutionary innovation and a blue-collar work ethic made it a manufacturing epicenter. When World War II erupted, its industrial leadership and workforce transformed factories into war production mode. That shift happened so quickly and effectively, it is easy to underestimate the herculean effort it required. A year before the Japanese attack on Pearl Harbor, Franklin Roosevelt had called upon the United States to become the Arsenal of Democracy. Detroit's populace assumed that role like no other community. By 1944, Ford's Willow Run plant alone was producing a B-24 bomber every hour.[4]

The latter half of Detroit's twentieth century was far less inspiring. The auto industry eliminated more than 300,000 jobs beginning in the 1940s. Property values fell by 77 percent. Riotous violence in 1943, and again in 1967, uncovered troubling racial divisions. Today, Detroit presents social scientists with a model for postindustrialization in the United States.

In his groundbreaking study of the city, *The Origins of the Urban Crisis: Race and Inequality in Postwar Detroit*, historian Thomas Sugrue distilled the complex interplay of forces that define contemporary Detroit. Sugrue argued persuasively that the loss of employment opportunity in the wake of deindustrialization, discrimination for the remaining opportunities, and racial segregation in the neighborhoods and suburbs all combined to undermine the once booming city. From its peak of nearly two million people in 1950, to its fall below three-quarters of a million sixty years later, Detroit can no longer claim a spot among the likes of Chicago, New York, Los Angeles, or Houston as a major urban center.[5]

Today that reality is illustrated by the abandoned factories, classrooms, theaters, and homes that have become a favorite subject for guerilla photographers. The cottage industry—referred to as "ruin porn" by Detroiters—presents gratuitous, haunting metaphors of urban decline. Already battling very real socioeconomic issues, the region bears the additional burden of an image problem. Detroit frequently served as a punch line, its complex story reduced to oversimplified explanations and blame. The perils of accepting an elementary understanding of Detroit's story are not limited to the future of southeast Michigan.

The implications, as Sugrue underscored, are much more broad. "Urban America," he wrote, "continues to be shaped by processes that have their origins deep in the mid-twentieth century. Coming to grips with that history is not a mere academic exercise. History is a process, ongoing, that at once opens up possibilities and constrains our choices in the present. To come to grips with the problems and promises of our cities, we must grapple with the past as a means to engaging with the present."[6]

Overcoming these currents and forging a new course has forced Detroit's citizens to negotiate the competing interests of its past to reimagine a bold future. In doing so, the region is once again working to craft a new identity.

In 2013, Detroit declared bankruptcy—the largest American city ever to do so. The path forward from that historic low held significant implications for museums. The state-appointed emergency manager called for an appraisal of city-owned collections at the Detroit Institute of Art. The prospect of selling collections to pay off the massive debt and fund city pensions raised enormous concern within the museum community. Ultimately, multiple foundations, the Detroit Institute of Arts (DIA), and the State of Michigan donated $816 million to reduce the impact on retiree pensions and establish the DIA as an entity independent of the city. With the "Grand Bargain" in place, the city emerged from bankruptcy in 2014.

As Sugrue documented, proponents in the wake of that agreement have offered visions of a new Detroit relying on a range of disparate strategies: farming and agricultural cooperatives, a resurgence of its industrial might, a white-collar business hub mindful of Pittsburgh's post-steel rebirth, and the gentrification of its historic districts with artists. The city has also worked to foster economic development through professional sports and casinos.

In *Reimagining Detroit: Opportunities for Redefining an American City,* John Gallagher underscored the importance of human geography in the equation. Gallagher pointed out that Detroit's sprawling footprint is larger than that of Boston, San Francisco, and Manhattan combined. With responsibility for such a massive infrastructure and a simultaneously dwindling population and tax base, Detroit found itself trapped in a vicious cycle. Gallagher advocated strategic downsizing that looks to Baltimore, rather than Chicago, for an aspirational model.[7]

While the solutions for charting its future are still fragmented, it seems clear that Detroit is in another pivotal chapter in its story. Just like the city's roles in previous eras, Detroit's navigation of its postindustrial existence has implications for the rest of the country. As a nation, we too are constantly evolving, embracing new opportunities, and reacting to forces beyond our control. Understanding these contemporary challenges and facing an unpredictable future require periodically rethinking our direction. In doing so, we rely on the past for context. The role of a public historian is especially critical during times of transition.

Yet within the contemporary public history profession, we are familiar with the concern that too many Americans don't know their history. Statistical and anecdotal evidence abounds. According to the U.S. Department of Education, in five surveys spanning twenty years, "A substantial majority of children in the assessed grades failed to demonstrate proficiency in U.S. history." In a 2012 study by Xavier University's Center for the Study of the American Dream, one in three native-born U.S. citizens failed the naturalization test given to immigrating citizens. Though purposeful in its provocation, former *Tonight Show* host Jay Leno regularly aired segments of the comedian asking people on the street basic U.S. history questions. Meant for comedic effect (and still available via a simple YouTube search), the segment is gratuitously depressing to those of us in the history field.[8]

Image 8.1. "The role of a public historian is especially critical during times of transition," wrote David A. Janssen, 2016 Annual Meeting program chair. *Source*: Brucemore, Inc.

This apparent deficiency is especially significant in the context of the current national climate. Angry histrionics within American political discourse are not a modern phenomenon. Still, the increasing polarization of the electorate in the post-9/11 United States is notable. A clear, reasoned understanding of historical context would seem most important as a stabilizing element during anxious debates about the future. In that context, a March 1, 2016, exchange between CNN political analysts Van Jones and Jeffrey Lord is illustrative. In their heated exchange, Jones characterized the Ku Klux Klan as a terrorist organization that he felt presidential candidates should rebuke as lustily as they do other violent extremists. Lord interrupted to assert the Klan as a "leftist terrorist organization" that "is part of the base of the Democratic party," admonishing Jones, "For God's sake, read your history!"[9]

Candidates who seek elective office and the pundits who support them regularly reference history. But what role do we have in providing context and interpretation, without necessarily taking sides? Do we have the capacity as a profession to inject ourselves formally into contemporary debates or do we cede that role to our colleagues in academia?

Another example—one that history organizations have indeed worked to address—is the debate over Confederate iconography. In the aftermath of a horrific shooting in 2015 at Mother Emanuel African Methodist Episcopal Church in Charleston, South Carolina, the long-simmering debate came to a boil. A national discussion ensued on the appropriateness of Confederate symbols and monuments in public or government spaces. Defenders of the symbols point to the Confederate imagery as acknowledgment of a people's heritage and preservation of the past. The countervailing argument, of course, is that much of the monuments and iconography emerged in direct response to swelling civil rights sentiment among African Americans, invoking the worst legacies of that heritage. Both sides use history as justification for their argument.

There is clearly an intersection between public history and contemporary politics. It is a concept championed by the History Relevance Campaign. Among the ways it is essential to our future, history "can clarify misperceptions, reveal complexities, temper volatile viewpoints, open people to new possibilities, and lead to more effective solutions for today's challenges." The significance in contemporary American society of knowing our past seems clear. Historical knowledge is a matter of the complex versus the simplistic; diversity of perspective versus divisiveness of intent; contextual breadth versus immediate reaction.[10]

If historical knowledge is a vital tool during times of transition, it follows that history organizations have a role to fill. To the extent that "all politics is local," there must be a corollary for history as well. While these debates play out on a national stage, they resonate locally. Like Detroit, the public history profession must take into account a changing reality. National Endowment for the Arts statistics on historic site visitation are indicative of the challenge. As people aged they were less likely to visit a historic site. In each of the three cohorts for which the most complete data are available, the drop-off in historic site visitation over the life course is at least 25 percent.

The data reveal generational differences with respect to Americans' tendency to visit historic sites. With each birth cohort, Americans of all ages have been less likely to visit historic sites. For example, those born from 1938 to 1947 had a 45 percent likelihood of having visited a historic site in the previous year when they were in their thirties and forties, while those born between 1968 and 1977 had only a 23 percent likelihood of having visited a historic site when they were the same age.[11]

As we advocate for the relevance of history, we must also assess our capacity to fulfill its potential—as individual organizations and as a broader profession. There are a number of issues to consider. Are the standard vehicles for disseminating our messages—tours, exhibits, lectures, articles, school programs—sufficient in the twenty-first century? There are some exciting things going on at many institutions addressing the differences in generational communication styles and the increased availability of technology, but those seem to be the exceptions rather than the rule. Are the messages we send truly pertinent to our diverse audiences and conducive to a shared understanding? Despite decades of talking the talk, we aren't yet walking the walk on integrating the experiences of all people into an inclusive, accurate narrative. The generational shift and the increasing diversity of the American populace impact our appeal and relevance. Data show that our audiences do not reflect the more heterogeneous America.

Moreover, how are we truly involving communities in the development of inclusive narratives and programs? This simple precept may often be overlooked in our zest for inclusion. We also need to do better at reaching audiences outside the walls of the museum. Many of us are still relying on quantitative attendance data without good qualitative measures of our success. We know we compete with social media and the Internet as go-to sources of history. How do we maximize our platform to disseminate good history to our publics?

The most salient question of our era may be whether we can provide historical perspective while avoiding political advocacy. How do we address timely and controversial topics without deterring visitors and donors? Ultimately we need to ask ourselves two essential questions: Are we serving our profession well? Are we serving our publics well?

Barge pilots on the Detroit River must navigate with a dual focus on the controls in front of them and the changing waterway in the distance. There is a time to concentrate on the task at hand. There must also be a time to assess the progress you are making, and the strategies you are using to further that journey. In the spirit of Detroit, we gather to celebrate our achievements, but with an eye on changing current questions, old models, and outdated strategies.

NOTES

1. Peter Gavrilovich and Bill McGraw, *The Detroit Almanac* (Detroit: Detroit Free Press, 2001), 29.

2. Ibid., 33. The site of Fort Pontchartrain, the original French settlement of Detroit, is currently the Crowne Plaza Hotel. It served as the headquarters hotel for the 2016 AASLH and Michigan Museums Association Annual Meeting.

3. Ibid., 71, 139, 289; Scott Martelle, *Detroit: A Biography* (Chicago: Chicago Review Press, 2012), 71.

4. Ibid., 140.

5. Details are from Thomas Sugrue, *The Origins of the Urban Crisis: Race and Inequality in Postwar Detroit* (Princeton, NJ: Princeton University Press, 1996).

6. Ibid., xliv.

7. See John Gallagher, *Reimagining Detroit: Opportunities for Redefining an American City* (Detroit: Wayne State University Press, 2010).

8. U.S. Department of Education, Institute of Education Sciences, National Center for Education Statistics, National Assessment of Educational Progress, *The Nation's Report Card: History 2014: Achievement Levels* (Washington, DC: U.S. Department of Education, 2014). Sam Wineburg points out the weakness that these studies rely on the one element of historic knowledge—the retention of basic facts— that is most readily available through objective tests. He also argues that the design and content of these tests are in the hands of statisticians, not historians. See Sam Wineburg, "Crazy for History," *Journal of American History* 90, no. 4 (March 2004): 1401–1414.

9. See http://on.aaslh.org/Jones-LordCNN.

10. History Relevance Campaign, "The Value of History: Seven Ways It Is Essential," www.historyrelevance.com.

11. National Endowment for the Arts, *Survey of Public Participation in the Arts* (Washington, DC: National Endowment for the Arts, 1982, 1992, 2002, 2008, and 2012). Estimates generated using the National Archive of Data on Arts and Culture.

Chapter 9

The Power of Possibility

Bob Beatty

One of the key tenets of the types of transformation Matelic, Durel, and Janssen reference is identifying and acting on possibilities. Leaders of these endeavors, wrote scholars James Kouzes and Barry Posner, "envision the future by imagining exciting and ennobling possibilities."[1] As one looks at the history endeavor today, it is certainly rife with opportunity.

Early in my career, Kent Whitworth, director of the Kentucky Historical Society and coauthor of the following chapter, shared a phrase with me that sums up this principle. "Stewardship is the open hand, not the closed fist." The phrase certainly has multiple meanings in multiple contexts. But as it pertains to our work in public history, it is a reminder of the obligation of history organizations to continue to keep in mind the opportunities to serve that our communities and stakeholders provide.

The history of Louisville, Kentucky, where AASLH met in 2015, inspired the *Power of Possibility* theme. One of the major cities of the upper South, Louisville was founded along the Falls of the Ohio, the only navigational hazard on the entire nearly 1,000-mile length of the Ohio River. About the Falls, Thomas Rodney declared in 1803, "I must now say a few words more about the Falls. They are a terrable [*sic*] place to pass through when the water is as low as now. . . . The rocks are so cragy [*sic*], the channil [*sic*] so crooked, and the water so furious and rapid that it requires the utmost care and dexterity to avoid the danger."[2]

Why is this important? Well, the Falls of the Ohio are precisely why Louisville was settled in the first place. As settlers and pioneers began the march West, a city developed to offer provisions, rest, trade, and help. Louisville's growth springs directly from these early visionaries who seized on the possibility the hazard provided.

This offers a model for the history enterprise as well. How can we see the issues that vex the field today—funding/sustainability, relevance, leadership, for example—as possibilities and opportunities? "We fail to thrive," 2015 program chair Kyle McKoy of the Indiana Historical Society and host chair Scott Alvey of the Kentucky Historical Society wrote, "when we limit ourselves to see only a choice between two options; public programs or academic research, contemplative or participatory experiences, content mastery or skills development, existing membership or new audiences."[3]

The key is in the simple difference in two phrases when making decisions. "If we truly are dedicated to not just survive, but to positively impact the future," they wrote, "we must reject the exclusionary 'either/or' and replace it with 'and.'" The power of possibility is a rethinking of our individual (and collective) modus operandi. "We can be simultaneously creative and disciplined, consistent and fresh, informative and fun. The challenging environment may or may not change, but our thoughts must."[4]

History professionals; teachers; public, avocational, and academic historians; and others present history in this manner on a regular basis. There are several hundred, probably thousand, examples of this happening at the very moment I write (and you read) this. People are engaging with history in ways that are meaningful, insightful, and even fun. The simple fact is, that despite how school-based history is often taught as rote facts, names, and dates, millions of Americans love history. This is the great possibility for the field of history.

There are countless examples of this principle in action. SUNY-New Paltz professor Sarah E. Elia uses local history as part of her English course with international students. "Teaching English through local history is not simply a means of learning a new language (though that is one of the chief goals of my programs and teaching)," she observed. "We are instead creating a host of skills and outcomes that make the students' experiences productive and memorable, those that develop skills of participation, partnership, and friendship with local communities."[5] For Elia and her students, the study of history offered possibility beyond studying English in a classroom.

The Oakland Museum of California offers another model. Its *Above and Below: Stories from Our Changing Bay* exhibit resulted from mitigation requirements of Section 106 of the 1966 National Historic Preservation Act.[6] Following the 1989 Loma Prieta earthquake, the California Department of Transportation (Caltrans) decided to replace a span of the Bay Bridge connecting San Francisco to Oakland. Because the bridge was constructed in 1936, its replacement had to adhere to Section 106.

Caltrans approached the museum to fulfill mitigation responsibilities in a very traditional sense, through a program. The institution saw much greater possibility and impact. It countered with a proposal to create a comprehensive exhibition that not only satisfied regulations but also helped the community wrestle with the vicissitudes wrought by a new bridge. The solution was not without complications, particularly with regard to the utilization of public money. "We were worried people would think [the exhibit] was a boondoggle," remembered Caltrans's Noah Stewart. "In the end, in the context of the criticism of the new bridge . . . this became a good news story for us. We have [the museum] to thank for pulling us down that route."[7]

Instead of a narrow focus on the history of the original bridge, the final exhibition used the past and present to contextualize change over time. It allowed the Oakland Museum of California to tell a more expansive story, one rooted in the community's dialogue and the institution's use of the latest historiography of environmental history. It emphasized the San Francisco Bay as a hybrid landscape, focusing on "the active role humans have taken, and will take, in shaping and stewarding the natural world." And it did so in a way that fit Caltrans's need (mitigation) with its own mission: "to inspire all Californians to create a more vibrant future for themselves and their communities."[8]

In this project, the museum exemplified another important role of the study of history: discovering the past and understanding it in a present context. This

Image 9.1. The exhibition *Above and Below: Stories from Our Changing Bay* at the Oakland Museum of California focused on the human impact on San Francisco Bay. Through a high-resolution aerial view, visitors were drawn to the places they know, their homes, and their routes to work in the context of the Bay itself. *Source:* Shaun Roberts

is where history institutions can do some of their most effective work. Not only do they uncover history within their communities or in their collections, they also interpret those histories in today's terms and share it with audiences. Effective history organizations show the historical process in action, asking questions of sources, and sharing conclusions with audiences, encouraging them to join the journey, by asking their own questions. Thus, audiences gain additional perspective. This is the power of possibility.

The near-bankruptcy of the Southern Oregon Historical Society inspired one final example of the power of possibility. The story began with a 2008 cut in funding that reduced the institution's budget by 100 percent. Stuck with financing a veritable history empire comprising facilities in three cities, including a historic farm, sixteen buildings, and more than a million artifacts, the institution and its board faced hard decisions. Change initiated with what then-director Allison Weiss called "an intensive community outreach program, through private meetings with opinion shapers and public town hall meetings." They asked, "Did anyone care whether or not the historical society closed for good?" Out of this, Weiss reflected, "We developed a guiding framework for decision making based on the principle that three elements are inextricably connected to the sustainability of the society, the Three R's: Relevance, Relationships, and Resources."[9]

"Feedback boiled down to this," Weiss recounted. "The historical society was no longer relevant to the community." The community's list of gripes was long. It routinely ignored offers to volunteer, disregarded community input, and operated its library at times inconvenient to researchers' work schedules.

In addition, the institution's hyper-focus on preservation of its archives rather than access to the material led it to ignore the significant opportunity the materials presented. In one of its community meetings, the all-volunteer Rogue Valley Genealogical Society suggested the historical society realign the priorities of its research library from conservation of the collection to its availability to researchers. The genealogists also offered a staffing solution. "Why don't you reopen the research library with volunteers?" they asked. Within three months, the dormant library was open four days a week. At the six-month mark, the historical society had hired its first professional librarian. Ultimately, the possibility posed by a community partner resulted in more than thirty-two volunteers working the equivalent of two full-time staff positions a week.[10]

The library is but one of several successful stories of the Southern Oregon Historical Society. The Society leased for ten times its market value its Hanley Farm property (which had been running a $70,000 deficit) to a national organic seed company, Seeds of Change.[11] It also partnered with a local children's museum to open an activity center in a portion of its 15,000-square-foot headquarters building, not only building a new relationship but also better utilizing its physical resources. Employing the three Rs—relevance, relationships, and resources—Weiss and her institution discovered true opportunities within what were devastating budget cuts. These opportunities exist throughout the field of public history.

Of particular note is Weiss's first "R," relevance. This has been a topic that has confounded history organizations for generations. But relevance is more than just the term "du jour." It is at the very core of the reason history institutions exist in the first place.[12] The issue of relevance, however, has become particularly troubling in the first decades of the twenty-first century as policy makers increasingly winnow history from the public school curriculum and politicians speak of academic study of the humanities with disdain.

There are literally millions of Americans who love history. How can we quantify this? One way is through examining history organizations in the United States. As previously noted, the cumulative number of history museums, historical societies, historic preservation organizations, and historic houses and sites exceeds 19,000 (55.5 percent of American museums).[13]

Image 9.2.   The Children's Heritage Fair is a popular annual event at the Southern Oregon Historical Society's Hanley Farm. *Source*: Allison Weiss

While visitorship numbers are elusive, we could estimate that 55.5 percent of the American Alliance of Museums' annual museum visitation (850 million people) are visiting history museums. The number of 471+ million visitors is surely high, but an inflated count of 100 or even 200 percent shows an abiding love of history as we presented in history institutions.[14]

There are other measures we can turn to measure people's love for history as well. Tens of millions of Americans research their family history and genealogy. Ancestry.com, perhaps the largest professional genealogy company, reports more than 2.4 million subscribers. While their methods and intent differ from traditional historians—genealogists are often mainly concerned with tracing family lineage and rarely with overarching historical context—they are nonetheless major players in the historical enterprise. There is tremendous possibility here for history organizations to create in-depth engagement and involvement in common histories. Thus, we move beyond the simple transactional activity of access to records to distinguishing ways to connect them to others with similar stories or pasts.

The National Register of Historic Places offers yet another way to enumerate connections to the past. The National Register lists more than 90,000 properties. These represent 1.4 million individual entities: buildings, sites, districts, structures, and objects. The National Park Service, the agency that administers the National Register, reports that nearly every county in the United States has at least one place listed.[15]

Certainly there are other ways to measure interest in the past (or lack thereof). Many can counter this admittedly facile analysis with data on ongoing funding challenges for museums and historic sites, declining enrollments in academic history programs, or a general national historical malaise, bordering on amnesia. All of these factors weigh considerably, and they very easily could tip the scales against the discipline. But consider again the title of this chapter: "The Power of Possibility." The public history profession simply must capitalize on the present opportunity.

Against this backdrop, a group of history professionals launched the History Relevance Campaign in 2012. The question that inspired the endeavor was "Why is history marginalized?" "Children are not expected to learn it in schools, community leaders rarely look to it to inform today's decisions, and national leaders select and distort facts to support their positions." For many, "engagement in history seems to be an occasional pleasant pastime, not something especially relevant to their lives. In contrast, those who are active in the practice of history—whether as professionals or amateurs—believe that history is central to their lives, and that it ought to play a greater role in the lives of our communities and nation."[16]

The relevance effort comes at a time when people's access to information is at an all-time high, a result of the ubiquity of the Internet. Closer to home, it is also because of massive digitization efforts of primary sources found in libraries, archives, and museums.

In addition, the division between amateur and professional historians is as blurred as it has been since the early days of the twentieth century. As historians David Kyvig and Myron Marty noted in *Nearby History*, we have more in common than not. "[A]ll historians shared a common curiosity. . . . All shared a desire to obtain the best information available so as to gain an understanding of a past that engaged them." Kyvig and Marty note only one distinction between amateurs and professionals, "Amateurs . . . may pursue history out of a simple love for it, while professionals expect to be financially compensated for their efforts."[17]

History is also an inherent human need. "We all need to know who we are, how we have become that person, and how to cope with a variety of situations in order to conduct our lives successfully," they avowed. "Organizations and communities require the same self-understanding in order to function satisfactorily."[18]

Public historian Darlene Roth expanded on this, identifying the following "Seven Reasons the Past Never Dies."

1. We need the past.
2. We live in the past.
3. We love the past.
4. We create the past.
5. The past lives in us.
6. We learn from the past.
7. The future has use for the past.[19]

In many ways, these seven statements point to the inherent possibility within the discipline. People are naturally attuned to history because it is meaningful to them. Many wrongly equate history with "memory" and "the past," and many more think of history as taught in school (typically rote memorization of facts). Roth argues that history is part of the human condition. It is so innate, perhaps, that it's easy to completely overlook its importance to our lives and understanding. This is why articulating of the value of history is so important.

The History Relevance Campaign has taken these principles and expounded upon them. It has articulated seven ways history is essential—history: (1) nurtures personal identity, (2) teaches critical skills, (3) adds to community vitality, (4) stimulates economic development, (5) fosters engaged citizens, (6) inspires leadership, and (7) provides a legacy.[20] Each of these values can surely stand on its own merit. But together, these values point to the critical role history plays in our individual lives, our communities, and to our future.

These seven values are not new. But their clear articulation is. The Value
of History statement offers not only a common language for the entire history
enterprise to address present (and future) challenges and possibilities but also
a fresh start for the discipline to document genuine, measurable change across
the profession and the public realm.[21]

Relevance is our existential crisis. As John R. Dichtl, AASLH president
and CEO, asserted, "As historians, we understand the power of possibility of
stories and the past resonating in the present, opening new ways of seeing and
solving contemporary problems." The History Relevance Campaign offers a
framework for articulating that power of possibility. "Maybe this is the best
moment in the past twenty or thirty years," wrote Dichtl, "to make sure we
each are ready, wherever and whenever, to make the case for historical understanding and the institutions, collections, landscapes, communities, and other
resources that keep the past alive."[22]

NOTES

1. James M. Kouzes and Barry Z. Posner, *The Leadership Challenge: How
to Make Extraordinary Things Happen in Organizations* (San Francisco: Pfeiffer,
2012), 17.

2. Indiana Historical Bureau, "Expedition Begins: September 28, 1803 through
December 5, 1803," accessed October 10, 2016, www.in.gov/history/2579.htm.

3. Scott Alvey and Kyle McKoy, "The Power of Possibility," 2015 American
Association for State and Local History Annual Meeting theme.

4. Ibid.

5. Sarah E. Elia, "International Students Encounter Local History," *History News*
71, no. 1 (Winter 2016): 25.

6. In short, Section 106 requires agencies that propose to adversely affect historic
properties to consult with the federal Advisory Council on Historic Preservation and
state historic preservation offices and find ways to avoid or minimize the damage,
commonly called mitigation in historic preservation circles. Full text of the National
Historic Preservation Act is available on the Advisory Council on Historic Preservation website, www.achp.gov.

7. Louise Pubols, *"Above and Below*: Exhibition as Mitigation," *History News*
70, no. 2 (Spring 2015): 13.

8. Ibid., 13, 14.

9. Allison Weiss, "Relevance, Relationships, and Resources: The Three R's of
Museum Management," *History News* 67, no. 3 (Summer 2012): 7–8.

10. Ibid., 9–10.

11. Seeds of Change also guaranteed an annual financial gift and the potential to
use the Hanley Farm name in a future marketing endeavor.

12. See the writings of Charles Willson Peale, John Cotton Dana, and Theodore
Low, for example.

13. Institute of Museum and Library Services, "Government Doubles Official Estimate: There Are 35,000 Active Museums in the U.S.," accessed October 10, 2016, www.imls.gov/news-events/news-releases/government-doubles-official-estimate-there-are-35000-active-museums-us. History museums probably constitute closer to 80 percent of American museums as the IMLS data recorded 33 percent of museums as "Unspecified or General," many of which certainly have a history-focused collection.

14. American Alliance of Museums, "Museum Facts," accessed October 10, 2016, aam-us.org/about-museums/museum-facts.

15. National Park Service, "National Register of Historic Places Program: About Us," accessed October 10, 2016,www.nps.gov/nr/about.htm.

16. History Relevance Campaign, "The Evolution of the History Relevance Campaign," accessed October 10, 2016, www.historyrelevance.com/the-evolution-of-hrc.

17. David E. Kyvig and Myron A. Marty, *Nearby History: Exploring the Past around You*, 3rd edition (Lanham, MD: AltaMira Press, 2010), x.

18. Ibid., 5.

19. Darlene Roth, "Seven Reasons the Past Never Dies," *History News* 68, no. 3 (Summer 2013): 14–18.

20. Adapted from History Relevance Campaign, "The Value of History: Seven Ways It Is Essential," www.historyrelevance.com/history-is-essential, accessed October 10, 2016.

21. Ibid.

22. John R. Dichtl, "Moving History from Nice to Essential," *History News* 70, no. 4 (Autumn 2015): 11.

Chapter 10

It's Possible

Kent Whitworth and Scott Alvey

Life in Kentucky's early days was much like what many of us might say about the history profession today—it was not for the faint of heart. Just as the settlers endured daily hardships in their struggle to survive, on many levels, this is true of what we have faced in the history world, too. Yet after a prolonged period of financial distress and seemingly lackluster audiences, we once again see opportunities for real impact.

Louisville was settled by indomitable pioneers who, when the Falls of the Ohio threw up barriers to their dreams of traveling west, found power in the possibilities presented by their new situation. Communities sprang up as these enterprising few shifted their westward thinking to settle by the falls and offer provisions, rest, trade, and help for people who followed. Life handed them lemons and they made bourbon!

In fact, the entire commonwealth is defined by people who recognized new opportunities and seized the power of possibility. From Henry Clay to Hunter S. Thompson, Carrie Nation to Tori Murden McClure, and of course "the Greatest" Muhammad Ali, Kentucky consistently has produced people who were the motivators and innovators in their fields.

Louisville is a good example of how this has played out. Perhaps Huston Quinn, mayor of Louisville from 1921 to 1925, said it best. "Louisville has the thrift of the East, the hustle of the North, the optimism of the West, and the hospitality of the South." Depending on your point of view, it's either the southernmost city in the North or the South's northernmost city. Louisvillians don't mind being called either because they know that both reflect how their city is an amalgamation of ideas, people, and interests.[1]

The same can be said of the history world. We are all facing a number of challenges and, depending on our perspective, an equal number of reactions to them. Most people address new challenges by tackling them head on or

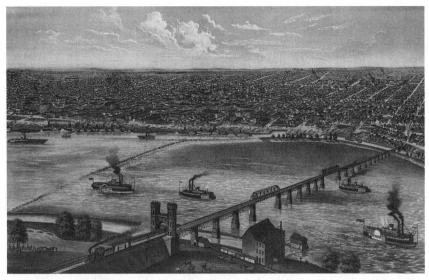

Image 10.1.   This circa 1907 Louisville postcard shows the Falls on the Ohio along with an inset drawing of the fledgling river town in 1778. *Source*: Kentucky Historical Society, Ronald Morgan Kentucky Postcard Collection

by circumventing them altogether. If we look to history and take the lead of Louisville's founders, however, the best approach is to not think in terms of challenges, but in terms of new areas of possibilities and opportunities. Rather than spend our days debating issues such as why STEM gets all of the public's attention and how to get people through our doors—saying the same things over and over again, just louder—we should instead be examining what we can do differently and more creatively in order to help address the needs of our audiences.

Where are the areas of possibility and opportunity that exist within what we're trying to accomplish through the study of history?

Look again at Louisville. It doesn't have the advantage of being either East Coast or West Coast—it's a landlocked city in a landlocked state in the center of the nation. But the city leaders long ago decided the location had the real opportunity, the real *possibility*, to become a logistical center. And that's just what Louisville became. And that's what we want people within our profession to learn to do—to see ourselves through the eyes of someone else and discover the opportunities that are there for the taking. As we've endured the past several years while riding the financial freefall, many of us have been fighting for our existence. But in the midst of that challenge there is real clarity. As Wendell Berry, renowned Kentucky poet and essayist wrote, "The mind that is not baffled is not employed. It is the impeded stream that sings."[2] In the midst of the obstacles in front of us, we saw the power of possibility.

There is more innovation now than ever because just maybe we were a little too comfortable in the past. Back then, we didn't have to ask if we truly were meeting real needs. We didn't have to think about, for instance, what the state is going to miss if the Kentucky Historical Society goes away.

Those are gut-wrenching questions, but they certainly bring clarity! Now the entire history field is trying to get these enormous issues right, and in the midst of that is unprecedented possibility. This topic is absolutely appropriate right now. In fact, it's essential, because as the economy gets better, we may get a little more comfortable again, and we'd better learn these lessons while we can.

We have an opportunity to transform the profession if, collectively, we examine the impact that we could and should have on society. How we react or don't react to this opportunity will in large part determine our relevance.

We know something about that in Kentucky. Looking back at the commonwealth in its pre–Civil War era, we were a leader in every sense of the word, from a business standpoint, an intellectual standpoint, and a political standpoint. Then we found ourselves in the backseat, got comfortable, and stayed there. Kentucky state historian Jim Klotter consistently challenges Kentuckians to rise above the lost opportunities of the late nineteenth and early twentieth centuries.[3] And now momentum is building on multiple fronts.

The history field is guilty of the exact same thing. We better get out of this backseat mindset and get out of it soon, because opportunity is knocking for us in a most unpredictable way. Who would have dreamed that yanking the rug out from under us financially would be the best thing that could ever happen? Yet we weren't going to come to grips with who we were and what we were really about until we were fighting for our lives and extinction was a real possibility. So what does this mean to someone from Iowa or Maine or Texas? How can they take the lessons we're learning in Kentucky and transfer them to their particular place and needs?

Kentucky's lessons aren't geographically bound. As a field, we lost track of who we were trying to serve. The shifting of the financial landscape didn't really tell us we must chop programs and activities. What it told us, emphatically, is that we need to concentrate on doing the *right* things. This is a challenge the entire field faces, not just folks in certain regions of the country.

This is where Stanford University professor Sam Wineburg's book, *Historical Thinking and Other Unnatural Acts*, can be a great guide. He says our work isn't just about *telling* history; it's about *teaching* history. It's about how we want to interact with our intended audiences. How do we want to see ourselves, and what is the real value that we bring to a particular need or situation? That's what each and every one of us needs to do. We must stop and ponder, "What do I want to accomplish?"

For us at the Kentucky Historical Society, this opportunity is about learning. It's about helping people engage with history and putting learning opportunities in their hands. Before the recent financial shakeup we were fairly passive in the way we wanted people to interact with us. But, look at Louisville's example once again. What really sets the tone is a focus on service. The city talks about how Louisville's citizens collectively make the difference, not just city government or certain individuals alone.

What about us in the history field? It's time we collectively begin asking our users, our visitors, our researchers, "What can we do for you? How can you participate in this learning environment?" We should not be dictating what that learning environment looks like and what we think people need to learn.

Most significantly, we've got to quit doing what we've often done: hope and wait for others to find us. We need to listen and to pay attention to the fundamental needs within our communities and then figure out what history organizations, with our suite of assets and expertise, can do to help resolve them.

In a 2001 interview Sam Wineburg said, "We need to raise citizens who ask themselves, 'Is this true? Who is saying so? What's the nature of the evidence?' Taught this way, history is a training ground for democracy." History could be poised to take its rightful place after all, but it will not come without its challenges.[4]

Several school systems nationwide are attempting, quite frankly, to dilute history by rewriting the Advanced Placement courses to focus only on the positive points of our nation's history and omit accounts of civil unrest. But of course civil disobedience is inherent in the very founding of our nation in the first place. This is where skills-based learning comes in; yet we've strayed from that. We deliver content, certainly, but teaching should not be about how you look up things in the stacks or how you write out notecards. Instead, it's about inquiry. How do we encourage people who want to better understand the news or the environment so they can ask the questions Wineburg raises? That's the skills-based process history research teaches. But as historical organizations, we must get to the kinds of activities that allow this to naturally happen.

The real irony of the situation is that while certain school systems are saying we've got to contain this content or it's going to get away from us, they also are acknowledging the power of history.

As Wendell Berry wrote in *The Art of the Commonplace: The Agrarian Essays*, "All good human work remembers its history." Our challenge is to refocus these school systems from trying to control history's content to instead seeing the great advantage of a next generation for which history has sparked curiosity, encouraged an inquisitive nature, one enhanced by the skills embedded in the historical process.[5]

Wineburg is right. *That* is the core of American democracy, and yet we're totally missing the point. We're afraid of tackling the controversial, potentially polarizing conversations.

How do we overcome this? We can start by creating dialogue around good information and solid research and by informing people. These conversations are tough, but they lead to constructive change. Research over the past fifteen to twenty years makes it clear that people trust museums when it comes to providing what they should know about the past. There's this unbelievable high ground just sitting there for the taking; yet many of us continue to play it safe. We're still reeling from budget cuts, and all the while we're often deaf to opportunity pounding on our doors.

Possibilities come in all shapes and sizes, and there is not a segment of our field that won't be directly impacted by this broader conversation that's taking place. As Carol Kammen writes in her introduction of *Zen and the Art of Local History*, "People come to local history from many different positions. Some just liked history, some wanted to understand place. Others came from an interest in architectural preservation, genealogy, or civic engagement— from other hobbies or pursuits. Some become interested because of a connection with community. There is no single path into local history." Hopefully you will find someone or something that resonates with you, and you'll be inspired by that insight.[6]

That's part of what the History Relevance Campaign is addressing. We're developing a common vocabulary that helps us explain who and what we are. We're also developing a common voice that tells people history is not just a body of knowledge, but that there is value to it for them personally, for their community, and for the future. If you would like to know more, please check www.historyrelevance.com.

In many respects, our role really hasn't changed that much over the years. It's just that we no longer can be so rooted in old behaviors that we lose sight of who we're trying to serve. We've always been places that gathered artifacts and information, and we talked about how to make it all accessible for people to use and gain knowledge. *But our audiences have changed:* from the way they want to use what we provide them and the way they want to make meaning out of things to how they want us to interact with them. So rather than existing in the traditional realm and hoping that maybe, if we keep doing what we've always done, one of these needs will intersect with our audiences, we should disengage from all of that and figure out what the needs truly are and plant the flag there. That's the power of possibility.

Kentucky is a great backdrop for how that is happening here and, in some cases, how it hasn't. Once again we're a microcosm for the field. None of us has a crystal ball, but we're all learning important lessons and we're having a greater impact collectively than ever before. We hope our colleagues will come and experience organizations of all shapes and sizes across the commonwealth and beyond that are working hard to help address the needs of our communities. We believe you will leave inspired and invigorated by the possibilities!

NOTES

1. Quoted in *The News-Herald*, Franklin, Pennsylvania, October 12, 1926.
2. Wendell Berry, "The Real Work," accessed February 17, 2017, on.aaslh.org/BerryRealWork.
3. Audio from Klotter's plenary panel with Wendell Berry is here go.aaslh.org/Plenary2015.
4. Judy Lightfoot, review of *Historical Thinking and Other Unnatural Acts*, on.aaslh.org/LightfootWineburg.
5. Wendell Berry, "Feminism, the Body, and the Machine," in *The Achievement of Wendell Berry: The Hard History of Love* by Fritz Oehlschlaeger (Lexington: The University Press of Kentucky, 2011), 13.
6. Carol Kammen, "Introduction," in *Zen and the Art of Local History*, eds. Carol Kamen and Bob Beatty (Lanham, MD: Rowman & Littlefield, 2014), xiii–xiv.

Chapter 11

The Whole Is Greater

Bob Beatty

In many ways, American state and local history reflects the founding principles of the nation. It is an example of democracy in action—people making decisions themselves, as a community rather than a dictate from above. In his treatise on the nascent American republic, *Democracy in America*, Frenchman Alexis de Tocqueville observed Americans' proclivity to work in concert in both the political sphere and in public life. "I have often admired," he commented, "the extreme skill with which the inhabitants of the United States succeed in proposing a common object for the exertions of a great many men and in inducing them voluntarily to pursue it."[1]

De Tocqueville called these activities "Public Associations in Civil Life." "Americans of all ages," he argued, "all conditions, and all dispositions constantly form associations. . . . associations of a thousand other kinds, religious, moral, serious, futile, general or restricted, enormous or diminutive. . . . If it is proposed to inculcate some truth or to foster some feeling by the encouragement of a great example, they form a society."[2]

In America, De Tocqueville discovered a nation of joiners. "Nowhere is this more evident," history and museum leader James M. Vaughan articulated in an essay response to a *History News* column of public historian Carol Kammen, "than in our efforts to save our local history and historic structures." "Soon after the creation of the republic," Vaughan continued, "community leaders and scholars organized themselves into state and local historical societies." De Tocqueville found this joining together as inherent in the American experiment of self-government. Americans clearly reflected this in their history organizations. As Vaughan noted, "Throughout the twentieth century, the pace of new historical and museum organizations steadily accelerated."[3]

There is little that stops the creation of a new museum or history organi-zation.[4] While there are certainly constraints precluding the activity, all in all, the founding of a new institution is pretty easy. It's the "keeping open" (sustainability) part that is hardest.

Thus far, this book has touched on issues of sustainability as they reflect entrepreneurship, change, transformation, and possibility. This chapter will focus on another of the sustainability tools: collaboration. It is thematically organized under Aristotle's famous precept, "The whole is greater than the sum of its parts."

Vaughan's essay highlights some of the challenges the history field faces in collaboration. "Our pride of independence coupled with our competitive spirit" counters the inclination to join others in a common cause. "These traits," he wrote, "become barriers to collaborations, partnerships, and merg-ers." Vaughan asked readers, "Can we learn to put the needs of our com-munities ahead of the more narrow needs of our own organizations?"[5] Many believe we can.

This idea builds upon that of one of America's greatest museum think-ers and leaders, John Cotton Dana. Dana set the stage for collaboration in his 1917 work *The New Museum*. "Learn what aid the community needs," he wrote, "fit the museum to those needs."[6] Dana wrote these words as he reflected on the principles he learned in establishing the Newark Museum. They are but a small part of a larger book that warrants reconsideration. Many would be wise to revisit this canonical text on an annual basis as Dana's philosophies and suggestions regarding the role and "place" of museums in a community are as relevant in 2017 as they were 100 years earlier, perhaps even more so.

In the pages that follow, Erin Carlson Mast, program chair of the 2014 AASLH Annual Meeting and CEO of President Lincoln's Cottage, aptly uses the "Stone Soup" folktale as an example of community collaboration. You'll need to read on for the specific context but the analogy works: history organizations are much stronger when they are meeting specific community needs rather than their own internal wants and desires.

"Nothing can replace the opportunities that arise when you intersect with people who come together around common goals and interests," Mast wrote with host chair Andrea Kajer in preparation for the 2014 AASLH Annual Meeting in St. Paul, Minnesota.[7] President Bill Clinton said exactly the same in an address at a conference at the Clinton Presidential Center in Little Rock, Arkansas. "Wherever [good] people are coming together with the aim of get-ting something done," he noted, "good things are happening."[8]

History organizations are one umbrella under which people gather together for a common goal. This service is at the heart of museum identity and mis-sion. Former museum director Barbara B. Walden found a direct parallel between the work of history organizations and local civic leadership. Both, she observes, "are dedicated to building a sense of identity and strengthening community connections," history organizations through the study of the past, civic leadership in service of the present. Collaboration is found at this intersection.[9] Like the characters in "Stone Soup," history institutions and community partners bring their own ingredients to the stew. "We must always turn to the needs of our local constituents when creating and strengthening our role within the community," Walden wrote. In turn, organizations will "soon discover the museum mission and the community mission are one and the same." This is important work. "It is about connecting the community and site in order to provide insight and inspiration to those who are seeking an experience that transcends the ordinary."[10]

What does this merging of institutional and community missions look like and how does it function? In 2016 authors Robert P. Connolly and Elizabeth K. Bollwerk documented much of this process in *Positioning Your Museum as a Critical Community Asset: A Practical Guide*. The book's opening distinguishes its approach. It is not meant to convince of the need for community integration. "We consider [that] a settled matter," Connolly and Bollwerk assert. Instead, the authors explicitly align themselves with John Cotton Dana, declaring, "We stand with . . . Dana's 1917 mandate for museums to act on their community's expressed needs."[11]

It's important for institutions to probe a bit deeper here. Most importantly, as Mast recently observed, "the expressed need may be different for different parts of the community. It's more about examining the different expressions of need and determining how your organization is best able to meet a deep, abiding need that is also true to its own mission/story versus chasing community needs and changing your organizational identity like a trend or fad."[12]

Connolly and Bollwerk; Mast and Kajer; and Vaughan, Clinton, and Walden all wisely advocate heeding Dana's words of a century ago. An effective museum, Dana wrote, "Examines its community's life first, and then straightaway bends its energies to supplying some of the material which the community needs, and to making the material's presence widely known, and to presenting it in such a way as to secure for it the maximum of use and the maximum of efficiency in that use."[13] Working together is Dana's underlying premise.

Some areas of collaboration are simple in their conception but incredibly complex in execution. Such is the case in the National Park Service (NPS) career of Gerard Baker, a member of the Mandan-Hidatsa nation. Baker served in a number of capacities in his career at the Park Service, including as superintendent of the much-contested Mount Rushmore National Memorial. He retired in 2010 as the highest-ranking American Indian in the National Park Service.

Image 11.1.   Gerard Baker, a member of the Mandan-Hidatsa nation, retired in 2010 as the highest-ranking American Indian in the National Park Service. *Source*: **American Association for State and Local History**

That same year Baker delivered the plenary address to the AASLH/Oklahoma Museums Association annual meeting.[14] In it he recounted much of his career of more than three decades at NPS, particularly as it related to including American Indian history into the sites he worked at. "One thing was [always] missing," he exclaimed, "the full story of the occupation of this country, from the American Indian side of things."[15] It was a glaring absence.

Baker sought to redress this situation. He recounts travels to Indian reservations of the Lakota, Oglala, and Crow nations to help reinterpret Little Bighorn Battlefield. "I invited them back to their national park, to their homelands," he said. Baker had to help overcome the fear some felt in returning. "If I come back there, you are going to arrest me, because it was my grandfather who killed George Custer," one stated. Baker assuaged his trepidation and his outreach resulted in not only Lakota and Oglala returning but also the collecting of stories from descendants of those whose great-grandfathers had fought at the battle.[16] This collaboration not only led to a more robust, thorough, and intellectually honest interpretation but also met the stakeholder needs.

Baker continued outreach in collaborations at Mount Rushmore, a site fraught with complexity for American Indians collectively and Baker individually. "It took me four days to accept the job. . . . What I did in those four days was not only pray about it, sit in some really good sweats with the elders, but I also started calling around. I asked, 'Should I go in here as an American Indian, knowing what happened to our people?' " He expected that many would call him a traitor. No one did. "Go there," the elders told him. Under Baker's leadership, Mount Rushmore took on a role as a place to start healing and creating a dialogue for American Indians. Baker's deep commitment to bridging these histories included visiting Indian reservations with his staff so the latter could better understand the former's culture, and vice versa. Baker also called together an Elder Summit at Mount Rushmore to further expand the park's interpretive story.[17]

In all this work, Baker utilized his position within NPS to collaborate with native peoples whose history was so affected, and absent, from traditional narratives. Expanding the interpretive narrative not only was the right thing to do but also provided a great service to the history field. "Our goal is that, when people leave this site, I don't want them to have all the answers. . . . I want them to leave with more questions than answers, because they are apt to come back, to do more research, to talk, and to listen," he stated. "That's what excites people about history."[18]

Baker's personal stories offer many lessons for our work. They remind us that it's important to look at the history of our own institutions, specifically how we've presented the past, and to acknowledge that sometimes we get it wrong or our entire premise was wrong. And it can be frustrating when people are hesitant to participate in our work, to be part of the whole. As historians, we need to dig deeper to understand the roots of this reluctance (e.g., because they were ignored or taken advantage of) and work through it with honesty of motives and integrity of action.[19]

Baker's long career reflects partnerships on a wide scale. Formal partnerships between two organizations in a local community are another example of why the whole can exceed the sum of its parts. Such is the case in a collaboration between the Indiana University of Pennsylvania and the Historical and Genealogical Society of Indiana County.

The project began with the university's history department recognizing a need to better align its public history curriculum with current best practice. This was important not only in building community alliances locally but also in, as Jeanine Mazak-Kahne writes, "fostering an understanding of how civic engagement contributes to the preservation and presentation of people, places, and memory."[20]

The university found a willing partner in this endeavor in its local history organization, the Historical and Genealogical Society. The seventy-year-old society was facing what many of its peer institutions grappled with: an all-encompassing mission fulfilled with one paid, half-time director and a cadre of dedicated volunteers. The institution maintained a historic house, a museum, a library, and an ever-growing archive. The latter, in particular, saw regular use. But as the archival collections continued to grow (a common issue across the nation), the collections inventory backlog expanded exponentially as well. This was the Historical and Genealogical Society's greatest need.

The university needed more impactful training for its graduate students; the historical society needed to improve its collections practices. A revised public history curriculum included a focus on archival management. The history department established a public history lab that allowed students to process and work with Historical and Genealogical Society collections in an environmentally controlled, secure location under professional supervision. What resulted was not only practical training for students (important enough in its own right). The coup de grâce is what the institution receives in return: a fully processed collection, housed in archival-quality materials, and prepared for researcher use.

The partnership had another benefit. It trained these new history professionals in the importance of community service. Mazak-Kahne shared the reflection of one student on the role of the public historian: "It is important for the upcoming generations of trained public historians to be active participants in the community. . . . One way to participate is through offering your skills and knowledge to help protect and preserve local history." Mazak-Kahne avowed that "the emergence of a spirit of civic engagement" continues to be the greatest outcome of the partnership.[21]

Other alliances are multi-agency and complex. Such is the case with a collaborative in Atlanta to purchase a collection of Dr. Martin Luther King, Jr.'s archives. It again started with a need, in this case, the desire of entities in the city of Atlanta to keep the King papers in Atlanta. King was born and grew up in Atlanta. He attended college at Morehouse, served as pastor at Ebenezer Baptist Church, and founded the Southern Christian Leadership Conference in the city. He is buried on the grounds of Atlanta's Martin Luther King, Jr. Center for Nonviolent Social Change. That this collection remained in the city was of paramount importance.

On June 8, 2006, Sotheby's announced an auction of 7,000 manuscript pages, King's working library of 1,000 books (with thousands of pages of marginalia), personal papers, and effects. Four days later, civil rights leader, former U.S. congressman, and former Atlanta mayor Andrew Young approached Atlanta mayor Shirley Franklin to acquire the papers. As F. Sheffield Hale reported, "Young's request set off eleven marathon days in which Franklin assembled a team to raise the necessary funds, determine the ultimate home for the papers, and negotiate with the King estate and Sotheby's to secure the collection prior to the auction date. . . . The King estate agreed to sell the entire collection for \$32 million if the funds were raised by June 23."[22]

One of the key collaborators in this endeavor was the Atlanta History Center. Mayor Franklin's office had negotiated with the institution to provide curatorial support and collection storage for the collection until the 2014 opening of the Atlanta-based National Center for Civil and Human Rights. Shortly after the purchase, the principals asked the museum for something else altogether: a debut exhibition of the papers. The institution opened the exhibition, one that would have typically taken several years of planning, in January 2007, less than six months later.

The exhibition *"I Have a Dream": The Morehouse College Martin Luther King, Jr. Collection* was the first and only full public exhibition of the King papers. It included more than 600 works: drafts of King's famous "I Have a Dream" speech, his 1964 Nobel Peace Prize acceptance speech, sermons from his ministry, and personal notes. It marked a truly remarkable moment not only for the institution but also for the Atlanta community.

Following initial processing by the Robert W. Woodruff Library of the Atlanta University Center, the papers are today held at Morehouse College. A collaboration between repositories of Dr. King's papers includes the Howard Gotlieb Archival Center at Boston University, the Martin Luther King, Jr. Research and Education Institute at Stanford University, and Morehouse College. And significant to Atlanta, the National Center for Civil and Human Rights has a permanent Martin Luther King, Jr. Collection gallery that features a rotating exhibition of items from Morehouse's King Collection.[23]

Altogether, these efforts reflect well Barbara B. Walden's commentary on the intersection of history organizations and the needs of civic and community agencies. This is how the whole becomes greater than the sum of its parts.

There is no clearer instruction manual for partnerships than that of the late Brian O'Neill. Like Gerard Baker, O'Neill worked at the National Park Service. He developed the most comprehensive list of how to ensure successful collaboration that I have ever encountered. They are listed here, as no chapter on partnership is complete without them. That said, it is imperative to read O'Neill's full description of each of these factors; the material is too important to overlook.[24]

"21 Partnership Success Factors"
by Brian O'Neill

1. Focus on important needs.
2. Make the partnership a win–win.
3. Adopt a shared vision.
4. Negotiate a formal agreement.
5. Ensure good communication.
6. Ensure the partnership is owned by your whole organization.
7. Maintain an environment of trust.
8. Leave your ego and control at the door.
9. Understand each partner's mission and organizational culture.
10. Utilize the strengths of each partner.
11. Find ways through the red tape.
12. Build step-by-step.
13. Strive for excellence.
14. Diversify your funding sources.
15. Constantly seek out and adopt best practices.
16. Always be courteous and diplomatic.
17. Honor your commitments.
18. Celebrate success.
19. Respect the right to disagree; act on a consensus basis.
20. Network and build relationships.
21. Put mechanisms in place to reinforce partnership.[25]

Greg Stevens, my fellow museum professional, good friend, and frequent partner-in-crime in getting things done, often says something he's adapted from the Judy Garland and Gene Kelly movie *Summer Stock*: "You've got a barn, I've got the costumes. Let's put on a show!" Greg's words are a witty way to remember the core elements of collaboration: meeting needs. In this analogy, the community need is an empty barn that needs filling (and entertainment), our institutional need is to put our costumes (historical assets) to use.

As you read the following from Erin Carlson Mast, keep these two sayings in mind: "You've got a barn, I've got the costumes. Let's put on a show!" It doesn't matter which of these you are, what matters is your desire to work together to create something greater than the sum of its parts. And as you do so, don't forget John Cotton Dana's proverb, "Learn what aid the community needs: fit the museum to those needs."

NOTES

1. Alexis de Tocqueville, *Democracy in Action: Part the Second, the Social Influence of Democracy*, translated by Henry Reeve, Esq., as revised by Francis Bowen, Phillips Bradley, editor (New York: Alfred Knopf, 1945), 106.

2. Ibid.

3. James M. Vaughan, "Call: The Future of Historical Societies," in *Zen and the Art of Local History*, eds. Carol Kammen and Bob Beatty (Lanham, MD: Rowman & Littlefield, 2014), 271.

4. New York is the only state that charters (incorporates) its museums and historical societies through its State Education Department. Other states treat these entities like any other nonprofit organization and incorporate them through their departments of state. As a result, New York State museums and historical societies must follow Board of Regents rules (written into state education law). See Museum Association of New York, "NYS Education Law Relating to Chartered Museums, Historical Societies, and Cultural Agencies," manyonline.org/professional-development/nys-education-law-relating-to-chartered-museums-historical-societies-and.

5. Vaughan, 272.

6. John Cotton Dana, *The New Museum* (Woodstock, VT: Elm Tree Press, 1917), 38.

7. Andrea Kajer and Erin Carlson Mast, "Greater than the Sum of Our Parts," 2014 American Association for State and Local History Annual Meeting theme.

8. Bill Clinton, "Wherever People Are Coming Together with the Aim of Getting Something Done, Good Things Are Happening," *History News* 69, no. 3 (Summer 2014): 19.

9. Barbara B. Walden, "Like a Good Neighbor: Community Advocacy for Small Museums," in *Small Museum Toolkit, Book 4: Reaching and Responding to the Audience*, eds. Cinnamon Catlin-Legutko and Stacy Klingler (Lanham, MD: AltaMira Press, 2012), 75.

10. Ibid.

11. Robert P. Connolly and Elizabeth K. Bollwerk, eds., *Positioning Your Museum as a Critical Community Asset: A Practical Guide* (Lanham, MD: Rowman & Littlefield, 2016), 1.

12. Erin Carlson Mast, email to author, December 23, 2016. She also offered this observation: "If at least some institutions were created to present one side of the story, an expressed need for one group, it's no wonder it's taken a tremendous amount of work and effort for those organizations to position themselves as indispensable to the whole community."

13. Dana, 32.

14. See chapter 1 for more on the theme for the meeting that Baker addressed.

15. Gerard Baker, "The Importance of the Human Story," *History News* 66, no. 1 (Winter 2011): 8,

16. Ibid.

17. Ibid., 9–10.

18. Ibid., 10.

19. From email communication with Erin Carlson Mast.

20. Jeanine Mazak-Kahne and Coleen Chambers, "A Town and Gown Partnership: Collaborative Learning in Indiana, Pennsylvania," *History News* 68, no. 4 (Autumn 2013): 7.

21. Ibid., 12.

22. F. Sheffield Hale, "'I Have a Dream': The Morehouse College Martin Luther King, Jr. Collection," *History News* 62, no. 4 (Autumn 2007): 8.

23. See www.morehouse.edu/kingcollection/index.php and www.civilandhuman rights.org/exhibit/martin-luther-king-jr-collection/.

24. Brian O'Neill, "21 Partnership Success Factors," accessed October 22, 2016, www.nps.gov/partnerships/oneill.htm.

25. Brian O'Neill, "21 Partnership Success Factors," *History News* 69, no. 4 (Autumn 2014): 17–21, available at resource.aaslh.org/view/21-partnership-success-factors.

Chapter 12

Greater Than the Sum of Our Parts

Erin Carlson Mast

You know the story. A poor and hungry stranger comes to a town and goes door to door asking for something to eat. Each household tells him they do not have enough food to spare. The stranger fills a large pot with water from a stream—or maybe it was a spring—and drops in a stone. Curiosity gets the better of the townsfolk and one by one they ask the stranger what he's making, to which he replies, "Stone soup." He muses aloud about what would make the soup better, and the townsfolk individually realize that they have something useful they can spare after all. The townsfolk moved past their mindset of scarcity, and found meaningful ways to contribute. Added together, the ingredients yielded a veritable feast, enough for everyone to enjoy. But they created much more than a meal; they created food for the soul, the establishment of a community.

A 2013 study could help explain the benefit of taking a step back and evaluating partnerships and collaborations that can alleviate resource concerns, rather than concentrating on the lack of resources you have to spare or contribute. In *Scarcity,* Eldar Shafir, a psychologist at Princeton University, and Sendhil Mullainathan, an economist at Harvard University, demonstrated that when we are constantly made aware that we have less time or resources than we need, it has a measurable, negative impact on our ability to solve problems. As NPR put in their review of the study, the impact of being reminded about resource issues causes people's performance on IQ tests to drop by "at least a quarter—or approximately the same mental hit a person takes after staying up all night." Thoughtful, strategic collaboration can help augment resources, freeing mental bandwidth to solve problems effectively.[1]

Of course, collaboration does not always yield a greater sum. To take the stone soup metaphor further, what elements of a collaboration support tasty soup, great conversation, and bonds that hold long enough to push the

125

equation from equal to to greater than? To find out, I turned to colleagues at National Trust For Historic Preservation sites for examples of how they have pushed their work to the next level through collaborations. It was a welcome opportunity to learn more about the work of people I seldom see. The examples that follow were selected from the many ideas they shared plus an experience from President Lincoln's Cottage.

I then contemplated what questions might help you find similar success. Before you dismiss the following examples as not applicable to your situation, forget what you think you know about National Trust sites. They come in all shapes and sizes, with and without endowments, from cities and towns of all shapes and sizes. There is a persistent myth that National Trust sites are centrally funded—they are not. They have different operational and governance structures. And they represent a range of physical, human, and financial resources. Please also note that while these examples are compatible with operating a historic site, they do not depend on it.

I have been privy to many conversations at the National Trust that dealt with scarcity in the field generally and at our sites specifically: lack of time, lack of staff, and lack of financial resources to address all the demands before us. Despite all that, passion for the work was always in abundance. Although that tension occasionally led to some hand-wringing, it has led to hard questions, trial and error, determination, and great successes.

As you read through these examples and questions, try to imagine your own organization, or institutions you've been affiliated with, and your own successes and challenges with forming alliances that become "Greater than the Sum of Our Parts."

CULTURE CHANGE—DRAYTON HALL

George McDaniel, who served for twenty-five years as the executive director of Drayton Hall in Charleston, South Carolina, is no stranger to grassroots advocacy efforts. Along with members of its community, Drayton Hall fought a mega-development that would have jeopardized its historic environs, replacing scenic drives with gridlock. In McDaniel's words, "Drayton Hall's past has been shaped by the fate of the Ashley River region, and so will our future. What happens 'upstream' affects us."

McDaniel was among the citizens who supported the designation of the Ashley River as a State Scenic River. Several years later, when the county contradicted a river management plan by refusing to buy land adjacent to the Ashley River to create a passive park, McDaniel and other members of the Ashley Scenic River Advisory Council went together to testify before the county council about the importance of purchasing the property. When they were told it was too late, they began a grassroots campaign. At the next county council meeting, 200 people packed the council rooms. Through the Advisory Council's combined efforts and the help of local council members, the Rosebrock Park (named after one of the councilmen) was purchased and created. In addition, further land diagonally across the river became the Ashley River Park.

By seeking out fellow, committed stakeholders; identifying and cultivating political allies; and using those combined networks to rally support, they succeeded in their conservation effort. That alone would have made the collaboration a success. But because of the inclusive nature of their work, they achieved something greater—culture change. According to McDaniel, the result of the successful campaign is that "a preservation ethos [now exists] in Dorchester County, which used to be hostile to historic preservation and environmental conservation." For Drayton Hall and its partners, creating culture change started with a structured advocacy effort.

Lesson Learned: A classic, "If you want to go far, go together."

Questions to consider:

- What are you doing to advocate on behalf of your institution or the field at the local, state, or national level?
- Are local, state, and national decision makers familiar with your organization and its impact? If not, how can you raise your organization's profile among these groups?
- What type of advocacy work are you engaged in? Is it consistent with your mission?
- If you are preparing to start an advocacy effort, how will you unite committed stakeholders on a specific issue?

NEIGHBORHOOD PRIDE—VILLA FINALE

Villa Finale is located in the heart of the King William Historic District of San Antonio, Texas. The Historic District predates the site's public opening but is closely connected to it. Walter Mathis, the last private owner of Villa Finale, was a driving force in local preservation. Villa Finale is continuing in Mathis's footsteps. According to Executive Director Jane Lewis, the site is very involved with the King William Association, a neighborhood group. Lewis noted, "Each year when the King William Fair—a giant street fair that covers the entire district—is held, Villa Finale is the VIP retreat for board members and top sponsors of the King William Association. Villa Finale members are also invited to enjoy the grounds of the museum during the fair."

By identifying that what they bring to the table is unique, and positioning itself as an asset to the lead organization, Villa Finale has established itself as a place of neighborhood pride and authority. Says Lewis, "This event is the largest annual fundraiser for the King William Association." There is a measurable, direct benefit to Villa Finale as well. The retreat-like atmosphere and behind-the-scenes exposure as the VIP retreat result in new members each and every year.

A leader in their neighborhood, Villa Finale also plays an active role in fostering state pride through preservation advocacy. They participated in the *I Love Texas Courthouses* campaign, a joint effort of Preservation Texas and the National Trust for Historic Preservation, and participate annually in Preservation Day lobbying activities in the state. "It expands our reach and engages us in more outreach programs within the state," said Lewis. "By expanding our 'presence' through these other organizations, we become more visible within the community." For Villa Finale and its partners, neighborhood and state pride are a proven formula for community and donor support.

Lesson Learned: What happens behind the scenes is as important as what happens out front; make the most of your role, whatever that may be.

Questions to consider:

- What resources are you willing to put toward a collaborative event or campaign?
- How is your organization uniquely situated to provide that added value?
- Do the tangible and intangible benefits of the event justify the investment?

ENLIGHTENMENT—MONTPELIER

For organizations in culture-saturated areas, partnership is both a necessity and an opportunity. According to Doug Smith, the director of the Robert H. Smith Center for the Constitution at James Madison's Montpelier located in Orange County, Virginia, "The sheer number of historic sites near Montpelier and related to the founding of the United States provides a unique opportunity where unified programming can create value for all partners." Sites in the region have made a concerted effort to complement—rather than compete with—one another's programming. "Montpelier, through its Robert H. Smith

Center for the Constitution, is a leading partner in the Presidential Precinct, a consortium uniting five landmark institutions," Smith noted. The institutions include three major presidential sites: Thomas Jefferson's Monticello, James Monroe's Highland, and Montpelier, as well as two major universities with direct connections to the history of the sites: the College of William and Mary, where Jefferson and Monroe studied the intellectual underpinnings of the American experiment in self-governance, and the University of Virginia, which Jefferson founded, with assistance from Madison and Monroe.

Smith explained, "The Presidential Precinct creates an environment that fosters inspiration and enlightenment, and provides a singular destination for international dialogue, critical thinking, and collaborative problem solving," in the heart of Virginia. "The goal of the Precinct is to advance the development of democracy around the globe. As a consortium, our institutions are able to leverage the strengths of each site." The sites have capitalized on the fact that they offer a concentrated store of knowledge about "three of the most formative leaders in American history and the principles of self-governance that they espoused." The power of the Presidential Precinct's concentrated, collaborative effort caught the notice of the White House. Smith noted that the Precinct "secured a financial commitment from the White House's Young African Leaders Initiative to train 225 leaders at sites in the Precinct over

Image 12.1.   Montpelier has hosted more than 130 government and civil society leaders through its Presidential Precinct collaborative, including many from the Arab Spring. *Source*: Presidential Precinct

a five-year period. One of the greatest legacies of sites like Montpelier is that we can continue to share the stories of our own founding period with domestic and international leaders actively forming constitutional democracies and building civil societies. The State Department and White House see tremendous value in our collaboration." For Montpelier and the other members of the Presidential Precinct, the power to inspire and enlighten today's leaders stems from their credibility as places that inspired enlightenment in past leaders.

Lessons Learned: The history of your organization may contain clues for meaningful collaborations with regional, national, or even global impact.

Questions for consideration:

- If your region is saturated with like-organizations, how can you position your organization as a distinct and desirable partner?
- If there is a dearth of like-organizations in your area, how might you connect to organizations with compatible missions or themes in other parts of the country or world?
- What is preventing you from partnering with certain competitors who have compatible missions or themes?
- Do you avoid partnering with larger organizations for fear of being steamrolled or, conversely, smaller organizations because you assume they have little to offer?

COMMUNITY VOLUNTEERISM—FILOLI

The centerpiece of Filoli in Woodside, California, is a 1915 mansion, but its assets extend well beyond that one building. Former executive director Cynthia D'Agosta emphasized, "Filoli's assets include many 'parts' that we consider and market as the whole, including the mansion and auxiliary buildings, the sixteen acres of historic formal gardens, over 200 varieties of heritage orchard trees, more than 660 acres of nature preserve, as well as a café and gift shop." It takes a considerable amount of human resources for Filoli to thrive.

Filoli has managed to engage a highly diverse and skilled network of volunteers who, in turn, support the site in a variety of ways beyond those who serve on its board and work at the site. Local environmental education nonprofit organizations provide input on Filoli's Nature Hikes, school visits, and educational curriculum. The institution has engaged MBA students from California College of the Arts to assess and make recommendations on Filoli's development strategies and ability to meet the demands of a new demographic in the area. Pro bono food service specialists advise on improvements to the café, catering, and hosting operations. And a local television station covers Filoli's biggest annual events, increasing visitation and exposure for the site while helping the station fulfill its community service needs. Taken separately, each volunteer or pro bono project has a specific purpose and benefit. Taken as a whole, Filoli's network of staff, volunteers, and pro bono partners result in an organization that is able to maintain infrastructure, vitality, and relevance to its community.

Lesson Learned: When it comes to volunteers and partnerships, you can only expect to get out what you put in to it.

Questions to consider:

- How are the physical assets at your organization marketed, supported, and utilized?
- If you have a volunteer program, how functional is it?
- How diverse are the opportunities for volunteering? Are you maximizing the skillset of your volunteers, or are their skills being squandered?
- If your volunteer program is nonexistent, what is holding you back?

CULTURAL CAPITAL—BRUCEMORE

If you visit Cedar Rapids, Iowa, and ask the locals what you should do while you are in town, there is a good chance the response will be "Go to Brucemore." For more than three decades, Brucemore has pursued a strategy that promotes the site as an authentic setting for "unique cultural experiences" in their region—experiences that draw approximately 40,000 people each year in a city of 200,000, according to Executive Director David Janssen. He explained, "Brucemore's broad and diverse menu of events has included almost every genre imaginable, from rock-and-roll to jazz and symphony to the Joffrey Ballet (twice). Brucemore also produces annual theater events on a natural slope near the estate's duck pond. Additionally, the site has hosted garden and art shows, Scottish heritage festivals, and old house fairs. In 2015 alone, the estate hosted or produced thirty-three performances as part of nine distinct programs."

Janssen shared, "The secret—and the challenge—is that none of these is a simple turnkey event. Each has unique challenges, cost centers, and audience appeal, requiring months and years of planning, trial, and error before they flourish. What they all have in common is a complex interplay among multiple stakeholders, including: cultural partners, food and service vendors (who often acquiesce with discounted rates), volunteers, sponsors, city leaders, and contractors. Each program relies heavily on collaborators motivated to supplement the capacity of site staff. None of the events would be possible to host or produce relying only on in-house resources."

Being a beloved cultural center in the region with a reputation for collaboration can make it difficult to say no or to sunset once-popular programs. After years of adding programs, Brucemore recently made the difficult decision to end a signature program known as "Bluesmore." While the decision to end the program and its associated partnerships wasn't easy, it was the right move to maintain the quality and integrity of programs with deeper support and broader interest. Brucemore's strategy has the annual impact of showcasing an attractive slate of differentiated events with a variety of partners, and the lasting impact of a regional reputation as the go-to place and partner for diverse cultural experiences.

Lesson Learned: Take the long view. Being a cultural pioneer with stick-to-it-iveness can result in true sustainability, as long as you are willing to make tough decisions.

Questions to consider:

- If a tourist asked a local in your area what attractions they should visit, what would be their first response? If you don't have public visitation, are you visible in other ways?
- How much time are you willing to give a collaboration to develop before you determine whether it's a success or failure?
- What is your exit strategy for a collaboration that has run its course?
- How can you create a culture of collaboration within your organization? Within your community?

BUILDING A FOUNDATION—PRESIDENT LINCOLN'S COTTAGE

The idea behind this story grew out of a lively panel developed first for the American Association for State and Local History's 2010 conference in Oklahoma City by the members of the Civil War Washington Museum Consortium: President Lincoln's Cottage, Ford's Theatre Society, Tudor Place Historic House and Garden, and Frederick Douglass National Historic Site.

Consortium members realized they were better together as a one-stop shop for teachers' Civil War Washington needs. As Callie Hawkins, associate director for Programs at President Lincoln's Cottage, recollected, "The consortium group had worked with several Teaching American History grants to create weeklong field experiences for national groups of teachers using our own model for the Civil War Washington Teacher Fellows. We were surprised when each of these groups remarked on how unique it was that four distinctive, yet alike organizations worked so well together to provide a seamless week of learning experiences for their teachers."

It is noteworthy that the teachers found the functionality and productivity of the cultural partnership so novel. According to Hawkins, prior to committing to the partnership, consortium members took a hard look at their resources, compatibility, and the program's objectives and needs. What they discovered was that when it came to needs such as physical space, expertise, staff resources, or budget, they each had an area of scarcity and abundance. They each contributed something unique. In short, they were near-perfect complements for the purposes of the teacher fellows program partnership. After comparing content and methodology, they discovered that not only

Image 12.2. President Lincoln's Cottage Associate Director for Programs Callie Hawkins facilitates a human timeline exercise with Civil War Washington Teacher Fellows participants. *Source*: President Lincoln's Cottage

were they able to offer a well-rounded perspective on the Civil War together, but that each site used different methods for engaging teachers, which ensured instructional variety. The group then agreed on the parameters of the partnership itself. Not only has the partnership endured and evolved, it has created a foundation of trust for additional collaboration as well.

Hawkins reported that when the consortium presented on their process and outcomes to the AASLH membership in 2010 and again through a different panel in 2011, responses were mixed. But in both cases, session attendees focused on the fact that the consortium members were fortunate that they had compatible personalities, expressing concern that if any of them left, the partnership would likely fall apart. The members of the consortium did not deny that individual personalities are a major factor in the success of any collaboration, but noted that since each of them were able to demonstrate the value of the collaboration with competitors, the organizations had come to regard the partnership as indispensable. Indeed, most of the staff members who carry out the program today were not part of the original collaboration in 2010. Yet the program continues to succeed. For President Lincoln's Cottage and the Civil War Washington Consortium, leading with friendship and an open mind paved the way for a collaborative peer network and invaluable partnerships that enhance resources and transcend individual personalities.

Lesson Learned: Partnerships will be more enjoyable if not more successful and enduring, if you are honest about what you have to offer and what you have to gain, and if you check your ego at the door.

Questions to consider:

- Is a potentially powerful partnership being sidelined due to personality conflict? What role do you play in the success or failure of that potential partnership?
- Are you realistic about what your organization has to offer?
- How will you determine who to have around the table?
- Are you prepared for the inevitable change in people involved?

The range of National Trust sites has many more examples of collaborations: from joint-ticketing ventures, to staff exchanges, to partnerships with universities, nonprofit organizations, and businesses that vary widely place to place, year to year. Partnerships and collaborations form the basis of our work. Not every partnership is desirable or destined to succeed, but each will contain valuable lessons and potential templates for future collaborations. There is no formula that will ensure successful, transcendent partnerships every time, and many of my colleagues were quick to offer words of caution, lessons they have learned and tested along the way. Partnerships need to be well structured. Diplomacy and honesty go a long way. Responsibilities and decisions need to be carefully articulated and agreements documented. And it never hurts to have a Plan B.

NOTE

1. Michaeleen Doucleff, "How Money Worries Can Scramble Your Thinking," August 29, 2013, accessed February 17, 2017, on.aaslh.org/ScarcityandThinking. See also Cara Feinburg, "The Science of Scarcity," *Harvard Magazine* 117, no. 5 (May–June 2015): 38–43.

Chapter 13

Crossroads: Exploring the Vibrant Connections between People and Place

Bob Beatty

"Place is at the heart of how we come to see the past." Thus said David W. Blight in his keynote address to the 2007 AASLH annual meeting.[1] One of America's most renowned historians, Blight is author of the 2002 Bancroft Prize–winning *Race and Reunion: The Civil War in American Memory*. He is an accomplished scholar. And he is one of us in that he understands the role particular places play in history.

Blight began his career in the 1970s as a high school history teacher in Flint, Michigan, where he'd take his students on trips to Civil War sites in the east: Gettysburg, Harper's Ferry, Antietam. These trips were powerful for both his students and Blight. "It is in that period of my life that I began to understand how important *place* was."[2]

Thirty-plus years later, Blight visited Elmina Castle, a Portuguese slave fortress in Ghana. In experiencing the "Door of No Return"—the infamous gateway that opens up to the beach where enslaved people were herded onto slave ships—he had a truly impactful, place-based encounter. "The most poignant moment . . . was when I was confronted by my own world-historical sensibility," he recounted. "I had written about Elmina Castle, and I had seen films about it. Now I was walking through the 'Door of No Return.'" Blight stepped onto a beach full of fishing boats. "In those fisherman's eyes," he wrote, "I saw the unbridgeable gulf that sometimes exists between past and present, between the meaning of a place and its long history." While clearly meaningful to him, the visit wasn't necessarily pleasant. "I was terribly uncomfortable, and it wasn't just about the slave trade. It was about somehow invading the space of these . . . fisherman."[3]

I suspect many of us have had similar experiences as Dr. Blight. History in books certainly piqued an interest. But for lots of us, myself included,

Image 13.1.   Historian David W. Blight gave the keynote address to the 2007 AASLH Annual Meeting, telling attendees, "Place is at the heart of how we come to see the past." *Source*: **American Association for State and Local History**

actually going to the places where history happened and/or terrific museums that display traces of the past added a new dimension to the past for us.

I use these two anecdotes because they offer two examples of how place can help instill tremendous meaning to the past. For Blight, the Civil War battlefields far from Flint, Michigan, no doubt inspired his later research and study of the Civil War, the most devastating conflict in American history.

And a visit to Ghana helped Blight better understand the power that place wields to those in the present.

Adam Goodheart called this "The Eloquence of Place." It is a term that resonates. Goodheart was specifically referring to Fort Monroe, decommissioned by the U.S. Army in September 2011 and designated by President Barack Obama as a national monument that November. Located on the James River near Hampton Roads, Virginia, Fort Monroe is at the site where African slavery first gained its foothold on the American continent in 1619. A little less than 250 years later, in April 1861, the fort became the site of the self-emancipation of three men: Frank Baker, Sheppard Mallory, and James Townsend. They were the first Americans to be known as "contrabands"— former slaves declared spoils of war by the U.S. Army during the Civil War. Their number grew to several hundred thousand by the war's end. Fort Monroe was significant to American history, Goodheart asserted. "Here, liberty as well as slavery began. Here," he argued, "African American history began. I hope it is a place where many future generations can come face to face with the American paradox of liberty and slavery, with the complications of both the past and the present."[4]

Place truly is at the heart of how we see the past. It's the very core of the discipline, and certainly is at the epicenter of local history. "Cities and towns have distinct voices," notes J. Dennis Robinson in his book on Strawbery Banke Museum in Portsmouth, New Hampshire. "Their neighborhoods, houses, and rooms tell tales; they hold deep impressions of their makers and their keepers."[5]

Local history is found at the intersection of people and place. These are the stories we share in tens of thousands of history organizations across the country and in the millions of historic places they occurred. This was the inspiration for *Crossroads: Exploring the Vibrant Connections Between People and Place*, the theme for the 2012 AASLH annual meeting in Salt Lake City, Utah.

"A crystal clear mountain lake, an American Indian cliff dwelling, a railway crossroad, a farmstead, your home," 2012 Program Chair Scott Stroh wrote. "Each evokes an emotional response; each stirs the human spirit; and each reminds us that history is, at its core, about the powerful connections between people and place." At this crossroads is "the sometimes empowering, sometimes challenging, but always special connection between people and place."[6]

And it is those who labor in place-based history (often, but not always local history) who truly engage in the magic that is place. "Local historians are a lucky group," Bruce Teeple writes. "We breathe life into the cast and characters who once inhabited our own backyards." He continues, "Every place and object, no matter how small or mundane has a story to tell, a story that is an integral part of the surrounding terrain."[7] Historian Joseph A. Amato agrees. "Working on the microcosmos, one discovers the power of locality in defining home, self, and communities. . . . Local history, in adroit hands, recaptures how peoples of a place and time experienced the world."[8]

There are thousands of examples of these principles in action each year across the United States. They happen in conversations between young people and their elders, they happen in classrooms, and, most importantly to us, they happen through the medium of public history. These are connections between people and place that create meaning and change, that make a difference in individual and community life. A few examples of this precept follow.

In 2006, the Ohio History Connection collaborated with an elementary and middle school in Columbus's Near East Side, a formerly thriving African American commercial and social hub. The area served as the center of African American life in Ohio's capital city until the building of interstate highways severed the community from the city's downtown. It is a story that is all-too-common in countless American communities.

The *Near East Side Community History Project* used student-led research projects to connect youth to their community's history. A study of the Great Migration placed the neighborhood in context. Students researched primary sources on area artists, churches, schools, and businesses, and conducted oral histories. Youth drafted text for historical markers and created a walking tour.[9] The project engaged students deeply and meaningfully in the discovery of their community. As one student reported, participation made her "feel like I was a special part in history."[10] Isn't that ultimately the goal we are all working toward?

Connecting people and place is often the very essence of the practice of local history. The creation of tangible products—markers, tours, exhibits, and the like—provides additional meaning for those participating in this process.

You can find history in less-likely locations as well. "Botanic gardens are for plants," George Longenecker, executive director of the West Virginia Botanic Garden in Cheat Lake, said to public historian Barbara J. Howe when she proposed using history in the garden's interpretation.

The site is truly significant to the region. It includes the reservoir that supplied water to Morgantown, West Virginia, from 1912 to 1969. Its land protected that water from pollution, a major problem throughout the nineteenth and early twentieth centuries. As local newspapers reported in 1885, the vote to develop a water works meant, "No danger of drinking nasty woolly water worms. . . . No more washing in wiggle-tail water now."[11]

Nature, water, pollution, plus a fantastic name (could *you* come up with "wiggle-tail water"?): the institution had all the elements of a connection between people and place. Ultimately, Howe convinced Longenecker and

Image 13.2.   The Ohio History Connection's *Near East Side Community History Project* used student-led research projects to connect youth to their community's history. *Source*: Stacia Kuceyeski

fellow board members to embark on a history-focused interpretation of the site. It allowed the site's visitors to enjoy it in a wider context than just a beautiful place in which to spend time in nature. The project also provided the opportunity to reach out to the community as it shaped this interpretation. Its work with daughters of the reservoir's only resident caretaker, West Virginia University faculty members, and other history organizations in the region and state helped strengthen the project and the institution's reach.

The ultimate interpretation included then-untold stories of African American history, the political power of women (who could not vote) in advocating for acquiring clean water, and the role of local government in setting rates and authorizing companies to supply water. The multifaceted history of place included stories of technology and engineering, of the laborers who constructed the water works system, and of the connection between clean water and public health. It addressed change over time in the importance of a clean, unimpeded water supply to the development and growth of nearby West Virginia University and addressed the threat of industrial pollution as well.[12]

The latter was unplanned, a fortuitous unintended consequence brought about as the present-day community grappled with the question of fracking locally. "I would like to think that some visitors . . . might make some connections themselves between industrial activity in the past and that happening now," Howe wrote. "If they do, then they might see that history can be relevant to public policy, both as they enjoy the scenery at the garden and as they turn on their faucets at home."[13]

Howe's reinterpretation project at West Virginia Botanic Garden presented history in an unexpected place. That is not the case with the Woodrow Wilson Family Home in Columbia, South Carolina. People expect to encounter the past when visiting a historic house museum. What they don't expect is a site that tells the story of Reconstruction, one of the most poorly understood, and highly significant, events in the American history.

The property has a very brief connection with the twenty-eighth president of the United States. Wilson lived there for only three years, from 1871 until 1874, when his father (a Presbyterian minister) moved the family from Augusta, Georgia. In 1928, generations after the teenaged future president left Columbia, preservationists saved his former home from demolition. It opened as a historic house museum in 1933. Seven decades later, Historic Columbia, the steward that managed the county-owned property, faced a dilemma that was as much a positive as a negative.

In 2005, Historic Columbia closed the house for much-needed capital repairs. This pause gave the institution the opportunity to rethink the site's interpretation. During restoration, staff worked with a team of scholars at the University of South Carolina to completely reimagine the site.

They chose to, in the words of Lana A. Burgess, director of the University of South Carolina Museum Management Program, "provide a fresh approach to the stagnant historical narrative of Reconstruction."[14] Reconstruction became the historical backdrop for this reinterpretation. As Wilson scholar Hendrik Booraem wrote, "Columbia's municipal government in the early 1870s . . . was controlled by freed African Americans and their white allies, a situation the Wilson family, like almost all white professionals, deplored and opposed more or less actively."[15] As this was the era in which the Wilsons lived in the home, it surely shaped the mindset and ideals of the future president.

The institution used the Wilson family's story as a springboard into discussions of the city and the state's wider story of the post–Civil War Reconstruction era. Central to that narrative is the experience of black South Carolinians. As John M. Sherrer, Historic Columbia's Director of Cultural Resources, noted, "Discussion of race, politics, in fact the very understanding of citizenship as we know it today, fueled the transformation . . . from a traditional historic house museum, into a twenty-first-century museum contained within a nineteenth-century residence." The house's setting in Columbia was essential in this new understanding. "It was here in Columbia," Sherrer wrote, "that Wilson experienced Reconstruction, where South Carolinians, black and white, were working out the meanings, ramifications, and potential of a society in which formerly enslaved men and women were now free."[16]

There is something significant in what Historic Columbia accomplished at the Wilson Home. Not only did the organization tackle a subject that is little understood and fraught with the complexity of racial tension and power relationships, it did so at a presidential site, a place where many visitors expect veneration and hero worship. What the organization accomplished in integrating a presidential site with a community museum of Reconstruction, historian Thomas J. Brown argued, "was a courageous and thoughtful undertaking." Brown wrote, "The topic commands national interest, but the selection of emphasis demonstrates Historic Columbia's commitment to local history by fitting its presentation of the president into the narrative most applicable to the community."[17]

The Wilson Home had a connection to President Wilson that was indisputable; what it lacked was a true "hook" between people and place. For Sherrer, the reinterpretation "became a pivotal moment in Historic Columbia's culture and the manner in which the organization's staff and volunteer interpreters were trained in facilitating engaging conversations at the site on topics that lie at the heart of so many current events, especially race." The house is "a nineteenth-century historic asset featuring a twenty-first-century approach to constructive conversations about what it means to be an American and how some of today's assumptions, aspirations, and concepts of citizenship had their foundations laid in Reconstruction."[18]

In understanding the possibilities inherent in the discovery of place, our institutions provide a truly valuable service. As Barbara B. Walden argued, "Museums have to identify what is distinct and unique about their shared story and, while continuing to preserve their community's collective narrative, create an environment that encourages and supports dialogue."[19] The Ohio History Connection accomplished this with student-led activities. The West Virginia Botanic Garden used environmental history in its interpretation and programming. And the Wilson House completed a reinterpretation of epic proportions. Each embodies an aspect of something Ralph Waldo

Emerson urged: "Know your own bone; gnaw at it, bury it, unearth it, and gnaw at it still."[20] History organizations would be wise to heed Walden's and Emerson's counsel and dig deep into possibilities and opportunities for connections with constituents.

In the next chapter, former AASLH Council chair David A. Donath shares additional thoughts on the intersection of people and place. As you read on, "Consider the meaning of place in your personal life," as Scott Stroh asked the field in 2012. "What are your special places? Why are these connections meaningful? How do they support and sustain you as an individual and your work in the field of history?"[21] One place immediately comes to mind as I read those words: the farm in Babson Park, Florida, where my father grew up—on Beatty Road, no less. It is a part of my family's history and legacy, one that I return to more than forty years after my grandmother sold the farm. What is that place for you?

Our connections to place might stop at that point were we not involved in the work of public history. "Think about your organization," Stroh expounded. "Is it representative of the values and distinctiveness of your place; how are these connections represented and are they fundamental to your institution? Consider your community: how is its story connected to your organization? . . . How can you and your organization support and inform your community?"[22]

NOTES

1. David W. Blight, "Place Is at the Heart of How We See the Past," *History News* 63, no. 1 (Winter 2008): 12.

2. Ibid.

3. Ibid., 12–13.

4. Adam Goodheart, "The Eloquence of Place," *History News* 67, no. 1 (Winter 2012): 9–11.

5. J. Dennis Robinson, *Strawbery Banke: A Seaport Museum 400 Years in the Making* (Portsmouth, NH: Peter E. Randall Publisher LLC, 2007), xvii.

6. Scott Stroh, "Crossroads: Exploring the Vibrant Connections between People and Place," 2012 American Association for State and Local History Annual Meeting theme.

7. Bruce Teeple, "Call Rethinking Local History," in *Zen and the Art of Local History*, eds. Carol Kammen and Bob Beatty (Lanham, MD: Rowman & Littlefield, 2014), 128.

8. Joseph A. Amato, "The Extraordinary Ordinary and the Changing Face of Place," *History News* 68, no. 2 (Spring 2013): 16.

9. For text of the markers, search "Mount Vernon" at http://remarkableohio.org/.

10. Stacia Kuceyeski, "Near East Side Community History Project," *History News* 64, no. 1 (Winter 2009): 29–30.

11. Barbara J. Howe, "'No More Wiggle-Tail Water': Interpreting the History of Morgantown's Water Supply at the West Virginia Botanic Garden," *History News* 67, no. 4 (Autumn 2012): 11–12.

12. Ibid., 14.

13. Ibid., 15.

14. Lana A. Burgess, letter of support in Historic Columbia, "Woodrow Wilson Family Home: A Museum of Reconstruction in Columbia & Richland County," Leadership in History Award Nomination, 2015.

15. Hendrik Booraem V, letter of support in Historic Columbia, "Woodrow Wilson Family Home."

16. John M. Sherrer, "From Historic House Museum to 21st-Century Museum," *Views from the Porch*, July 20, 2015, accessed October 23, 2016, http://blogs.aaslh.org/from-historic-house-museum-to-21st-century-museum/.

17. Thomas J. Brown, letter of support in Historic Columbia, "Woodrow Wilson Family Home."

18. Sherrer.

19. Walden, 75.

20. Borrowed from my colleague Colleen Dilenschneider's excellent blog, *Know Your Own Bone*, http://colleendilen.com.

21. Stroh.

22. Ibid.

Chapter 14

Explorations in Place and Time: A Personal Journey

David A. Donath

INTRODUCTION

In 2012, I was State Historic Preservation Officer and Director of Historical Resources for the State of Florida. Florida is a place that is very different from the Vermont described here, but a place, like Vermont, that is rich in natural beauty, diverse cultural landscapes, distinctive historic sites, and powerful human voices and stories.

Shortly after arriving in Tallahassee, one place particularly captivated my heart, mind, and spirit. Known as The Grove, it sits on ten oasis-like acres in the heart of Tallahassee, Florida's capital city, and served as home for two of its governors. Charged with transforming this place into a public museum, the question facing our organization was: what would this place become? Do we create a historic house museum, embrace living history, fill the place with exhibits and displays, or do we create something else? As you will read on, and undoubtedly know from your own work, these are not new questions. The only differences are the places being considered.

It was at this moment that, perhaps for the first time, I really began to think about place in the broadest possible sense. I thought about place in a way unencumbered by physical, intellectual, and/or chronological boundaries. I thought about places of importance to me, why they were important, and how this value manifested itself in my life and work. And, I thought a lot about The Grove as a place rich in history, stories, and the context of the past. More importantly, I began to think about The Grove's true and authentic wealth as deriving from its place as more than a museum destination, but as a starting point for personal and communal journeys in which the historical context of a place is used to foster, facilitate, and nurture something bigger, something more powerful, and something more meaningful than a singular understanding of the past.

Much of the inspiration for this new way of understanding and exploring place originated and developed through conversations and interactions with David Donath. And as I learned more about Salt Lake City itself, a theme bubbled to the surface that connected the city's history with the needs of history organizations and their paid and unpaid staff—*Crossroads: Exploring the Vibrant Connections Between People and Place.* This theme focused so specifically on connections between people and place that I immediately thought of David to provide significant insight into our personal and organizational relationships with *place* and *places*.

Although introduced as a personal journey, David Donath's words offer much more. David's expression of his own experiences offers a thoughtful reflection and analysis about topics and issues of significant importance to our communities, our institutions, and our places. In so doing, he provides a powerful example of an individual's and several organizations' inspiring efforts not only to preserve places and teach history but also to change the world and lift the human spirit through deeper connections with place.

—*Scott Muir Stroh III, 2012*

If you don't know where you are, you don't know who you are.

Wendell Berry quoted by Wallace Stegner (1992)

Like Wallace Stegner before him, Wendell Berry is a leading voice among our great environmental writers. Berry primarily was talking about understanding our places in nature. But I apply Berry's observation also to understanding our place in time—to knowing where we are in history as well as on the ground. Both of these concepts are core to our work in the field of state and local history. They are also core to our roles as citizens in our communities, to our personal identities, and to our human wellbeing.

To develop and function as healthy human beings and citizens, we need to be grounded in place and time. We need to appreciate where we are, where we have come from, and how we got here. Our identities depend on our ability to navigate time and place. Our productive roles as members of communities and of society as a whole depend on our working sense of our place in the world and in its historical processes.

These needs also apply to communities and governments. To be healthy, they need perspective. In the history field we call this context, meaning perspective on our locales and their relationships to past and present. Former U.S. Speaker of the House Tip O'Neill famously quipped, "All politics is local." He understood that over time our community relationships form the roots both of politics and of culture. These are all good reasons why we should care about something we call local history.

As I reflect on a forty-year career in the vineyard of history, I see my personal journey as a quest for identity and context. First enticed by the chestnuts of civics and American history that I learned in public school, I delved deeper into understanding my place in nature, geography, and time. Initially groomed to be an engineer, I chose to study history instead. Eschewing the political and economic history that seemed fashionable in my graduate seminars, I chose historical geography and its social and cultural corollaries. Most of all, I was interested in the stories we tell that help us to understand our places in nature, culture, and history, the stories that lend our places authenticity. About the time I completed my ABD (all but the dissertation), I fled the academy for the more tangible world of historic preservation—then to the field of historic sites and outdoor museums. I never looked back, but I never stopped studying, learning, and searching.

I left the classroom during the heady time of the U.S. Bicentennial celebration. Despite the national traumas of Vietnam and Watergate, popular fascination with American history was at a high tide. I wanted to embrace our history, immerse myself in past life, and engage a public that shared my hunger for historical experience and enlightenment. After a brief sojourn in the Wisconsin state historic preservation office, I directed one of the state's historic sites, and then its array of six sites scattered around the state. The then New Social History and a related quest for period authenticity defined our gold standards as we revised our sites according to careful material culture research. We sought seamless restorations, furnishing plans, and interpretive scripts as if such perfection were possible. We also revised our sites' tired Eisenhower-era presentations, finding them all too often "phony-colonialized," triumphalist conflations of the American story. We sought authenticity by perfecting accurate social history time capsules that we thought would have the power to transport our visitors into past lives and places through the transformative power of living history. We were passionate storytellers as well as righteous iconoclasts, but I confess that after a few years of this, I grew restless and a bit cynical. A decade later I would give a talk at an Association for Living History Farms and Museums conference entitled "Is There Life after Living History?"

I moved on—to an outdoor museum that addressed four centuries of history of a single place—an ancient neighborhood on the New Hampshire Seacoast. The Strawbery Banke Museum was experimenting with a range of approaches to interpreting place over time. Taking inspiration from the neighborhood's rich layering of architecture, artifacts, and stories, Strawbery Banke sought an understanding of the past in its complexity and anachronisms.

Forget the historical time capsule. In the Puddle Dock neighborhood, four centuries of change lie side by side and juxtaposed, one on top of the other, often with multiple generations revealed in the same historic building. Imagine a late eighteenth-century merchant mariner's residence with its east half restored to the 1790s era of Captain Shapley, and its west half restored to the 1950s era of its working-class tenants. And next door, the postmedieval 1690s house of John and Elizabeth Sherburne dissected as an architectural artifact; or a 1720s house restored to its 1940s form as the neighborhood's mom-and-pop Abbott Store—all in the same historic neighborhood, little more than a block apart.

Image 14.1, Image 14.2, Image 14.3.   Strawbery Banke Museum, in the Puddle Dock neighborhood of Portsmouth, New Hampshire, demonstrates four centuries of change over time, often with multiple generations revealed in the same historic building.

Source: Strawbery Banke Museum/John Dunkle and Strawbery Banke Museum/Crowley Collection

At the time, Strawbery Banke seemed to verge on historic site heresy. By our earlier lights, we'd assumed visitors could be hopelessly confused by the depiction of multiple periods and themes all assembled chock-a-block on a single site. Rather than a neat historical time capsule, had Strawbery Banke assembled a Tralfamadorian mélange where Billy Pilgrim indeed had come unstuck in time and ambled the streets of Puddle Dock? But our visitors weren't perplexed, they were intrigued, and they navigated our anachronisms with amazing adroitness. Rather than seeking chronological timelines, some found the past easier to approach from the vantage of the present—from finish to start, so to speak. People who might have hated history in the classroom loved rediscovering it on the ground as it offered new ways to appreciate a place over time—or a place caught up in time. We saw that many visitors understood history as generational rather than chronological. Grandparents could show their grandchildren places of their own pasts alongside places depicting other periods, and then they might leap back another century and recall the pasts of their own grandparents or great-grandparents.

Strawbery Banke's profound strength lay in its stratigraphy of multiple generations, all encapsulated in a single compact neighborhood. Layer upon layer, generations of people of multiple callings, ethnicities, and circumstances had laid down the evidence of their lives in this single place. Layer upon layer, we were picking it apart so visitors could see it, touch it, hear its stories, and form insights into their own pasts and their own places. Asked what they thought was best about the experience, many answered, "Its authenticity."

But today, many historic sites and outdoor museums are troubled. While Strawbery Banke, Old World Wisconsin, and many others remain interpretively rich, they face severe financial challenges. Critics argue that America has too many historic house museums. The impulses that created them have shifted, their audiences are slipping away, and only the strongest of them may prove sustainable long into the future. Today, even the strong are struggling. Authenticity needs to join forces with purposeful societal relevance.

There's truth embedded in these critiques. Most of our classic outdoor museums developed during the post–World War II era of prosperity, a time when automobile tourism was a mainstay of American family vacations and entertainment. Many historic sites and outdoor museums grew up as roadside attractions or park-like destinations, complete with convenient parking lots, clean restrooms, ubiquitous gift shops, and perimeter fences. Fences were essential to define the bounds of the site, the historic zone, or the time capsule. Also, fences controlled access, limiting entry to only those who bought an admission ticket. Pragmatically, success (or failure) became measured by increasing (or declining) ticket sales, and the "show" inside the fence defined the program. At Strawbery Banke, continually mending and painting of its in-town fence proved a major effort and expense, while interpretive and administrative staff members remained frustrated by gatecrashers. At the same time, staff from other fenceless outdoor museums bemoaned the unticketed masses that invaded the *sancta sanctorum*, interested only in a quick snapshot, a visit to the restroom, and perhaps a trinket from the gift shop.

Automobile-borne visitors often engaged this new kind of museum as onetime vacation pilgrimages, rather than regular visits. Economic necessity drove sites to focus their attention on visitors who paid admission and came inside the fence. Historic sites and outdoor museums operated like theme-park attractions, although they saw themselves as more profound and beyond the attractions' pale. They were authentic—emphasizing historical accuracy and education while flirting with a blend that they called edutainment. Never mind that theme parks possessed their own brands of authenticity, some-times even rooted in popular history, and that other businesses increasingly branded themselves as themed entertainment, engaging customers in authentic experiences.

Today's historic sites and outdoor museums indeed face real challenges as they must produce and most importantly sustain an expensive product even while they increasingly lack the ability to differentiate themselves effectively from encroaching leisure-time competition. Audiences move on while costs relentlessly grow out of reach. Travel patterns and visitor expecta-tions change. Audiences find satisfying experiences in new places, including cyberspace. Too often, the time capsule or the fenced-in historic zone simply lacks its former competitive edge.

After my inspiring sojourn at Strawbery Banke, I returned to my home state of Vermont to lead the development of a new outdoor museum in Woodstock. I went to Billings Farm & Museum in 1985 at the start of its third operating season, and I've been there ever since. Billings incorporates a 140-year-old fully operational dairy farm together with conventional historical museum exhibits, a living-history restoration, and an active film program. And yes, it has a fence, it sells admission tickets, and I confess to often opening board meetings with reports on how attendance is doing.

But Billings Farm is not a conventional outdoor history museum. Its audi-ence often first discovers it as a tourist destination, but many become regular visitors and longtime members.

Billings incorporates a full-scale dairy farm operation with a world-class herd of Jersey cows and that produces fluid milk and (recently) artisanal cheese, and that markets high-end livestock and genetics. Since 1871 it has remained an outstanding farm of roughly the current scale in terms of herd and cropland. In terms of production, in Vermont and nationally, it has long been a prominent agricultural model. In 1893, Billings Farm won top prizes at the World's Columbian Exposition in Chicago. Today it wins comparable honors as among the three best Jersey dairy farms in North America.

But today Billings is not only a farm. It is an outdoor museum with a core purpose of place-based education and immersive interpretation. Every year its 60,000 visitors engage the farm and its animals up close and personal, and they participate in a lively array of historical programs and activities. Its engaged audience includes a growing membership with a high rate of repeat visitation (averaging five visits per year).

Billings Farm also helped to create the Marsh–Billings–Rockefeller National Historical Park, which is Vermont's sole unit of the National Park System, dedicated to the theme of conservation stewardship. In addition, the Farm's parent institution, the nonprofit Woodstock Foundation, also owns a separately governed for-profit subsidiary, the Woodstock Inn, a venerable four-diamond resort that includes ski areas, a golf course, a spa, and other recreational facilities. In addition to the Farm's and Park's educational and conservation missions, with the resort, they help to anchor the community of Woodstock environmentally, aesthetically, historically, recreationally, and economically as an internationally known destination. The mission of the Woodstock Foundation and its combination of sister entities is indeed all about place.

In the mid-1990s, at the time that plans for Woodstock's National Park were taking shape, the then acting director Denis Galvin challenged the National Park Service to work beyond its individual parks' boundaries. He challenged them to connect the dots, developing linkages between parks and their neighbors, communities, and landscapes, including cultural resources such as museums. Rather than focus exclusively on their own enclaves, parks should inspire visitors to explore their historical, cultural, and environmental contexts lying outside of park boundaries. The big story could be found in the connective tissue that lay beyond the boundaries, and parks would not fully achieve their programmatic potentials until they engaged it. This advice resonated with the museum.

At Billings we'd long held a collaborative attitude, seeing our place as part of a web of kindred places across Vermont and beyond. We saw our role not only as an engaging educational farm and museum but also as an inspiring gateway and guide. We embraced the role of helping visitors (whether tourists or residents) to appreciate the agricultural working landscape of Vermont. We also took a leading role in advancement and stewardship of Vermont both as a national treasure and as a world-class destination. We didn't think in terms of competition with other places. Instead we focused on gateways and networks.

Billings Farm & Museum originally had defined its interpretive mission as exploration of the rural, agricultural life of east-central Vermont in the century after the Civil War. This was a time frame that coincided with the history of the farm itself, a nineteenth-century gentleman's estate handed down and modernized through subsequent generations. A bit like Strawbery Banke, Billings Farm & Museum presented historical anachronism, with its modern evolved gentleman's farm juxtaposed against an exhibit about Vermont's hill-farming families whose lives were at the other end of the social and technological scales. By the 1980s Vermont's traditional farm life was growing scarce, and the museum initially tended to gloss over social and technological distinctions in favor of a simpler interpretation that celebrated farm life and farm work. But within its first decade it embraced the Billings Farm's site-specific history, adding a documented restoration of its 1890 Farm House. This illuminated the gentleman's farm of the period, and highlighted its social and technological counterpoint to Billings's hill-farm contemporaries. It also explored the historical origins of the current farm. But was Billings Farm fulfilling its potential to engage and interpret the life, work, and sustainability of Vermont's evolving working landscape?

True or not at the time, we said we were. In 2002 we inserted an epigram on the back of our holiday greeting card dubbing Billings Farm as the "Gateway to Vermont's Rural Heritage." We thought this slogan justifiable—after all, nobody else claimed such a distinction. A handful of our longtime Vermont colleagues raised their eyebrows. "What makes you so special?" they asked. The following summer, as Billings celebrated its twentieth anniversary as an outdoor museum, we invited the then governor Douglas to give a keynote address. We encouraged him to speak about agriculture, always a good topic in Vermont, and we hoped he might mention Billings Farm's role as a rural heritage gateway. He said,

> If farming is to have a future in this state, indeed if Vermont is to have a future with farms, the Billings Farm & Museum will help to lead the way. As a gateway to our rural heritage it shows thousands of visitors and students every year where rural Vermont has come from and why it is so important. . . . It shows how generations interact with the places they inhabit and the places from which they draw their sustenance, how generations can care for the places they pass on to their children. In so many ways the Billings Farm represents the best of Vermont past, present and future.

With the governor's endorsement of our mission, we grappled with the question of what this really meant for the presentation of the Billings Farm.

What indeed? Our program was inside the fence, concentrated in a rich, multifaceted farm experience. But our historical context and much of our real subject matter were immersed in what lay beyond the fence, in the living farm countryside all around us. As we embraced our identity as a heritage gateway, opportunities emerged that we otherwise might not have recognized.

In 2004 and 2009 the National Geographic Society's *Traveler* magazine published lists of the world's greatest destinations, ranked by both their attractiveness and their integrity. The Vermont countryside scored in the top tier of both rankings, very high among the world's great, unspoiled destinations. Vermont's world-class ranking surpassed that of any other place in the United States, as well as most of the truly famous destinations on the planet. Vermonters were astonished. "What made us so special?" But our astonishment and pride were laced with hints of dread. What did it really mean to be a world-class destination? Did Vermonters really want to become the objects of mass tourism? Maybe Vermont could make money on this somehow, but could it protect itself from the inevitable changes that might spoil our cherished place? Good questions all.

We went back to our friend Governor Douglas and proposed a conference on the issue. He agreed, and in 2005 Billings Farm & Museum hosted a Governor's Summit on the Vermont Destination. On the table were the issues of opportunity and threat inherent in Vermont's world-class destination status. Around the table were thirty-eight of Vermont's most effective leaders: entrepreneurs, tourism operators, hoteliers, conservationists, preservationists, educators, museum people, artists, legislators, and governmental officials. Two days of provocative, sometimes intense, deliberations produced a statement of core values and a report. These in turn informed discussion and policy making about Vermont's future, and the story continues to unfold.

Billings Farm & Museum had entered a new arena. No longer just an outdoor museum delivering a program inside the fence, it had engaged the geographical and historical context beyond its immediate place. And it had also become a vocal advocate for Vermont's working landscape. Doing so might lie within the mission of the Woodstock Foundation, but what were the implications for the Farm & Museum? What did the heritage gateway role really imply? Where did museum interpretation merge with advocacy, and did that matter? What did these things imply for our relationships around the state? What about our audiences? How might this change visitor experiences inside the fence? Could it help engage them and thereby enrich their experience?

We appreciated that our purpose was to educate and interpret through immersive place-based programs. Our visitors wanted rich engaging experiences.

Ours were authentic, and we made an immersive farm experience the core of our program for both visitors and schoolchildren. Our visitors responded. Many were inspired toward further exploration; some even toward action. Funders took an interest as well.

For the Woodstock Foundation and the Billings Farm & Museum, this redefined role seemed to reinforce its mission, vision, and place in the larger communities of Woodstock and Vermont. These ideas resonated with the philosophy of its founder Laurance S. Rockefeller, who believed that places possessing a strong combination of natural beauty, environmental quality, heritage, culture, recreational opportunity, and civic vitality *had the power to lift the human spirit*. This seemed to mirror National Geographic's criteria for great, unspoiled destinations. And it echoed Vermont's own brand identity: "A place that conveyed a profound sense of well-being."

We had found a great fit. How would it sugar off into the interpretation, exhibits, and programs of Billings Farm & Museum? What stories would we tell? What would make this authentic for the lives of our visitors? We took our ideas to the National Endowment for the Humanities (NEH), where we found program officers who shared our enthusiasm for an outdoor museum that extended its program beyond its fence. With consultation and planning grants from NEH we took our staff on the road to explore other potential gateway sites across the country and then assembled scholars and practitioners to help us think through our own potential. We conceived of the outdoor museum both as an immersive onsite experience and as a portal for exploring its surrounding countryside. Quite different from a time capsule, we began to think of our place as an air lock or a decompression chamber. Our aim became using our onsite experience to inspire visitors to fully explore the countryside beyond the fence; to delve deeply into the working landscape, its history, and its culture. We began to think of ourselves as an interpretive concierge for Vermont's working landscape and rural countryside.

Vermonters, wary of the impact of mass tourism on their state, warmed to the idea of a place where visitors might be inspired to appreciate the state's fragile working landscape and to use it sensitively. They liked the idea that through deep exploration of the Vermont countryside, existing tourists might spend more time there, leading to more tourism revenue, increasing "heads in beds" without adding hordes of new tourists. Vermonters themselves appreciated Billings Farm as a place where they and their families could learn about their cherished home state, taking heightened sensitivity back to their individual home places. At Billings, tourists and residents alike could find inspiration toward broader explorations of Vermont, deepening their experiences and their appreciation of this authentic place—a real place in nature and in history. And through appreciation and inspiration, their spirits might be lifted and they might grow in their personal senses of stewardship.

Like most big undertakings, ours remains a work in progress. But we are grounded in our place, both spatially and in time. Knowing where we are helps us to know who we are—and to figure out where we may be heading.

Chapter 15

Turning Points: Ordinary People, Extraordinary Change

Bob Beatty

The history of Birmingham, Alabama, directly reflects one of the most important aspects of local history: the roles individual communities and people play in the historical narrative. In this case, the city is probably most known for its role in the modern civil rights movement. In September 2013, AASLH met in Birmingham. It was a significant year, the fiftieth anniversary of the (in)famous Birmingham Summer. September (and the very week hundreds of history professionals were in town for the AASLH conference) marked the fiftieth anniversary of the tragic bombing of Birmingham's Sixteenth Street Baptist Church.

The summer of 1963 events in Birmingham were a turning point in American history. Nonviolent protests led by the Southern Christian Leadership Conference (SCLC) sought integration of what was then the most segregated city in the South. Protests sought not only to break segregation's stronghold in the city but also to reinvigorate the civil rights movement itself and, according to author Steven Kasher, "Stimulate a national reawakening of conscience."[1]

Reverend Fred Shuttlesworth was a longtime leader of Birmingham's civil rights efforts. Founder and head of the Alabama Christian Movement for Human Rights, he was also a founding member of the SCLC (which Dr. Martin Luther King, Jr. led from its founding until his death in 1968) and the man primarily responsible for the organization's presence in Birmingham in 1963. Like many of the watershed events of the civil rights movement, the Birmingham campaign (dubbed "Project C" for "confrontation") was an exemplar of everyday people facilitating truly extraordinary change. In this case, hundreds of ordinary African Americans—including children—endured death threats, beatings, police dogs, fire hoses, bombings, arrests, jail, and murder in order to overcome the stultifying oppression of the Jim Crow South.

Image 15.1.   Reverend Fred Shuttlesworth, longtime leader of the civil rights movement in Birmingham, beside his statue in front of the Birmingham Civil Rights Institute.
Source: Wayne Taylor/Creative Commons

But, like many local history events, Project C wasn't just about Birmingham. "We wanted confrontation, nonviolent confrontation, to see if it would
work on a massive scale," Shuttlesworth noted. "Not just for Birmingham—
for the nation. We were trying to launch a systematic, wholehearted battle

against segregation which would set the pace for the nation."[2] To Fred Shuttlesworth, "Victory in Birmingham, Alabama, itself meant victory to the nation."[3]

The SCLC protests in Birmingham produced one of the most enduring documents of the civil rights movement: Martin Luther King's "Letter from a Birmingham Jail." In it, King fiercely answered a letter—thinly veiled as an "open" letter but actually directed at King and the SCLC leadership—from eight white Alabama pastors. He excoriated the pastors' call for "our own Negro community to withdraw support from these demonstrations."[4] He wrote,

> We know through painful experience that freedom is never voluntarily given by the oppressor; it must be demanded by the oppressed. . . . For years now I have heard the word "Wait!" It rings in the ear of every Negro with piercing familiarity. This "Wait" has almost always meant "Never." We must come to see, with one of our distinguished jurists, that "justice too long delayed is justice denied." We have waited for more than 340 years for our constitutional and God given rights. The nations of Asia and Africa are moving with jetlike speed toward gaining political independence, but we still creep at horse and buggy pace toward gaining a cup of coffee at a lunch counter. Perhaps it is easy for those who have never felt the stinging darts of segregation to say, "Wait."[5]

King's stirring letter spelled out the suffering African Americans endured in Birmingham, the South, and throughout the United States. And the events in Birmingham did much more than give us an enduring, iconic argument for civil rights. The protests fulfilled Shuttlesworth's goal of invigorating the cause for justice nationwide and inspired more than 1,000 demonstrations in more than a hundred cities throughout the South. In June 1963, President John F. Kennedy sent to Congress his proposed civil rights bill (it eventually passed the following year). And on August 28, more than 250,000 people participated in the March on Washington, a watershed moment in the civil rights movement that culminated in Martin Luther King, Jr.'s famous speech, "I Have a Dream."

Thousands of books have been written about the civil rights movement. Many reference the role ordinary people, black and white, played in the movement: from Rosa Parks in Montgomery to the Little Rock Nine; from the Greensboro Four, who inspired the sit-in movement, to the Freedom Riders; and from the brave marchers from Selma to Montgomery. And within or outside of these famous events of the modern civil rights movement, everyday citizens fought for civil rights as well. These ordinary women and men, children and adults, were the foot soldiers of the African American freedom struggle.

Fred Shuttlesworth exemplifies these ordinary people leading extraordinary change. As historian Andrew Manis writes, "Shuttlesworth emerged from a relatively impoverished southern rural working-class family. He possessed

neither the high-caliber education nor the rhetorical polish of King. Shuttlesworth better exemplified the poorer backgrounds of most southern blacks in
the civil rights era." Manis continues, "His actions inspired the courage and
confidence of ordinary blacks who loved and adored him."[6]

Today, the Birmingham airport bears Shuttlesworth's name. A statue of
Shuttlesworth has been on display outside of the Birmingham Civil Rights
Institute (BCRI) since its opening in 1992.[7] In 2002, the BCRI established its
annual Fred L. Shuttlesworth Human Rights Award for a person who embodies the principles of the American civil rights movement and Shuttlesworth's
life: "A philosophy of nonviolence and reconciliation; courage, both moral
and physical, in the face of great odds; humility; leadership by example; and
an established commitment to human-rights activities."[8]

Much of this activity reflects the discipline's turn toward the activities of
everyday people in the construction of the narratives of the past. It is history
organizations that care for and interpret many of the primary sources that
make up these histories. With this in mind, program chair Katherine Kane
and Liz Silkes of the International Coalition of Sites of Conscience wrote the
following in anticipation of the Birmingham gathering of hundreds of history
professionals on the fiftieth anniversary year of Project C. It widens the perspective from the lesson of Fred Shuttlesworth and the civil rights movement.
It challenged public history professionals to closely examine their own work
with Birmingham's lessons in mind. "If history is the example, the provoca-
teur, and the context," they resolved, "how do we best use it today? How can
we build programs that deal directly with issues, making history interesting,
relevant, useful, and human? How do you take the history your organization
uses and connect it to people's lives? How is change reflected in your institution's programs?"[9]

Keep these questions in mind as you read Max A. van Balgooy's chapter
that follows. Think about ways you can shed light on the important everyday
people and events and how they demonstrate change over time. Van Balgooy
articulates three turning points for history organizations: (1) doing history
with a passion, (2) making history meaningful, (3) pursuing an aspirational
vision. These three elements, he argues, can turn the ordinary into the extraordinary for our institutions.

Passion comes first, I believe. If you've read this book chronologically,
you'll note that the situation can appear somewhat dire for the discipline.
I strongly believe that if you lack passion for history and for our work, you're
probably in the wrong field. There are many days when passion is what carries us through.

Leadership is one of the ways history is essential. The discipline provides
inspiration for leaders and role models for meeting the challenges that face
our communities, our nation, and the world.[10] In history we find countless

actors who passionately believed their endeavors and offer us examples to follow in our personal and professional lives. It's more than okay to carry with us love for a particular person and/or event from history. Our visitors will relate to this and it may inspire them as much as it has inspired your own pursuit of history.

One example is Founding Father George Mason. "As a citizen and public servant," writes Scott Stroh, director of Gunston Hall, "Mason passionately and diligently worked to ensure that the rights of the people were central to government and that the government did not infringe on these inherent rights." In Mason's time, as in ours, Stroh continues, "The topic of rights and freedoms, governmental authority, the role of the people in government and society, citizen engagement, and the freedom of the press were front-page stories."[11]

Although Mason advocated for the abolishment of the slave trade at the 1787 Constitutional Convention and his writings unambiguously condemn slavery as an institution, one certainly cannot separate Mason the slaveholder from his own words in the Virginia Declaration of Rights. "All men are born equally free and independent," he wrote in 1776.[12] Clearly, Mason's definition of "all" did not include African Americans (and his use of "men" excluded women as well). Yet one of history's paradoxes is how the actions or words of flawed individuals spur the thinking of succeeding generations. George Mason's Virginia Declaration of Rights inspired later documents expressing the universal right of freedom: the Declaration of Independence, the Bill of Rights, the French Declaration of Rights, and the U.N.'s Universal Declaration of Human Rights. The Virginia Declaration of Rights also indirectly inspired Elizabeth Cady Stanton's Declaration of Rights and Sentiments. Stanton and her contemporary Lucretia Mott presented the Declaration of Rights at the first women's rights convention in Seneca Falls, New York, in 1848.

Three years later, in 1851, Stanton, Mott, and abolitionist Susan B. Anthony formally joined forces in the fight for women's rights. Anthony's impassioned advocacy on behalf of women inspired a similar ardor in journalist Lynn Sherr. "The modern women's movement," she said in 2008, "has brought about some of the greatest social transformations in our lifetimes. It also led me, and so many others, to women's history, a subject that did not exist when I was growing up." In contemplating the work of Anthony and her comrades in the women's movement, Sherr notes, "Their circumstances seemed unimaginable to me. And yet their boldness in fixing the problems was inspiring." Anthony's fervor for the cause instilled in Sherr a passion for history. "Learning about Anthony and her colleagues was a revelation. Passing on to others what I had learned became my mission."[13]

Mason's passionate articulation of the rights of man (and to be perfectly clear, this did not include women or enslaved peoples) inspired other, similar declarations. One of these, the Declaration of Sentiments, launched the woman's rights movement. These primary sources not only reflect the time in which they were written but endure today as well.

The second of van Balgooy's turning points is making history meaningful. Consider again the charge to attendees in Birmingham. How do we best use the lessons of history to build activities that directly confront issues, those that make history interesting and relevant and useful, and human? "How do you take the history your organization uses and connect it to people's lives?"[14]

An anecdote from Barbara Franco exemplifies this struggle: "My first job was as a decorative arts curator in a house museum in Utica, New York. One day as I was painting teeny tiny accession numbers on teeny tiny dollhouse furniture, I sat back and asked myself, 'Who cares?' The answer to that question has helped guide me throughout my entire career. In the end, what we do is important, not for itself, but because people must and do care about the past."[15]

Steve Elliott, former chair of the AASLH Council and current CEO of the Minnesota Historical Society, addressed this challenge. "Ours is a unique value proposition," he maintained. "We have . . . all kinds of stuff. But it's what we *do* with our stuff that matters. Our wedding dresses, forts, and moccasins in and of themselves aren't valuable unless we make them meaningful." "Our stories may be local stories," he continued, "aggregated they may be part of larger, sweeping narratives. But our stories of struggle, success, and failure; triumph and tragedy; and progress are not merely interesting, or just instructional, well-selected, and compellingly interpreted. They can be transforming." That transformation ultimately comes down to creating significance. "It's up to us to use our stuff to tell stories that connect today and have meaning for tomorrow," Elliott concluded.[16]

Bill Tramposch, recently retired as director of the Nantucket Historical Association, calls this "Making a Place for the Magic." To do so, he implores us to "Tell stories that connect and reveal. . . . All of our efforts should strive to pull and envelop the learner into the experience, and experience that is as rich in the affective voice as it is impeccable in the cognitive." "Watch and trust the power of imagination," he beseeches. Our institutions "are places where key reconnections are made." We should not forget that "they are sanctuaries . . . transformative in their ability to take us away from our normal lives and return us again, with fresh perspective. They cause us to forget where we are while helping us remember who we are and who we can be."[17] This is the essence of making meaning.

The last element van Balgooy identifies is the importance of an institution pursuing an aspirational vision. This makes the work of history much more important than simply preserving the past. History plays a role in connecting individuals to each other. In his outgoing council chair's address at the 2006

AASLH Annual Meeting, David Crosson stated his aspiration for the field. "We have to accept the vision of historical salvation, that [history organizations] do not exist for the sole purpose of imparting historical information . . . but we actually have a meaningful role to play in changing people's lives." He cited the United States Holocaust Memorial Museum as an example of this principle in action, a museum that "should, and could, move visitors to lamentation, contemplation, repentance, and perhaps even action."[18]

Crosson's call permeates much of the conversation about the discipline of public history. "Doing public history well delights and enriches private lives," Denny O'Toole, former coordinator of the long-standing Seminar for Historical Administration, stated at the 2011 Leadership in History Awards Banquet. "It provides context and perspective for understanding events of the moment and helps inform and add ballast to the ideas and opinions we all bring to our lives as citizens of this republic."[19]

Museum leader Nina Simon proffers another example of this aspiration, tying it to the omnipresent theme of relevance. According to cognitive scientists Deidre Wilson and Dan Sperber, "relevance 'yields positive cognitive effect.'" "Something is relevant," Simon posits, "if it gives you new information, if it adds meaning to your life, if it makes a difference to you. . . . Relevance leads you somewhere. It brings new value to the table." Wilson and Sperber assign a second criteria: effort. It is critically important to know "how much effort is required to obtain and absorb that new information," Simon explains. "The lower the effort, the higher the relevance."[20]

Simon adds a twist to the equation, a vision she urges for her institution and for the field. These conclusions should be top of mind as history institutions ponder their own present (and futures). "If we want our work to be relevant, we need to satisfy both criteria," she notes. We need to "stimulate a positive cognitive effect" for stakeholders, "to yield new conclusions that matter." And we need to do so with minimal effort on their behalf. "If it's easy to visit, and the experience yields value," she concludes, "your work is bound to be relevant." If you meet neither of those criteria, she asks, "Why would anybody care to try?"[21]

As van Balgooy writes in the next chapter, extraordinary organizations pursue aspirational visions. The specifics must relate to an individual institution's assets, of course. Steve Elliott expresses this precept well. "It's time we recognize the vital role we play in today's shrinking world: helping our fellow Earth travelers to understand each other, and consequently saving the planet. History . . . is the starting point. And the future."[22]

In their book *Nearby History: Exploring the Past Around You*, historians David E. Kyvig and Myron A. Marty quote historian Robert Kelley about the importance of the study of history. Kelley's words articulate van Balgooy's arguments—why it's important that history professionals and institutions

exude passion for the discipline, offer opportunities for meaningful engagement with the past, and aspire to a vision for improving society:

> It is our discipline that asks the question, how did the subject of concern evolve
> over time into its present condition? Other disciplines, as in economics, engi-
> neering, political science, and sociology, are concerned with the dynamics of
> the existing situation. The examples of badly formed policies which would have
> escaped that condition had some attention been paid to the history of the issue
> at hand, or of the problem or situation, are endless. Historically grounded poli-
> cies, in small and large settings, cannot help but be sounder in conception, and
> they are likely to be more effective, consistent, and, one hopes, more aligned
> with human reality. In the long run, they should be less costly to administer.[23]

Perhaps O'Toole best sums up these principles. History, he said, "is important work. I hope . . . that you continue to find your work deeply satisfying
despite the heavy challenges that face you. . . . The civic well being of the
communities you serve depends on it."[24]

NOTES

1. Steven Kasher, *The Civil Rights Movement: A Photographic History, 1954–68*
(New York: Abbeville Press, 1996), 88.
2. Ibid.
3. Andrew M. Manis, *A Fire You Can't Put Out: The Civil Rights Life of Birmingham's Reverend Fred Shuttlesworth* (Tuscaloosa: University of Alabama Press,
1999), 335.
4. C. C. J. Carpenter, D.D., L.L.D.; Joseph A. Durick, D.D.; Rabbi Milton L.
Grafman; Bishop Paul Hardin; Bishop Nolan B. Harmon; George M. Murray, D.D.,
L.L.D.; Edward V. Ramage; and Earl Stallings, "Letter from Alabama Clergy, 1963,"
360.
5. Martin Luther King, Jr., "Letter from a Birmingham Jail," in *Major Problems in the History of the American South, Volume II: The New South*, eds. Paul D.
Escott, David R. Goldfield, Sally G. McMillen, and Elizabeth Hayes Turner (Boston:
Houghton Mifflin Company, 1999), 363–64.
6. Manis, 4.
7. Incidentally, the institution sits at 520 Sixteenth Street North, across the street
from both the Sixteenth Street Baptist Church (where four African American girls
lost their lives in a bombing on September 15, 1963) and Kelly Ingram Park (the site
where many civil rights demonstrators were attacked by dogs, police, and fire hoses
in the summer of 1963).
8. Birmingham Civil Rights Institute, "Annual Fred L. Shuttlesworth Human
Rights Award," accessed October 11, 2016, www.bcri.org/events_activities/annual_
events/shuttlesworth_awards.html. Recipients have included Shuttlesworth himself,

eminent historian Dr. John Hope Franklin, Congressman John Lewis, SCLC Education Director Dorothy Cotton, and journalist and author Charlayne Hunter-Gault.

9. Katherine Kane and Elizabeth Silkes, "Turning Points: Ordinary People, Extraordinary Change," 2013 American Association for State and Local History Annual Meeting theme.

10. Adapted from History Relevance Campaign, "The Relevance of History: Seven Ways It Is Essential," accessed January 8, 2017, www.historyrelevance.com/value-statement.

11. Scott Stroh, "Foreword to the Second Edition," in *The Five George Masons: Patriots and Planters of Virginia and Maryland*, eds. Pamela C. Copeland and Richard K. MacMaster (Fairfax, VA: George Mason University Press, 2016), x.

12. Copeland and MacMaster, 175.

13. Lynn Sherr, "Rochester and Its Environs Truly Did Transform Nineteenth-Century America," *History News* 64, no. 1 (Winter 2009): 8.

14. Beatty, Kane, Silkes, "Turning Points."

15. Barbara Franco, "History and the Long Now," *History News* 62, no. 1 (Winter 2007): 18.

16. Stephen Elliott, "History Is the Starting Point (and the Future)," *History News* 68, no. 1 (Winter 2013): 13.

17. Bill Tramposch, " 'That Would Be Good Both Going and Coming Back," *History News* 68, no. 1 (Winter 2013): 17–18.

18. David Crosson, "Ingsoc, Dog Food, and Holy Water," *History News* 62, no. 1 (Winter 2007): 15.

19. Dennis A. O'Toole, "This Is a Worthy Thing to Do with One's Working Life," *History News* 67, no. 1 (Winter 2012): 21.

20. Nina Simon, *The Art of Relevance* (Santa Cruz, CA: Museum 2.0, 2016), 29, 32.

21. Ibid., 32, 35.

22. Elliott, 13.

23. David E. Kyvig and Myron A. Marty, *Nearby History: Exploring the Past Around You*, 3rd edition (Lanham, MD: AltaMira Press, 2010), 13–14.

24. O'Toole, 21.

Chapter 16

What Kind of Ordinary Will You Be?

Max A. van Balgooy

"The next time it may be you, or your daughter or mother," warned the mimeographed leaflets, urging "every Negro to stay off the buses Monday in protest of the arrest and trial."[1] The previous Thursday, December 1, 1955, Rosa Parks had been arrested on a city bus in Montgomery, Alabama, for refusing to give up her seat to a white man. It became a turning point for civil rights, triggering a 380-day bus boycott that lasted until the U.S. Supreme Court ruled in *Browder v. Gayle* that segregation, even outside public schools, violated the Fourteenth Amendment.

Rosa Parks is often portrayed as a tired and ordinary black seamstress who quietly took a stand against segregation by sitting down. Delving deeper into the story, you quickly discover that Parks was actively involved as a leader in the civil rights movement, investigating and documenting cases of abuse against African Americans and women and participating in a national network of people who were fighting for reforms through lawsuits, bus boycotts, and other strategies for decades. Parks did not plan to be arrested that cold December day, but when the opportunity arose, she seized it. Her motivators were the heart-wrenching crimes against Recy Taylor and Gertrude Perkins and the tenacity of E. D. Nixon and Jo Ann Robinson.[2] Her success was neither accidental nor exclusive. She was one of many seemingly ordinary people whose aspirational vision, contemporary relevance, and personal passion overcame seemingly impossible situations, finding a way where there seemed to be no way. They looked and lived like many of their next-door neighbors, but they made extraordinary and meaningful changes to the everyday lives of Americans.

Parks's actions inspire us today, a reminder of the tremendous changes that are behind us and an encouragement for what we face ahead. Museums, historical societies, and historic sites are filled with stories of people like her that can inspire and inform our visitors. For example, Frieda Fromm-Reichmann pioneered the humane treatment of mental illness, and Vivian Simpson forced the University of Maryland to end discrimination against women, but few people in my hometown of Rockville knew these women were part of our community until the local historic preservation organization published a booklet about them a couple of years ago.[3]

Rosa Parks's experience can inspire history organizations, which are also in the midst of extraordinary change, albeit of a very different kind. The economic downturn that began in 2008 threatens many museums, historic sites, and historical societies, even those that have large endowments and attendance. But the change is bigger than the current economic recession. National Endowment for the Arts surveys over the past three decades show attendance rates at historic sites have fallen from 37 percent in 1982 to 25 percent in 2008 and that it has accelerated in the last decade. We're not alone, however. Similar declines are occurring at concerts, dance performances, craft fairs, and sporting events.[4]

Some scholars attribute the decline to the shift in educational policies in the 1980s that began to eliminate history, music, art, and sports from the curriculum. The reduced exposure to these activities as children resulted in reduced participation as adults.[5] Political scientist Robert D. Putnam sees something larger and more pervasive. In *Bowling Alone,* his best-selling study of community, he showed that "For the first two-thirds of the twentieth century a powerful tide bore Americans into ever deeper engagement in the life of their communities, but a few decades ago—silently, without warning— that tide reversed and we were overtaken by a treacherous rip current."[6] The growing pressures of time and money on two-career families, the social isolation that comes with suburbanization, and the privatization of leisure time due to electronic media (e.g., television and the Internet) have played a role, but more significant is the replacement of the "long civic generation" by their less-involved children and grandchildren. The "long civic generation" was one of the results of the progressive movement, urbanization, and the civil obligations induced by several wars. With their slow disappearance, people visit less, join less, volunteer less, give less, trust less, and vote less. During the past fifty years, America passed through an extraordinary change that is undermining the foundations of our communities, including history organizations.

Although the trends are headed down, it doesn't mean we're out—yet. Even though visitation is declining, Americans have a broad interest in heritage and regularly participate in historical activities, such as taking photographs to preserve memories, watching movies about the past, or attending family reunions.[7] Tourism is a major industry in the United States, and most adults include a cultural or historical activity while traveling.[8] Our shared identity as Americans serves as stronger bond than occupation, religion, race, and ethnicity, suggesting that history organizations have enormous leverage.[9] Even outdoor enthusiasts stated that after their top choices of walking and jogging, they most enjoyed visiting historic sites.[10] Indeed, ordinary museums, historical societies, and historic sites can be the tipping point in our communities to improve civic engagement and increase the quality of life. Valuable opportunities await us if we are willing and able to grab them.

A dozen years ago, Richard Moe as president of the National Trust for Historic Preservation asked if there were too many historic house museums.[11] It's an intriguing question, but it hasn't generated the right kind of debate. Instead it's prompted discussions about how and when to launch a national "spay and neuter" program for historic sites and avoided more important questions. If history and heritage are important to our society, why are so many history organizations struggling? If museums, historical societies, and historic sites are part of a basic educational network that includes schools and libraries, wouldn't our nation be better off if there were more?

Every history museum, historic site, and historical society is ordinary—it's just that each chooses what kind of ordinary it wants to be. One definition is to have "no exceptional ability, degree, or quality." In that sense, when history organizations are unable or unwilling to make a difference in their communities, there are too many of them. Living in the doldrums, they are content to be superfluous. The other definition is "commonly encountered; usual." When a history organization is a vital and everyday part of its community, it can be encouraging, strengthening, and transformative. We need more of these.

History organizations choose the impact they want to make. Sometimes the choice is intentional and brought in by a visionary leader or strategic plan, but it can also come about through organizational confidence and maturity. These transitions can occur quickly or over many years, and, unlike with puberty, there's no guarantee that an organization won't return to its previous condition. In my work with dozens of history organizations over the past thirty years, I've witnessed three typical turning points that resulted in extraordinary activities and programs.

DOING HISTORY WITH PASSION

The first turning point occurs when history organizations practice history. If we are in the "history business," history should permeate and inspire everything we do. Fifty years ago, historian Barbara Tuchman asserted that "Being in love with your subject . . . is indispensable for writing good history—or good anything, for that matter."[12]

How do we know a group is in love? Observe what members say and do. Do they talk about history with feeling and interest? Do they spend time with history actively and joyfully? Does history influence their thinking, and do they want to learn more? Now evaluate your organization's staff, volunteers, and trustees, particularly those in high-level positions: Are they passionate about history? Certainly we need skilled attorneys and financial managers, but we also need to sustain and grow the enthusiasm for history. If it's impossible to find someone who is both a whiz at finances and a history buff, don't place them in a position where they make strategic decisions about the organization. They will be tempted to do what's best for the bottom line, not what's best for the mission. Likewise, a board can't be filled solely with historians; they need to bring other needed skills to the table.

Practicing history isn't just collecting objects, verifying facts, and presenting anecdotes about the past. It's an investigation to answer a question—an "inquiry" that cracks open the etymological nut at the source of the word "history." Are your events, exhibits, programs, and publications answering questions that intrigue your visitors and addressing issues in your community? Are your activities producing some thoughtful leaders or only consumers and followers?

Embracing scholarship and original research should be an ordinary part of our work as history institutions. Although the past doesn't change, our understanding of it does. Bringing a different perspective or question to well-worn sources can result in entirely new revelations, as demonstrated by Laurel Thatcher Ulrich's study of a community through a midwife's seemingly mundane diary or Doris Kearns Goodwin's examination of Abraham Lincoln's presidency through his everyday relationships with his Cabinet members.[13] By working with outside experts, you can assess your public programs to keep them sharp, identify the needs and opportunities for research, and mine your collections to find the significant stories of the ordinary people who worked and lived in your community.[14] Don't hesitate to ask professors, authors, or curators for help—they welcome the opportunity to work with others who care about their subject and to get an opportunity for a behind-the-scenes peek at the collections.

The award-winning books *A Midwife's Tale* and *Team of Rivals* wouldn't have been possible without the staff and collections of many state and local libraries, museums, historic sites, and historical societies, so the second step is increasing access to your collections. Historical societies have amazing collections, but much is unknown because inventories and finding aids aren't available. Cataloging all those collections to make them intellectually and conveniently accessible is ideal but often out of reach. Tackle this project methodically by identifying the specific collections that will be valuable to most researchers, and then process them in ever-deepening levels, starting with a simple description of each group and eventually describing each item. In the meantime, simple resources such as a footnoted timeline, a bibliography of best books and articles, and a guide to archives for your site or community provide a springboard for researchers studying a topic and using your collections. Today's digital age has made it much easier to share

Image 16.1. In *A Midwife's Tale: The Life of Martha Ballard, Based on Her Diary, 1785–1812*, historian Laurel Thatcher Ulrich used the seemingly mundane diary of an eighteenth-century New England midwife to craft a book that won the 1991 Pulitzer Prize. *Source*: American Association for State and Local History

the collections with much less impact on the organization, so consider sharing frequently requested documents and photographs online, perhaps even your entire catalog. Indeed, humdrum records contain a "powerful history," according to Ulrich: "Martha Ballard's diary forced me to reassess [conventional] history. In some ways, it turned the story upside down."[15] That mundane midwife's diary in the Maine State Library also earned her a Pulitzer Prize, a Bancroft Prize, and six other national awards.

MAKING HISTORY MEANINGFUL

The second turning point occurs when history organizations become more meaningful and relevant to their audiences. Good writers always have the reader in mind and are continually asking, "Will they turn the page?" History organizations can ask similar questions such as: Will they return? Will they recommend us to their friends? Will they be convinced to support our organization? That means understanding your visitors, a knowledge that continually changes because visitors are continually changing.

Recording attendance is a good place to start, but that information often lacks sufficient detail to inform decisions. It's like a restaurant noticing that sales are down but not knowing whether it's happening at breakfast, lunch, or dinner or due to the food, service, price, or neighborhood. Attendance statistics are more valuable when we capture a visitor's demographics and behavior (e.g., age, residence, repeat visit) against all of an organization's programming (e.g., tours, events, site rentals, website) consistently over several years.

While museums and historic sites often claim to know their visitors, they typically have only a superficial understanding of the public's interests, motivations for visiting, and preferences for learning. Boards and directors bemoan the lack of response to exhibits, events, and programs but fail to remember a key principle: people build relationships with people, not companies, brands, products, or organizations. Use the wrong message or medium, and you'll be ignored.[16] Visitor research helps find the connections between what you offer and what your audience wants. For example, a San Francisco Travel Association's study showed that historic sites are the most important destination for heritage travelers, but more important to tourists are affordability, variety, beauty, relaxation, and food.[17] Armed just with that knowledge, your museum or historic site could be more attractive by relocating seating, improving the appearance of your site, or building relationships with nearby restaurants and attractions to offer discounts to your visitors.

Being relevant also means helping people make decisions or developing a better understanding of the issues that face them every day. They want to know how they fit into the places and times that surround them—and we have the ideal tool in our hands. The best kind of history explains the past and informs the present. For example, what does the history of a popular park or neighborhood event tell you about your community? If there's a troubling national issue, such as unemployment, political corruption, racial conflict, or gang violence, how has it been handled locally over time? No doubt you'll find some ordinary people who took risks and some extraordinary turning points that changed the outcome. You'll also bond neighborhoods and build understanding by sharing the lives of fellow citizens, past and present, familiar and unknown.

History and history organizations make this possible by exploring varied sources, weighing evidence, coming to conclusions, and, most important, providing an interpretation. That means a thesis, a proposition, or an opinion that people can accept or reject. Exhibits, tours, and websites often shy away from rendering an explanation because it can provoke conflict or controversy, but as Barbara Tuchman noted, "There is no such thing as a neutral or purely objective historian. Without an opinion a historian would be simply a ticking clock, and unreadable besides."[18]

Our visitors need to develop these skills as well, so they can be informed citizens and make wise decisions. Educational psychologist Sam Wineburg found that student and teacher perceptions of historical research are quite different from what historians actually do. Students are trusting and will read a document without question from start to finish, assuming it's accurate and authoritative. Historians are skeptical and instead scan the text to get their bearings, then spend much more time questioning the source, its purpose, and its connections to people, places, and events. For historians, he wrote, "Texts come not to convey information, to tell stories, or even to set the record straight. Instead they are slippery, cagey, and protean, reflecting the uncertainty and disingenuity of the real world."[19]

As part of our work to make history meaningful, we need to make historical thinking visible. At museums and historic sites, visitors enjoy tours, exhibits, lectures, and books—the end products of history. Visitors rarely experience the uncertain process of sifting and weighing evidence that goes on beforehand. Science museums routinely teach visitors not only about the facts and theories of science but also how to observe and study natural phenomena to generate those facts and theories. Indeed, the popularity of "citizen science" suggests that ordinary people not only want to *learn* science but *do* science as a means of civic engagement.[20] Is such a thing as "citizen history" possible? Can residents of our communities be actively involved in the scholarly work of historical research and analysis? Absolutely.

Much of the work in historical thinking has been focused on students in the classroom using documents. Among the leaders in the field are the National

Image 16.2.   It is important, Sam Wineburg believes, that we teach how to evaluate sources by asking questions about authorship and context, and by raising questions about other supporting evidence. *Source*: Stanford News Service

Park Service, National Trust for Historic Preservation, Wisconsin Historical Society, and History Education Group at Stanford University.[21] These efforts are increasingly joined by projects where historical thinking includes adults, occurs outside the classroom, and uses artifacts, buildings, and landscapes as evidence.[22]

Archaeological excavations attract crowds of people who wonder what's being discovered and even volunteer to sit for hours moving gallons of dirt by the teaspoonful. The Hampden Community Archaeology Project in Maryland took it a step further by linking the history of a nineteenth-century industrial village to current urban issues by involving local residents (particularly teen-agers) in the excavations, collection of oral histories, documentary research, and interpretation.[23]

On the other side of the country, the Washington State Historical Society launched a *Civil War Read-In*. Public historian Lorraine McConaghy worked with hundreds of amateur historians around the state to better understand the territory's role in the Civil War. These volunteers carefully read a newspaper, a manuscript collection, or a county history and then entered the evidence they found into a database maintained by the historical society. According to McConaghy, the *Read-In* built capacity in historical research, developed a new resource, and helped her curate an exhibition, *Civil War Pathways*.

Historical thinking is also found on television. Over more than a dozen seasons, *History Detectives* followed the twists and turns of research into intriguing objects owned by ordinary people, along with explanations of methods and sources. The companion website is rich with excerpts from the show, videos of "detective techniques," a blog that followed up on stories, and lesson plans and rubrics for teachers.

These are extraordinary and magical efforts. They shift the visitor experi-ence from passive to active, getting people up close to historical artifacts and documents to encounter eureka moments and practice history. Essential to success are passionate historians, curators, and other subject experts. Like the experienced chef in a kitchen, they provide directions, demonstrate techniques, make connections, ask questions, and suggest alternatives. In the end, they share delicious discoveries and create history enthusiasts. The joy we experience in our archives, collections, and places is contagious and shouldn't stay under glass or behind velvet ropes.

Finally, engagement relies on a masterful use of language, so we shouldn't shy away from techniques used for centuries by poets and storytellers in our tours, programs, and exhibits. Rather than efficiently saying that "Just after my mother turned sixteen in 1959, she took the train from Mississippi to Cali-fornia," see how much more powerfully this idea can be shown in the hands of poet Natasha Trethewey:

> In 1959 my mother is boarding a train.
> she is barely sixteen, her one large grip
> bulging with homemade dresses, whisper
> of crinoline and lace, her name stitched
> inside each one. She is leaving behind
> the dirt roads of Mississippi, the film
> of red dust around her ankles, the thin
> whistle of wind through the floorboards
> of the shotgun house, the very idea of home.[24]

Through carefully crafted histories, the past can be a compelling and enthrall-
ing experience in the hands of Liaquat Ahamed, Ron Chernow, David Hackett
Fisher, Annette Gordon-Reed, Alex Haley, Laura Hillenbrand, Walter Isaacson, Erik Larson, Jill Lepore, David McCullough, Jon Meacham, Rebecca
Skloot, Barbara Tuchman, and Isabel Wilkerson—many of whom are not
classically trained historians.[25] These stories are carefully constructed narratives with a clear beginning, middle, and end; follow a protagonist through
conflicts and resolutions; call on the five senses; and rely on action verbs to
drive the story.[26] The opening sentences of Thomas Jefferson's biography by
Jon Meacham provide a taste of this engaging type of history:

> He woke at first light. Lean and loose-limbed, Thomas Jefferson tossed back the
> sheets in his rooms at Conrad and McMunn's boardinghouse on Capitol Hill,
> swung his long legs out of bed, and plunged his feet into a cold basin of water—
> a lifelong habit he believed good for his health.[27]

Well-written books can be more than entertainment—they can also invoke
extraordinary change. Harriet Beecher Stowe, Helen Hunt Jackson, and
Upton Sinclair turned statistics into stories, revealed hidden perspectives, and
humanized ordinary people, such as enslaved Africans, Native Americans,
and immigrant workers, demonstrating through *Uncle Tom's Cabin*, *Ramona*,
and *The Jungle* that literature can transform a nation. Yet these novels were
caricatures of reality, giving history organizations a distinct advantage: They
are society's bastions of the real and authentic. These documents, artifacts,
and places should not only be preserved within our walls but also shared
beyond them to allow extraordinary things to happen.

PURSUING AN ASPIRATIONAL VISION

The third turning point for history organizations occurs when they adopt an
aspirational vision for improving society. Imagining a better America, museums, historic sites, and historical societies can follow examples set by such
visionaries as Ann Pamela Cunningham. She believed that George Washington's exemplary service during the nation's formation would urge a "bond of
Union and political regeneration" during a period of increasing conflict in the
1850s and that the preservation of Mount Vernon would "commence a new
Era in our political life as a Nation."[28] Sadly, Cunningham's grand vision of
preserving the Union was delayed by the Civil War. But her impact was long-
lasting in that the creation of one of the nation's first historic house museums
prompted the formation of many others in the century that followed.
	Many historic sites, historical societies, and museums have aspirational
visions within their founding DNA, but these hopeful images may have been

forgotten over time. That passion can be restored, however. Museums are already considered the most trustworthy places to learn about the past and serve as a common place for learning and discovery.[29] By using diverse collections and perspectives, history organizations build bridges among various groups and encourage mutual understanding. By exploring shared histories through exhibits, programs, events, websites, and publications, they engage people in many ways. By focusing on the local and nearby, they strengthen connections among neighbors. By saving significant places in their community, they publicly demonstrate a commitment to their own heritage. These are exactly the characteristics that are essential for building strong communities— an aspirational vision I hope all history organizations share.

One piece, however, is often missing: a gutsy vision. The typical mission of collecting, preserving, and interpreting is not sufficient. Those are methods, tasks, jobs, works, or actions that define a purpose and explain "how" it will be accomplished. Needed is a goal, a destination, a target, the ends, an idealized description of the future that explains "why." To borrow from grammar, it needs a transitive verb—a verb that requires one or more objects. What's the object or purpose of collecting, preserving, and interpreting? As you fulfill your mission, what do you want people to know, feel, or do? What impact do you want to have on your community? How can you do history in the public's interest? Every history organization will answer these questions differently because every community is unique, but ultimately, the struggle to answer them will result in a clear (and hopefully inspiring) vision.

As management guru Peter Drucker reminds us, the nonprofit organization's "product is a changed human being. Nonprofit institutions are human-change agents. The 'product' is a cured patient, a child that learns, a young man or woman grown into a self-respecting adult, a changed human life altogether."[30] It is incredibly difficult for history organizations to have a courageous vision. To suggest how the future could be better or different suggests we've judged the present to be bad or incomplete; it's so much easier to avoid controversy or debate. An honest exploration of history won't allow us to escape difficulties and contradictions. History is the study of people, who are often complex, intricate, irrational, interwoven, and knotty. Strip out the difficult parts, and history loses its power to inform, educate, and inspire because it becomes less authentic, truthful, and human.

History organizations can be aspirational and seek to improve their communities, as witnessed in these two mission statements:

> The Harriet Beecher Stowe Center preserves and interprets Stowe's Hartford home and the Center's historic collections, promotes vibrant discussion of her life and work, and inspires commitment to social justice and positive change.
>
> The Anne Frank House cares for the Secret Annex, the place where Anne Frank went into hiding during World War II and where she wrote her diary. It

brings her life story to the attention of people all over the world to encourage them to reflect on the dangers of anti-Semitism, racism, and discrimination, and the importance of freedom, equal rights, and democracy.

Harriet Beecher Stowe and Anne Frank continue to inspire history organizations and their visitors. It may seem impossible to be inspirational if your museum or site isn't focused on an extraordinary person or event, but consider the history you preserve and interpret: Why is it significant and important? In your community's history, what were the turning points? Who was involved? As decisions were made, what alternatives were rejected? What are the challenging issues today? How did they come about? What happened before and after? Who was involved? Every community has ordinary people who have made and are making extraordinary changes—we need to find them in our collections and embody their spirit in our organizations.

LESSONS FOR ORDINARY PEOPLE AND ORGANIZATIONS

Turning points require extraordinary change in ourselves and in our organizations, but they are essential to our success and progress. As an example, let's look at the largest expansion of civil rights in American history—the granting of woman suffrage in 1920, which affected more than half of the population.

The first turning point occurred in 1848, when the first women's rights convention was held in Seneca Falls, New York. A male chaired the convention (and thus followed the social mores of the era), but it did give women the new opportunity to speak in public. As confidence grew, the next turning point occurred in the 1870s, when women tested the law by voting in elections (Susan B. Anthony being the most famous test pilot) or advocated for changing the law (including an amendment to the Constitution). The movement then stalled for several decades. Despite the proliferation of state and local suffrage organizations, little happened except more meetings, training workshops, and behind-the-scenes advocacy. Only after divisions within the movement and the encountering of continuing defeats did middle- and upper-class women change tactics in the 1910s by introducing the suffrage parade and partnering with working women.[31]

Parades seem unremarkable today, but a century ago, they were a bold and dramatic act for women. The parades moved women from private parlors to public streets and mixed the social strata. Marching, speaking out in public, and associating with lower classes were undignified and unladylike for the upper class. Yet thousands of ordinary women stepped out of their ordinary roles to make the extraordinary happen. Seeking the vote, more than 20,000 women marched with 57 bands, 74 horses, and 145 decorated automobiles in New York City in 1915. The 1913 suffrage parade in Washington, DC, prompted a riot, but it also introduced parades as a form of protest in the nation's capital. Soon the extraordinary suffrage parade became an ordinary event around the country, prompting more confidence and new tactics, including White House pickets, arrests, and hunger strikes. Without the parade as a turning point, women might still be unable to vote.

Ordinary people can inspire us through their brave and courageous actions, and in every community, their impact can be felt even if their names have been forgotten. As history organizations, one of our roles is to remember their contributions. Museums, historic sites, and historical societies can also have an extraordinary effect. As University of California, Berkeley, professor emeritus Randolph Starn observed, "It is no stretch, except perhaps for our professional egos, to suppose museums actually deliver more history, more effectively, more of the time, to more people than historians do. My guess is that many historians first got the itch for history from museums, surely more than from the textbooks they read in school."[32] Let's give our communities the itch for history every day.

NOTES

1. Jo Ann Gibson Robinson, "Jo Ann Gibson Robinson on the Montgomery Bus Boycott, 1955," in *Major Problems in the History of the American South, Volume II: The New South, Paul D.* Escott, David R. Goldfield, Sally G. McMillen, and Elizabeth Hayes Turner, eds. (Boston: Houghton Mifflin Company, 1999), 359.

2. In 1944, six white men raped Recy Taylor in Abbeville, Alabama; in 1949, two white police officers raped Gertrude Perkins in Montgomery, Alabama; E. D. Nixon was head of the Montgomery chapter of the NAACP and president of the Alabama branch of the Brotherhood of Sleeping Car Porters; Jo Ann Gibson Robinson was an English professor at Alabama State University and president of the Women's Political Council. Danielle McGuire, *At the Dark End of the Street* (New York: Vintage Books, 2010), 84–134.

3. Mary A. van Balgooy, *Women Who Dared* (Rockville, MD: Peerless Rockville, 2010).

4. Sunil Iyengar, Tom Bradshaw, and Bonnie Nichols, *2008 Survey of Public Participation in the Arts* (Washington, DC: National Endowment for the Arts, 2009).

5. Nick Rabkin and E. D. Hedberg, *Arts Education in America: What the Declines Mean for Arts Participation* (Washington, DC: National Endowment for the Arts, 2011).

6. Robert D. Putnam, *Bowling Alone: The Collapse and Revival of American Community* (New York: Simon and Schuster, 2000), 27.

7. Roy Rosensweig and David Thelen, *The Presence of the Past: Popular Uses of History in American Life* (New York: Columbia University Press, 1998), 234.

8. Travel Industry Association of America, *The Historic/Cultural Traveler* (Washington, DC: Travel Industry Association of America), 2003.

9. Harvard Kennedy School, *National Social Capital Community Survey* (Cambridge, MA: Harvard Kennedy School, 2006).

10. Osiris Group, Inc., *Think Outside: Promoting Natural Assets and Experiences in the Philadelphia Region* (Philadelphia, PA: Greater Philadelphia Tourism Marketing Corporation, 2005).

11. Richard Moe, "Are There Too Many Historic House Museums?" *Forum Journal* 16, no. 3 (Spring 2002): 4–11.

12. Barbara Tuchman, *Practicing History* (New York: Ballantine Books, 1982), 14.

13. Laurel Thatcher Ulrich, *A Midwife's Tale* (New York: Vintage Books, 1980); Doris Kearns Goodwin, *Team of Rivals* (New York: Simon & Schuster, 2005).

14. AASLH can help you do history more effectively. Look for inspiration in Carol Kammen's "On Doing Local History" column in *History News* or, if you're ambitious, complete the Standards and Excellence Program Workbook (StEPs).

15. Laurel Thatcher Ulrich, "Change Is a Crossroads," *History News* 68, no. 1 (Winter 2013): 8.

16. Karen Freeman, Patrick Spenner, and Anna Bird, "Three Myths about What Customers Want," *HBR Blog Network*, May 23, 2012, accessed May 30, 2012, hbr.org/2012/05/three-myths-about-customer-eng/.

17. Destination Analysts, *San Francisco Arts and Cultural Travel Study* (San Francisco: San Francisco Travel Association, 2010).

18. Tuchman, Practicing History, 29.

19. Sam Wineburg, *Historical Thinking and Other Unnatural Acts* (Philadelphia, PA: Temple University Press, 2001), 66. See also *Historical Thinking Matters*, a website produced by the Roy Rosenzweig Center for History and New Media at George Mason University and the School of Education at Stanford University.

20. Caren B. Cooper, "Links and Distinctions among Citizenship, Science, and Citizen Science," *Democracy & Education* 20, no. 2 (2012): 1–4.

21. Charles White and Kathleen Hunter, *Teaching with Historic Places: A Curriculum Framework* (Washington, DC: National Trust for Historic Preservation, 1995); Nikki Mandell and Bobbie Malone, *Thinking Like a Historian* (Madison: Wisconsin Historical Society Press, 2007); Sam Wineburg, Daisy Martin, and Chauncey Monte-Sano, *Reading Like an Historian* (New York: Teachers College Press, 2011).

22. AASLH focused heavily on this area in the 1980s with the publication of *Nearby History* by David Kyvig and Myron Marty (Nashville, TN: AASLH, 1982) and James B. Gardner and G. Rollie Adams, eds., *Ordinary People and Everyday Life* (Nashville, TN: American Association for State and Local History, 1983).

23. Robert C. Chidester and David A. Gadsby, "One Neighborhood, Two Communities: The Public Archaeology of Class in a Gentrifying Urban Neighborhood," *International Labor and Working-Class History* 76 (Fall 2009): 127–46.

24. Excerpt from "The Southern Crescent" from *NATIVE GUARD: Poems* by Natasha Trethewey. Copyright © 2006 by Natasha Trethewey. Used by permission of Houghton Mifflin Harcourt Publishing Company. All rights reserved.

25. Liaquat Ahamed, *The Lords of Finance* (New York: Pengu in Press, 2009); Ron Chernow, *George Washington: A Life* (New York: Penguin Press, 2010); David Hackett Fisher, *Washington's Crossing* (New York: Oxford University Press, 2003);

Annette Gordon-Reed, *The Hemingses of Monticello* (New York: W. W. Norton, 2008); Alex Haley, *Roots: The Saga of an American Family* (Garden City, NY: Doubleday, 1976); Laura Hillenbrand, *Unbroken* (New York: Random House, 2010); Walter Isaacson, *Benjamin Franklin: An American Life* (New York: Simon & Schuster, 2003); Erik Larson, *Devil in the White City* (New York: Crown, 2003); Jill Lepore, *New York Burning* (New York: Vintage Books, 2005); David McCullough, *The Path Between the Seas* (New York: Simon & Schuster, 1977); Jon Meacham, *Thomas Jefferson: The Art of Power* (New York: Random House, 2012); Rebecca Skloot, *The Immortal Life of Henrietta Lacks* (New York: Crown, 2010); Barbara Tuchman, *The Guns of August* (New York: Macmillan, 1962); Isabel Wilkerson, *The Warmth of Other Suns* (New York: Random House, 2010).

26. To learn more about narrative techniques, see Mary Carroll Moore, *Your Book Starts Here* (San Francisco: Riverbed Press, 2011) and Nancy Duarte, *Resonate: Present Visual Stories That Transform Audiences* (Hoboken, NJ: John Wiley & Sons, 2010).

27. Meacham, 1.

28. Patricia West, *Domesticating History* (Washington, DC: Smithsonian Institution Press, 1999), 15.

29. Rosensweig and Thelen.

30. Peter Drucker, *Managing the Nonprofit Organization* (New York: HarperCollins, 1990), xiv.

31. Holly J. McCammon, "Out of the Parlors and into the Streets: The Changing Tactical Repertoire of the U.S. Women's Suffrage Movements," *Social Forces* 81, no. 3 (March 2003): 787–818.

32. Randolph Starn, "A Historian's Brief Guide to New Museum Studies," *American Historical Review* 110, no. 1 (February 2005): 68.

Chapter 17

Commemoration: The Promise of Remembrance and New Beginnings

Bob Beatty

Commemoration is one of the most important tools in the toolkit of a public historian. First, honoring anniversaries is part of our institutional job description. As history professionals, the community looks to us to help mark the passage of time. Second, commemorating the past is also good business. Compared to many of the things we do, anniversaries are a relatively easy sell. It's much easier to cut through the noise of daily life with something that has brand recognition of some sort already. For example, most people know there was a War of 1812 or World War I. They may not know when it happened or who fought in it—but there's a very good chance it won't be a completely new concept. History organizations are wise to pay attention to these opportunities and maximize them.

Historian Seth C. Bruggeman calls commemoration "the *lingua franca* of public memory. It encompasses," he continues, "the various ways we have imagined—in monuments, ceremonies, festivals, pageants, fairs, museums, reenactment, and more—to conjure deep regard for the past. Unlike history, which is concerned primarily with circumstance, commemoration dwells almost entirely in feeling. It is for this reason that we all recognize commemoration, and understand it for the most part, even when it doesn't speak directly to us." The emotive aspect of commemoration, Bruggeman argues, is what separates commemoration from other programmatic activities. "The incredible diversity of rituals, objects, and customs that we associate with commemoration are all intended to give public feeling to otherwise private memories."[1]

It's important to keep in mind that commemoration and anniversary celebrations are related, yet distinct, ways history organizations present the past. Julia Rose, 2011 Annual Meeting program chair; chair of AASLH Council from 2014 to 2016; and author of *Interpreting Difficult History at Museums and Historic Sites*, sees a sharp distinction between the two activities. Rose ties commemoration with learning. The "informational and educational aspect of commemoration," she posits, "fuels how learners, participants, and observers value their engagement with the commemoration experience."[2]

While this chapter delves more deeply into commemoration, do not overlook the importance of anniversaries. As Kimberly A. Kenney, curator at the McKinley Presidential Library and Museum, notes, they provide "a great reason to install a magnificent exhibition, plan a spectacular series of programming, or host one grand signature event. You can use an anniversary to launch a fundraising campaign, preserve a historic building, or reach a new audience. Anniversaries can do all these things and more, as long as you seize the opportunity."[3]

Kenney's ideas support the conclusions of Bob Enholm, former director of the Woodrow Wilson House in Washington, DC. Enholm noted four categories of commemorations in the most succinct articulation of commemorative possibilities I have yet encountered. They are commemorations of anniversaries with broad social influence, narrow historical events, more whimsical anniversaries, and solemn remembrances. For centennial events of the Wilson presidency, these ideas played out as follows:

1. Broad social commemorations such as the Nineteenth Amendment. Enholm warned that these are sometimes so big that history organizations sites can get lost in the shuffle of broader activities.
2. Narrower historical events—for example, the centennial of Woodrow Wilson's signing the National Park Service Act in 1916. It's a significant happening, but the challenge was in discerning how wide the interest in that particular event would be.
3. Historical highlights. Enholm sees these as hooks for community building with people who know of and care about sites and history in general. The Wilson House hosted a Speakeasy Bash to honor Wilson's attempt to veto Volstead Act and promoted the centennial of Mother's Day.
4. Solemn commemorations. These are what many of us think of when we ponder commemoration. In Enholm's case, these were the centennial of World War I and Armistice Day, or the day Edith Wilson died.[4]

More important, though, commemoration offers the opportunity to reflect, to look deeply at change over time. Whereas anniversary celebrations highlight the event itself, commemoration looks at what has changed in the intervening years. This may be one of the most significant components of the endeavor—understanding where things have been, where they are today, and why.

In this way, commemoration highlights two of the seven values of history. First, it brings to the fore how the study of the past is valuable to communities. "History lays the groundwork for strong, resilient communities. No place really becomes a community until it is wrapped in human memory: family stories, tribal traditions, civic commemorations. No place is a community until it has awareness of its history. Our connections and commitment to one another are strengthened when we share stories and experiences." Second, through commemoration, history helps create and nurture engaged citizens. "History helps people craft better solutions. . . . By bringing history into discussions about contemporary issues, we can better understand the origins of and multiple perspectives on the challenges facing our communities and nation. This can clarify misperceptions, reveal complexities, temper volatile viewpoints, open people to new possibilities, and lead to more effective solutions for today's challenges."[5]

As one of the most noteworthy ways to engage the public, commemoration poses challenges as well. I learned that firsthand as curator of Education at the Orange County Regional History Center in Orlando, Florida. Beginning in 2001, I and colleagues from the University of Central Florida (UCF) began to plan for the fiftieth anniversary of the groundbreaking *Brown v. Board of Education* decision. That *Brown* had little immediate impact on Central Florida was immaterial (Orange County schools did not fully integrate until sixteen years after the decision). It was one of the most significant Supreme Court decisions in history and a watershed event in American history.

The anniversary provided the community the opportunity to reflect on and acknowledge change over time. As Spencer Downing of the UCF History Department and one of the event's co-organizers, recalled, "We expected [*Brown, Black, and White: A Community Remembers* Brown v. Board] would provide numerous occasions to consider how far we had come in five decades. . . . We had faith that the story of overcoming Jim Crow segregation would be compelling enough to unite even the most disparate and distrustful groups."[6]

The project was a success by all measures, and was a great way to rally the community around a single focus. But the most important thing I carry with me is a lesson I learned early in the process: the difference between "celebration" and "commemoration." It's an important distinction.

Early in the process, Downing, former county mayor Linda Chapin (also of UCF), and I hosted a meeting at the local black history museum to discuss our nascent plans for a celebration of the anniversary. Attendees pushed back. "As people lived it," Downing recounts, "not all of it was worth celebrating. Change had been slow and often painful. There had been losses as well as gains." African Americans at the meeting lamented the unintended consequences of integration and the loss of important community institutions, particularly the closure of black neighborhood schools and the decimation of the community's black business district. Most important, "celebrating" connoted that the work of *Brown* and the civil rights movement was finished. Together with the community, we adopted the term "commemoration" to denote our work. As Downing succinctly puts it, "We changed not because we were appeasing self-involved complainers. Instead, we realized that doing relevant public history means responding to the community's real needs."[7] Ultimately, our audience taught us what it sought from us, and we fit our activities (in this case our language) accordingly.

And unlike the more personal nature of celebration, commemoration hearkens a communal pursuit. In *Interpreting Anniversaries and Milestones at Museums and Historic Sites*, Kimberly A. Kenney quotes the British Imperial War Museum: "'To commemorate' . . . indicate[s] an activity that is a shared, perhaps civic, event." Celebration, in contrast, is a "personal, internal act of thinking, remembering, or paying respects." "It goes without saying that a commemoration should never be referred to as a celebration," Kenney concludes.[8] Historian Charlie Bryan, CEO emeritus of the Virginia Historical Society, agrees with Kenney. "'[C]elebrate' connotes a joyous event," he writes. "'Commemorate,' meaning to honor the memory of, is much more appropriate."[9]

In 2009, AASLH began preparations for its 2011 Annual Meeting, to be held in Richmond, Virginia, the former capital of the Confederacy. The upcoming Civil War Sesquicentennial provided an obvious thematic focus for the conference. The emphasis would be on commemoration and what it means to the field and to our audiences. As a tangible reminder of change over time, something everyone can relate to, commemoration is one of the field's most relevant activities. "We, as a profession," program chair Rose wrote, "are on a continuing quest to make collections and sites of commemoration meaningful and relevant; to increase their relevance to an ever-broadening and diverse audience; to meet the challenges of changing forms of communication and changing economy; and to take advantage of constantly emerging technologies."[10]

Commemoration is an active process, Rose reminds us: "The promise of remembrance and new beginnings is inherent in . . . commemoration, a core promise that energizes our investigations and innovations in the work of history."[11] "New beginnings" is an important part of the equation. It's not enough to simply share that something happened in the past. History organizations must help people understand the significance of the event to the present day as well. "The lessons from commemorations hold infinite possibilities, which are as varied as the multiple viewpoints learners bring to a particular commemorative representation," Rose writes in her 2016 book

Interpreting Difficult History at Museums and Historic Sites. "The act of collectively remembering," she notes, "is imbued with a promise to teach others and a promise to keep learning." Community is at the heart of the venture, she professes. "This can contribute greatly to building a sense of community and nationhood."[12]

Commemorating events with this in mind, therefore, highlights the essential nature of history to the present and future. History inspires leadership by demonstrating how people met the complex challenges of the past. History inspires leaders who in the present must now meet challenges once seen in the past. Through the study of history, we leave a foundation upon which future Americans can build.[13]

Rose finds these elements in commemoration. "The work of commemoration [is] the responsibility to mark, research, and teach the meanings of our ancestors' achievements and afflictions. . . . The process . . . demands reflection, discussion, and planning." The ultimate goal of commemoration reflects the goal of the study of history: to make meaning of the past. This

Image 17.1.   Public historian and past AASLH Council chair Julia Rose places emphasis on the educational aspects of commemorative activities. *Source:* **Charlie Champagne**

helps, Rose asserts, in "creating identities, from personal affiliations to global identification."[14]

This again links the concept of commemoration to another value of history: the nurturing of personal identity. A focus on change over time—rather than a simple anniversary celebration—enables people to discover their own place in the present as they learn stories of those who have come before them and shaped the world in which they live. Because commemoration often sheds light on stories of freedom and equality, injustice and struggle, loss and achievement, and courage and triumph, attention to these events helps communities and people to create value systems that guide their approach to life and relationships with others.[15]

Commemoration was the theme for the Richmond meeting in 2011, because it connected the conference with the 150th anniversary of the Civil War. The field had high hopes for the Civil War Sesquicentennial because of the enduring popularity of the war in the nation's consciousness. While our nation's public memory of the Civil War is perhaps the most contested in American history, the Civil War is familiar to a vast majority of Americans. The war's sesquicentennial offered the history profession a tremendous opportunity to deeply engage the public in a subject with which it was familiar.

The field was very concerned that the 150th anniversary not be a repeat of the war's centennial, which occurred against the backdrop of the Cold War and focused almost exclusively on themes of national unity and the soldiers' bravery. Worse, it ignored the central role that slavery and emancipation played in the war, a particularly galling error since the centennial was concurrent with many significant events of the modern civil rights movement.[16]

Fifty years later, these events were celebrating their own important anniversaries. As Rick Beard wrote, "The Civil War's impact stretches well beyond the events of 1861 to 1865, up to and including the early twenty-first century as Americans continue to wrestle with such long unresolved issues as the politics of federalism, contested regional heritage, race, and civil rights."[17] The latter two were of particular relevance, for the sesquicentennial would coincide with the fiftieth anniversaries of significant events from the civil rights movement: the Freedom Rides, James Meredith's integration of Ole Miss, the Birmingham Summer and the March on Washington, the Selma to Montgomery March, and the passage of the Civil Rights and Voting Rights Acts.

Beard was prescient in assessing commemorations in general. "Our intentions to use America's historical anniversaries as opportunities for education and commemoration have often proven frustrating and disappointing." "More often than not," he reported, "efforts . . . have failed to attract the funding . . . and proven unable to capture the public's attention for more than a few moments."[18]

Image 17.2.   The Civil War Centennial commemorations coincided with many events of the modern Civil Rights Movement. Pictured here are students from Kentucky's Berea College participating in the Selma to Montgomery March in 1965. *Source:* Michael Clark

Beard's words proved prophetic. The Civil War Sesquicentennial ended up being nowhere near the national, keynote historical commemoration many of us expected. Congress never formally established a national commission. In that absence, states throughout the nation filled the void, creating sesquicentennial commissions that engaged in a variety of commemorative activities.[19]

Many of these states constructed their work around a set of four guiding principles that Beth Hager of the Pennsylvania Heritage Society/Pennsylvania Historical and Museum Commission drafted following discussions at the 2007 AASLH Annual Meeting. Hager's recommendations gave form to many Civil War Sesquicentennial commemorative efforts.

1. Emphasize 150 years, not the 150th anniversary. With the emphasis shifted from the four years of war to the causes and consequences of that war, we can discuss its relevance to our various and diverse audiences today.
2. Local museums and historical organizations should make themselves available as centers for open discourse about the war and its legacy. Our institutions have a responsibility to provide historical context in an effort to foster deeper understanding for our communities.

3. The field should make stronger efforts to provide evidence about the causes and effects of the Civil War by sharing primary sources with the public. Make the human drama of 1861 relevant by going back to the original records, revealing the causes of the Civil War.
4. Respect, hear, and engage all groups.[20]

There are parallel themes with the commemoration of the centennial of World War I in the United Kingdom. Fought from 1914 to 1918, the First World War affected Europe far more greatly than it did the United States. The war is ever-present, typically in monuments and memorials found in towns throughout the British Isles. The Great War is as much a part of the public consciousness in Britain as the Civil War has been in the American South. It plays a very prominent role in public memory.

And like the Civil War, this presents challenges, challenges more easily overcome due to the attention the commemoration brings with it. Kate Tiller of the British Association of Local History documented three such possibilities for the war's centennial in the United Kingdom: understanding the war's impact beyond the military engagements, revisiting the meaning of the war, and providing greater historical understanding.

First, she writes, is

> the need to investigate and understand the war more widely, recognizing the importance of perspectives not previously considered significant and turning attention to the home front; to the wartime experiences of women and children; to the economic, social, cultural, and political consequences of the war; to the experiences of empire and dominion; and to military events beyond the Western Front.

Second, like Hager's call for a reexamination of the causes of the American Civil War, Tiller notes the need to "revisit and scrutinize deep-rooted, existing assumptions about [World War I]." The war was ultimately "a futile sacrifice, a bitterly costly conflict that failed to end all wars and led to another, more clearly justifiable world war only twenty-one years later." This revision of the historiography is an important outgrowth of the World War I centennial. And, last, is the importance of local history to the historical narrative. "Amid the growing hype, threatening at times to tip into unreflective cliché or event centenary celebration," she writes, "local history has a special and important part to play. . . . Returning to local experience and using and integrating the rich, direct contemporaneous evidence enables realities of wartime throughout British society to be rediscovered." "Doing so," she concludes, "moves us on to combine remembrance with greater historical understanding."[21]

Hager calls for an emphasis on change over time; for institutions to serve as a space for discourse and discussion; and to respect and engage others' voices. Tiller urges us to expand the story beyond the obvious, reevaluate historiography, and to use local history as a basis for historical understanding. Both encourage the use of primary sources in understanding history. Each observation is as relevant to complex discussions of the Civil War and World War I as for commemorations of less-complicated events. Public historians would be wise to keep them in mind as they develop commemorative activities.

There is one last thing to remember about commemoration; it is an important consideration. Commemoration often says much more about the present day than it does about the past. As Ann Toplovich writes, "Commemorative events in the United States have always tended to be more about the issues in the country at the time [of the commemoration] . . . than celebrating the past." This can be problematic to those laboring in public history as we seek to help our communities develop a shared understanding of the past. Toplovich warns against this. "Keep in mind," she notes, "that we can make a valiant effort to shape the public's collective memory of the past but we cannot dictate that memory to individuals. When it comes to commemorative events, we may have messages we want to share but we should not fault

Image 17.3. Kate Tiller, emeritus fellow and director of studies in local history at Oxford's Kellogg College, has written on the academic practice of local history, with current interests in local histories of the twentieth century and of remembrance and community. *Source:* Kate Tiller

ourselves if we cannot convince every single member of the public to accept our historical view."[22]

Edward T. Linenthal, the dean of American historians of commemoration, offers his own thoughts on the subject in the chapter that follows. Much of Linenthal's work examines larger commemorative stories: the Holocaust Museum in Washington, DC; the Smithsonian's *Enola Gay* exhibition; and his work at the site of the 1995 terrorist bombing of the Alfred P. Murrah Federal Building in Oklahoma City and with the Flight 93 Memorial Commission. Yet Linenthal also acknowledges the impact and importance of the commemoration of more quotidian events.

Linenthal agrees that commemoration is important work. It is one of the best weapons in our arsenal as public historians. And it is something our public expects from us. As Toplovich writes, "Each generation looks to historical organizations for guidance in commemorations, and each generation marks those events in different ways and for different purposes. With planning and a willingness to trust the public . . . organizations will find that honoring anniversaries is some of the most significant work we can do."[23] Or as historian Edward Ayers said about the Civil War Sesquicentennial, "We will do our best to take full advantage of this responsibility and . . . we will connect our local stories and our state stories to these big stories, so that the full significance of their meaning is recognized and preserved for all of us."[24] This is our charge as we engage in commemoration.

NOTES

1. Seth C. Bruggeman, *The AASLH Guide to Commemoration* (Lanham, MD: Rowman & Littlefield, 2017), 1.

2. Julia Rose, email message to author, January 9, 2017.

3. Kimberly A. Kenney, *Interpreting Anniversaries and Milestones at Museums and Historic Sites* (Lanham, MD: Rowman & Littlefield, 2016), 1.

4. Bob Enholm in "Anniversaries and Commemoration: The Responsibilities and Promise of Presidential Sites," session at the Presidential Sites and Libraries Conference, Little Rock, Arkansas, June 2014. Accessed February 17, 2017, http://resource. aaslh.org/view/anniversaries-and-commemoration-the-responsibilities-and-promise-of-presidential-sites/.

5. History Relevance Campaign, "The Value of History: Seven Ways It Is Essential," http://www.historyrelevance.com/value-statement, accessed December 13, 2016.

6. Spencer Downing, "Not for a Test, but History for Life," in *Zen and the Art of Local History*, eds. Carol Kammen and Bob Beatty (Lanham, MD: Rowman & Littlefield, 2014), 5–6.

7. Ibid., 6.

8. Kenney, 3–4.

9. Charles F. Bryan, Jr., *Imperfect Past: History in a New Light* (Richmond, VA: Dementi Milestone Publishing, 2015), 15.

10. Julia Rose, "Commemoration: The Promise of Remembrance and New Beginnings," 2011 American Association for State and Local History Annual Meeting theme.

11. Ibid.

12. Julia Rose, *Interpreting Difficult History at Museums and Historic Sites* (Lanham, MD: Rowman & Littlefield, 2016), 53.

13. Adapted from History Relevance Campaign, "The Value of History: Seven Ways It Is Essential," http://www.historyrelevance.com/value-statement.

14. Rose, *Interpreting Difficult History*, 53.

15. Adapted from History Relevance Campaign, "The Value of History."

16. For an excellent history on the Civil War Centennial, see Robert J. Cook, *Troubled Commemoration: The American Civil War Centennial, 1961–1965* (Baton Rouge, LA: LSU Press, 2011).

17. Rick Beard, "From Civil War to Civil Rights: The Opportunities of the Civil War," *History News* 66, no. 3 (Summer 2011): 12.

18. Ibid.

19. Most were poorly funded or not funded at all. The Virginia Sesquicentennial of the American Civil War Commission was the most well resourced. See Cheryl Jackson, "The Civil War Sesquicentennial Commemoration in Richmond, VA: Living Out the Promise of Remembrance and New Beginnings," *History News* 66, no. 1 (Winter 2011): 26–27.

20. Beth Hager, "The Civil War Sesquicentennial: Seeking Common Ground," *History News* 63, no. 1 (Winter 2008): 18.

21. Kate Tiller, "Anniversaries, War, and Local History," *History News* 70, no. 4 (Autumn 2015): 15. See also Carol Kammen, "On Doing Local History: Wilson's Ghost," *History News* 69, no. 4 (Autumn 2014): 3–4.

22. Ann Toplovich, "Anniversaries Are about Today: Commemorating Transformative Events," *History News* 64, no. 1 (Winter 2009): 22.

23. Ibid.

24. Edward Ayers, "We Will Do Our Best to Take Full Advantage of This Responsibility," *History News* 67, no. 1 (Winter 2012): 18.

Chapter 18

Public History and the Challenges of Commemoration

Edward T. Linenthal

Over the past thirty-five years I have had the opportunity to write about processes of veneration, defilement, and redefinition at some of our most iconic battlefields; followed the creation of the United States Holocaust Memorial Museum in Washington, DC; examined the ill-fated *Enola Gay* exhibition scheduled to open in 1995 at the Smithsonian's National Air and Space Museum; and explored how citizens of Oklahoma City—and other Americans—responded to the April 19, 1995, terrorist bombing of the Alfred P. Murrah Federal Building. As a member of the Flight 93 Memorial Commission, I had the opportunity to witness from the inside, the creation of an important memorial site. Most recently, I have been a member of a small advisory group in conversation with Norwegian colleagues regarding the memorial process in response to the terrorist attack in July 22, 2011, on the island of Utøya, where sixty-nine Labor Party youth were murdered.

While my writing has focused on these big sites and stories, the work of public history—from everyday interpretation to commemorative production—proceeds effectively and often unobtrusively in every nook and cranny of culture. Archivists, interpreters, docents, rangers, scientists, and others all enrich our understanding of local, regional, national, and transnational pasts. They model for a diverse public the art and craft of engaging the past, from the smallest local sites to the attention-grabbing spectacle sites.

I have mixed feelings about commemorative occasions. I do not think the torrent of commemorative rhetoric that emerged in response to the horrors of the Oklahoma City bombing or the 9/11 attacks, for example, has helped us grapple with the toxic after-effects of such violence. Instead, the endless parade of words is often a strategy of containment, in which words used far too easily—the "triumph of the spirit," "closure," "healing process," and the like—offer cheap grace in the guise of profound commemoration. Is the rush to commemorate before the depth of the wound even registers a form of commemorative forgetting? Is there too often a desire to create a memorial so that we do not have to actively engage these shattering events but consign them to the "memorial bookshelf" and expect the memorial to do our remembering for us?

Think, for example, of the formulaic phrases "Never Forget" or "Never Again" that have been attached to our responses to the Holocaust. Is there really any stable meaning to this feeble attempt at commemorative profundity? Does "Never Forget" mean "We should always remember the historical roots of the rise of National Socialism, the mix of religious, racial, and pseudo-scientific anti-Semitism that was an essential part of its worldview, the reality of war that fueled what became the inexorable move toward the Final Solution?" (I don't think so.) Does it mean we should "Never Forget" those millions who were murdered? (Perhaps, but since few of us knew them, what does it mean to never forget them?)

When I am confronted by the *Tower of Faces* in the United States Holocaust Memorial Museum with photographs of those murdered in the Polish village of Ejszyszki (many of them looking directly at me), I think of the overwhelming power of evil to take lives that can never be recovered, of members of future generations never born, and I feel an incredible impotence to do anything about any of it. This, to me, is an appropriate response, one that I must struggle with in any subsequent shaping of a personal and public response to the Holocaust. And, finally, when we use the phrase "Never Again," don't we consign genocide to one place, one time, one regime? It ignores the harsh reality that the work of genocidal regimes has moved easily into the twenty-first century. A more honest, but more troubling, commemorative question is "Will it ever stop?" Further, as historian Peter Novick asked in his important book *The Holocaust in American Life*, if an event does not rise to the level of the "holocaustal," is it unworthy of our attention? Dark brooding, however, is not often the popular choice for commemorative production. Must commemorative production be necessarily inspirational? Can it engage difficult, even indigestible memories? And lest we assume that the work of remembrance is healing by definition, in my experience, intense remembrance can be divisive as well as unifying, subversive as well as inspirational.

Too often, the reassuring language of preferred narratives dominates commemorative rhetoric, stories that impoverish our moral imagination and contribute to commemorative forgetting. For me, a revealing example was President Bill Clinton's speech at the dedication of the Oklahoma City National Memorial on April 19, 2000, five years after the bombing. In *The Unfinished Bombing: Oklahoma City in American Memory*, I noted that Clinton said, "There are places in our national landscape so scarred by freedom's sacrifice that they shape forever the soul of America—Valley Forge,

Image 18.1. The *Tower of Faces* exhibit at the United States Holocaust Memorial Museum features images from Ejszyszki, Lithuania, a small town with a vibrant Jewish community that an SS mobile killing squad massacred in 1941. The exhibit reminds us of the power of difficult history in commemorative practice. *Source*: United States Holocaust Memorial Museum, Photo by Max Reid

Gettysburg, Selma. This place is such sacred ground." In response I wrote, "These people's lives were not given in an act of conscious sacrifice for their nation; they were taken in an act of mass murder. The landscape to which Oklahoma City is connected is not Valley Forge, Gettysburg, and Selma, but sites of political terrorism and mass murder: the Sixteenth Street Baptist Church in Birmingham, Alabama, the McDonald's in San Diego, and Columbine High School."[1]

Often, changing interpretations, clashing narratives, and voices excavated from a forgotten past threaten comfortable stories that had gone unchallenged. These stories remained uncontested for so long that, for some, they became self-evident, primal truths that seemed a constitutive element of the natural world. (This, I think, is the conviction behind the expression, "It's a well-known fact.") If not quite natural, these sacred stories are guarded with fierce conviction by those resistant to the notion of history as an enduring argument. Interpretive change—often expressed through commemorative production—is attacked as revisionism, which, in the eyes of the attackers, signifies a crass surrender to the whims of current social or political fashion, and an irresponsible, almost criminal, willingness to jettison what they consider to be true history.

Such attacks are bolstered by the moral odium revisionism acquired when linked to those who denied the reality of the Holocaust. These people are not, however, revisionists; they are deniers. But the accusation of revisionism remains, lamentably, an effective rhetorical weapon to hurl at those who want to talk about slaves, for example, instead of servants during tours of plantations, those who want to look beyond the iconic mushroom cloud of the atomic age into the consequences of the use of nuclear weapons, those who want to spur our moral imagination by moving beyond comfortable and comforting narratives and engage visitors more thoughtfully.

It is crucial for public historians to articulately, passionately, and directly confront this attack. Commemorative occasions offer an ideal opportunity to do so. We can use, to good effect, the thoughtful words of historian Patricia Limerick, who writes, "Every normal human being is forever recalculating, reorienting, reorganizing information and reaching for new understanding. Thus, if you know a historian who is not a revisionist, indeed, if you know any human being in any line of work who is not rethinking, reappraising, and revising her or his previous assumptions, then charity requires you to summon the paramedics and get that non-revisionist examined fast, on the chance that there might still be time to get this party's heart restarted."[2] Or we could turn to the words of John Dower, who writes that his fellow historians "regard the past with greater detachment, knowledge of long-term legacies, and the fuller understanding that derives from accounts by participants and access to private papers and hitherto secret documents. Bias may color judgments, and controversy is predictable, but in any case knowledge becomes thickened and understanding altered."[3]

Would we, for example, expect historians who focus on the Holocaust to turn away from newly opened archives in various eastern European countries after the breakup of the Soviet Union? Wouldn't we look at them oddly and think them betraying their professional research obligations if we heard one of them say, "I would love to go and immerse myself in the archives just opened, because they contain documents that will shed light on issues we do not yet understand so well. Alas, I can't do it, because that might cause me to revise our understanding of the Holocaust . . . and that would make me a revisionist, and we all know how horrible that is!" Commemorative occasions offer valuable openings to begin to counter this insidious definition of revisionism, a characterization that continues to impoverish a thoughtful appreciation of the historian's craft, and one that marks the vast gulf that separates that craft from the boosterism of heritage production.

I have quite mindfully used the phrase *commemorative production* in this chapter. Official commemorative events are owned and operated for specific purposes by particular interests. There are often, of course, counter-interests that contest the official production in any number of ways. In the 1970s, the People's Bicentennial Commission offered visible protest against what it saw as an uncritical, triumphalistic, corporate-infected commemoration of the American Revolution; numerous commemorative events at Gettysburg celebrated what former Virginia governor Angus W. McLean called, in 1929, a "golden mist of American valor." All too often—and this is a story now well told—that golden mist obscured more than it revealed, erasing from dominant narratives the centrality of slavery in the coming of the war, how African Americans served as crucial actors rather than passive recipients of white largesse during and after the war, and the enduring legacies of the war. Not without controversy, the National Park Service's (NPS) *Rally on the High Ground* initiative has moved interpretation beyond the golden mist to a much richer understanding not only of Civil War battles but also of the many reasons that armies came to these killing fields in the first place.[4]

At the Little Bighorn, without question the most controversial historic site in the nation until fairly recently, commemorative productions expressed a patriotic orthodoxy that centered on George Armstrong Custer and the men of the 7th Cavalry. Through commemorative rhetoric, theater, poetry, art, and film, the dominant interpretation was that Custer and his men died a sacrificial death and that their blood helped open the American West to civilization. The Sioux, Cheyenne, and Arapaho existed only at the margins of commemorative production—as "savages" raging against the inexorable force of civilization.

After the volatile centennial events in 1976, however, when Native Americans staged demonstrations and produced their own commemorative events, the National Park Service, stewards of the site since 1940, confronted a host of razor's edge issues. How, for example, could NPS transform what had been a shrine to Custer and the cavalry into a historic site that offered responsible interpretation of all Americans who fought there? And how could this be accomplished when the focal point of the battlefield was Last Stand Hill? (For a short time, NPS offered visitors bus tours of the site of the massive Indian village in the valley, which allowed for a very different appreciation of the battle. Where one stands, after all, helps determine what one sees.) Numerous other changes spurred the transformation from shrine to historic site. After years of argument, the site's name was changed from Custer Battlefield National Monument to Little Bighorn Battlefield National Monument. More importantly, the dedication of the Indian Memorial took place on the anniversary of the battle, June 25, 2003, grounding a more inclusive appreciation of the battle and the many Americans who fought there.

Sometimes, commemorative production does not necessarily evolve into more inclusive ritual, but lurches back and forth between exclusivity and inclusivity. In 1985, at the fortieth anniversary of the battle of Iwo Jima, American and Japanese veterans of the battle gathered on the island and in the final ceremonies, often shook hands and even embraced. Marine veterans spoke of the courage of their enemy. Yet, at the fiftieth anniversary ceremonies at the USS *Arizona* Memorial in Pearl Harbor, State Department representatives, who had taken over planning from the National Park Service, deemed it too controversial to have American and Japanese school children walk together at the memorial and place flowers in the harbor. And yet, immediately after the formal commemorative ceremonies at the USS *Arizona* Memorial concluded, American and Japanese veterans of December 7, 1941, gathered for a conference in Honolulu. I participated in this conference, and learned that sometimes the most profound commemorative events are unplanned and spontaneous. "By the end of the conference," I wrote, "the audience—never as large as had been expected—had thinned. But the approximately 100 people still in attendance got to witness, quite unexpectedly, an extraordinarily moving event. The Punahou School Chorale ascended the stage and sang the beautifully haunting Civil War song 'Tenting on the Old Camp Ground.' As the refrain 'many are the hearts that are weary tonight, wishing for the war to cease; many are the hearts that are looking for the right, to see the dawn of peace' hung in the air, American and Japanese veterans walked slowly—some with canes—to the stage area to stand together and exchange farewells as the audience joined the choir in singing 'God Bless America.' It was a majestic moment in our commemorative history."[5]

Some years from now, when historians compare the sesquicentennial years of the Civil War to the centennial events, what will they learn? Will the evidence suggest that in contrast to the centennial years, commemorative production offered a nuanced, thoughtful, inclusive, and challenging understanding of the causes and consequences of the war that stands still at the center of American history? Will future commemorative energies of 9/11 respond to the hope envisioned by the great Chilean expatriate writer Ariel Dorfman, a hope that still seems, sadly, far from being realized? Might those of us, Dorfman asks, living in "the most modernized society in the world . . . be able to connect, in ways that would have been unthinkable before September 11, 2001, to the experience of so many hitherto inaccessible planetary others"? How will we respond to this challenge, "To find," Dorfman writes, "ways to make this new global tragedy draw us all closer to each other, not because we can now kill one another more easily and with more devastating effects, but closer because we share the same need to mourn, the same flesh that can be torn, the same impulse toward compassion"?[6] I thought about these words often during the evolution of the Flight 93 memorial project, a memorial that can, potentially, offer commemorative occasions that respond directly to this hope and this challenge.

NOTES

1. Edward T. Linenthal, *The Unfinished Bombing: Oklahoma City in American Memory* (New York: Oxford University Press, 2001), 234.

2. Patricia Nelson Limerick, *Something in the Soil: Legacies and Reckonings in the New West* (New York: W. W. Norton, 2000), 17.

3. John W. Dower, *Cultures of War: Pearl Harbor, Hiroshima, 9–11, Iraq* (New York: W. W. Norton, 2010), 221.

4. An interesting collection of essays is James Oliver Horton and Lois E. Horton, editors, *Slavery and Public History: The Tough Stuff of American Memory* (New York: The New Press, 2006).

5. Edward Tabor Linenthal, *Sacred Ground: Americans and Their Battlefields*, second edition (Urbana: University of Illinois Press, 1993), 243.

6. Ariel Dorfman, *Other Septembers, Many Americas: Selected Provocations, 1980–2004* (New York: Seven Stories Press, 2004), 9–10.

Chapter 19

Inclusion Is Active

Bob Beatty

"Everyone makes history. Relevant history is inclusive history," thus wrote AASLH president and CEO John Dichtl to the organization's membership in November 2016.[1] Dichtl's words reflect one of the central precepts in public history today. They not only provide guidance for AASLH as an organization but also offer insight into how the field itself is progressing and responding to community needs. Simply put, American history organizations must address issues of diversity and inclusion in an intentional, systematic, and thoughtful way. And they must do so now.

Why is this important? More than anything, it's the right thing to do. Organizations should strive to represent the entirety of their communities' pasts, to be welcome to the various narratives that comprise their histories. As Dichtl asserted, "State and local history is about telling the stories of individuals and communities contextualized in the history of the nation and internationally, and immigrants and cultural exchange have always been vital to American community."[2]

Beyond that, diversity and inclusion is inherent to the practice of public history. The American Alliance of Museums' (AAM) 1992 publication *Excellence and Equity: Education and the Public Dimension of Museums* provides one of the most succinct calls for these principles in our work. An outgrowth of the organization's 1984 *Museums for a New Century* report, *Excellence and Equity* links two concepts vital to the American museum and public history community: excellence in all services and inclusiveness that embraces the cultural diversity of modern-day America. The report, moreover, emphasized three key ideals: a commitment to education is our central public service; our institutions must become inclusive places that welcome diverse audiences; and dynamic and forceful leadership is key to fulfilling a public service role.[3]

Excellence and Equity challenged the field to provide its "most fruitful public service . . . by fostering the ability to live productively in a pluralistic society and to contribute to the resolution of the challenges we face as global citizens." Commitments to both excellence and equity obligate institutions to make decisions about collections, exhibitions, and programs supported by scholarship and to show respect for the various cultural and intellectual viewpoints of the community. Museums influenced by these concepts "have the potential to nurture an enlightened, humane citizenry that appreciates the value of knowing about its past, is resourcefully and sensitively engaged in the present, and is determined to shape a future in which many experiences and many points of view are given voice."[4]

Diversity and inclusion is our mandate as history professionals, but it is also a matter of survival. Population demographics reflect that the American populace will be "majority minority"—in which no single race or ethnicity formulates the majority of the population—by 2040. This is a tremendous change in less than 100 years. From 1900 to 1970, the U.S. population was between 87 and 90 percent white, non-Hispanic. By 1990, that figure dropped to 80 percent, and in 2015 it was six in ten. By 2040, only half of the population will be white, non-Hispanic. This statistic is particularly troublesome because currently 80 percent of our visitors are white, non-Hispanic. If we want to best meet our missions to serve the community, we must improve upon this number.[5]

Setting aside the justness of the cause of more inclusive histories, these demographics are not favorable for sustainable institutions or the field in general. Looking at numbers alone, at least 38 percent of our visitors today should be people of color.[6] In less than twenty-five years, that number should really be closer to 50 percent. History organizations, as community leaders, bear the responsibility to close these gaps.

This is not a new discussion and has been a part of regular field-wide conversation since at least the advent of the New Social History movement of the 1960s. But it has evolved into a more active pursuit. This is the biggest change I've seen in my nearly two decades in the history profession, the move from the term "diversity" to "inclusion."

"Diversity" is a term with which most are familiar. It is the ideal I pursued in my early career directing education programs at the History Center in Orlando, Florida. We sought to engage the diverse elements of our public, starting with the local African American community, that had long had fraught relationships with the institution. We did likewise with the local Hispanic community and offered targeted activities on women's history, among other topics.[7] These activities were not one-offs and I worked hard to follow John Cotton Dana's mantra, "Learn what aid the community needs: fit the museum to those needs."[8] Evaluations and informal conversations with stakeholders reflected people's general pleasure with our efforts. But if I'm being honest about my own journey toward diversity and inclusion, I'm not sure these activities moved the needle all that much. They had great results in short-term engagement but not necessarily in building long-term relationships.

I've since come to the realization that diversity is a passive exercise. As Chris Taylor, chief inclusion officer of the Minnesota Historical Society, observes, "Diversity tends to be more about the number of programs aimed at 'diverse audiences' and the number of 'diverse attendees' to our programs."[9] This often gives institutions and history professionals cover for a field that is 90+ percent white and whose exhibitions, programs, and activities have often skewed toward that demographic as well.

Speaking of my own experience at AASLH, I can remember my own frustration about why people hadn't applied for a diversity fellowship we offered for our SHA program, or why so few people of color engaged with the organization. I believed my heart was in the right place, and that our board and staff were supportive of diversity. So why, then, were we doing so poorly in this area?

Image 19.1.   As chief inclusion officer of the Minnesota Historical Society, Chris Taylor is charged with developing internal and external strategies for diversity and inclusion, including programming; creating authentic, sustainable relationships with communities; increasing staff cultural competency; and working to create a more diverse staff through recruitment and retention. *Source*: Chris Taylor

Images 19.2 and 19.3.   Joan Baldwin (above) and Anne Ackerson (below) address diversity and inclusion in their book *Leadership Matters*. Their current research examines gender equity and museums. *Source*: Jonathan Doster and Linda B. Norris

Enter "inclusion," an active pursuit that makes it incumbent upon the institution to reach out and actively seek to make connections, to make people feel more a part of the work we are doing. Ultimately, as Taylor notes, inclusion signifies "feeling safe, engaged, respected, and valued."[10] And while he's specifically referring to inclusivity as it relates to an institution's internal operations, I believe it applies to our organizations' external focuses as well.

AASLH has taken a very public stance on diversity and inclusion over the past several years. In June 2016, its Governing Council adopted a Diversity and Inclusion statement that starts with the quote that began this chapter, "Everyone makes history. Relevant history is inclusive history."[11] With this in mind, Dichtl avowed, "It is especially crucial that our association and its member organizations are institutions of openness, dialogue, and engagement across all the borders that divide us. Historical organizations' role as trusted interpreters of the past, inclusive institutions in their communities that foster honest discussion" is more important than ever.[12]

Along with a better understanding of the importance of the activity of inclusion rather than the passive quest for diversity, the field has begun focusing on a wider diversity spectrum, one that includes factors beyond race/ethnicity. In her 2016 revision of *Museum Administration 2.0*, Cinnamon Catlin-Legutko wrote that "Diversity sensitivity extends beyond culture concerns when gender, sexual orientation, and range of ability and age are included."[13] Anne W. Ackerson and Joan H. Baldwin, authors of *Leadership Matters*, agree. "Demographic diversity, in all its permutations—race, age, gender, economics, and so forth—is considered to be as critical to the history ecosystem as the diversity of types of institutions." They continue, "It's the whole spectrum of race, class, and gender that marks our place and time in the twenty-first century. We find diversity in the digital divide, the unemployment line, among college acceptances, and the stock market average."[14]

Ackerson and Baldwin also highlight an additional troubling trend of gender equity and its relation to wages. "Women dominate the history and cultural heritage museum workforce," they write, "causing researchers and pundits to believe they are the primary reason salaries and wages have remained low and benefits minimal in comparison to other educational institutions and female-dominated fields." The result? The American Alliance of Museums reported that "women museum directors/CEOs earn seventy-eight cents for every dollar earned by their male counterparts."[15] Sadly this reflects national trends as well.

So what can history organizations do, and what should they be expected to do, about all of this? In 2017, Katherine Kane, chair of the AASLH Council from 2016 to 2018, shared five ways the organization seeks to build diversity and inclusiveness. Public historians would be wise to consider applying these statements to their own efforts as well.

AASLH acts to build diversity and inclusiveness (as it):

1. Finds the creativity, the resources, and the will to change (internally) and advances diversity and inclusiveness in the history field.
2. Recognizes and defines the inequities in the history/cultural profession and addresses them by dedicating intellectual, financial, emotional, and structural resources for building a diverse and inclusive field.
3. Seeks to develop the capacity of member organizations and for itself to build relationships based on mutual trust, balance of power, and recognition of expertise within diverse communities to democratize the historical narrative and sustain the relevance of history organizations to a rapidly changing demographic.
4. Collaborates with organizations that have successfully developed inclusive policies and programming.
5. Encourages telling the stories that have not been told.[16]

Kane's second point just mentioned reminds us that inclusion is about more than just audience; it should also be reflected within our institutions as well. As Catlin-Legutko wrote, "A critical step in meeting the diverse needs of the community is a diverse staff that reflects its community and understands the larger societal realities."[17] Cynthia Robinson of Tufts University emphatically agrees:

> A successful museum's culture is one where leadership is mindful of history and inequities, and thus sets a tone that says that sexist and racist behavior and attitudes in the workplace, in interpretation, and in interactions with visitors will not be tolerated, and who helps staff understand the far-reaching impact of colonialism and of the importance and challenges of creating an organization that truly serves a multicultural audience.[18]

Ackerson and Baldwin note how this extends to organizations' governing bodies as well. "The boardroom is still male (but just slightly so), and most of them are white. On this score, many directors and trustees remain puzzlingly defensive, saying things like 'our small, rural community is not racially diverse' or simply 'we just cannot find diverse people to serve on our board.'"[19] This has long been the field's excuse for a lack of diversity. We must recognize that these statements (which are all too common) reflect a lack of inclusion. "Inclusion is a verb," Chris Taylor reminds us, "in that 'to include' requires action."[20] Our institutions should consciously reflect our communities, Ackerson and Baldwin maintain. "Board and staff leaders owe it to the future health of their institutions to put in motion strategies that create pathways to attract volunteer and paid talent that better mirrors the communities they represent."[21]

With this, however, institutions need to recognize the inherent challenges for people of color joining our staffs. Taylor writes, "Increasing staff diversity" (the noun) "does nothing for the organization if that organization is not able to retain diverse staff or to create a space where diverse perspectives and experiences are embraced" (the verb, or the action of inclusion).[22] Dina A. Bailey uses a succinct example, "You might have one Asian American person on staff and consider yourself to have a diverse staff. However, if you do not practice inclusion, that staff member might soon leave and your organization will be homogenous again."[23]

The active process of inclusion connotes intentionality. The field has long understood the moral imperative of diversity, inclusion, and equity. But that has not been enough for us to change the dynamic, Taylor observes.

> We cannot continue to allocate minimal resources, in terms of money and time, and really believe that we can be different organizations. . . . We have to begin to recognize inclusion as a business imperative. . . . It must be treated as a strategy that will continue to keep your organization relevant ten, fifteen, twenty years from now.[24]

Taylor and Bailey both ultimately remind us that diversity and inclusion is both an internal and an external activity. In addition to recruiting more people of color to work in our institutions, Bailey underscores, "We need to focus on talent management, cultural competency trainings, implementing specific diversity and inclusion strategic plans for policies and procedures, and developing and maintaining staff development." External efforts are important as well. "We need to strengthen existing relationships with diverse communities," she continues, "and build new ones and we need to develop and implement programs specifically for target audiences."[25]

In these external activities, we must actively engage our friends in the communities we want to serve. "More often than not," Taylor posits, "they want you to be successful as much as you do when it comes to inclusion." Ask how your institution can best engage these communities; learn directly from them how your institution can be inclusive. But, Taylor urges, we must also bring these partners into the conversation from the beginning. Consider The Platinum Rule (an update to The Golden Rule, one of the oldest maxims in the world): Treat others as THEY would like to be treated. "You cannot know how members of under-engaged communities want to be treated until you ask," he states. "You develop relationships and you work in partnership. True partnerships, not paternalistic or transactional partnerships, but authentic transformational partnerships. And what you will find is that more often than not, the transformation in that partnership happens for you more so than your partner."[26]

Inclusion is not an accident. Therefore, if we haven't yet formed relationships, it is incumbent upon us to make them. It is an intentional act on the part of history organizations and professionals to create a culture where as many people as possible feel like they belong and are a part of our work. And we must acknowledge that this change will not magically happen overnight. Taylor again provides insight,

> Groups that have had their cultures marginalized since the inception of this country will not all of the sudden decide to patronize our organizations. It is up to us to create spaces that have value for members of these communities. We need to make sure they see themselves represented in our archives, collections, and programs. They must feel like we value their cultures as much as any other culture. But most of all, they must feel like they can truly be stakeholders, and have a say in what we do.[27]

We are far from the final pages in the chapter of the field's efforts toward diversity and inclusion. In fact, I'd argue that we are actually only now writing the foreword. Bailey believes, as do I, that "The public history field is making strides to become more inclusive. Efforts are being made in terms of interpretation, collections, programs, and hiring. The next step is to work on making these strides sustainable. Diversity and inclusion must infiltrate all aspects of museums." This includes holding ourselves and our leaders accountable in pursuit of this goal.[28]

Finally, diversity and inclusion is a key element of our institutions and our work being truly relevant. As John Dichtl wrote, "'promoting history relevance,' also implies [actively practicing] inclusive history, thinking anew about how to engage a variety of audiences in finding meaning in the past." Dichtl concludes, "I think we all want the result of our efforts at inclusion around the subject of history ultimately to be that 'people will value history for its relevance to modern life and use historical thinking skills to actively engage with and address contemporary issues.'"[29]

In the chapter that follows, Dina A. Bailey, program chair for the 2017 AASLH Annual Meeting in Austin, Texas, shares additional thoughts on these issues. Dina and I first became acquainted when she was at the National Underground Railroad Freedom Center in Cincinnati. She has since founded her own company, Mountain Top Vision, LLC, a consulting firm that focuses on working with organizations in the area of change management and strategic initiatives in order to embrace diversity and inclusion in communities.

NOTES

1. John R. Dichtl, "Letter from the President: On Being an Inclusive History Organization," *Broadside*, November 2, 2016, accessed February 8, 2017, blogs. aaslh.org/letter-from-the-president-on-being-an-inclusive-history-organization.

2. John R. Dichtl, "AASLH Responds to President's Executive Order Restricting Entry to U.S.," *Broadside*, February 1, 2017, accessed February 8, 2017, blogs.aaslh. org/aaslh-responds-to-presidents-executive-order-restricting-entry-to-u-s.

3. Robert L. Beatty II, "Legacy to the People: Community and the Orange County Regional History Center" (master's thesis, University of Central Florida, 2002), 22–23. See also American Association of Museums (AAM), *Excellence and Equity: Education and the Public Dimension of Museums, A Report from the American Association of Museums* (Washington, DC: American Association of Museums, 1992).

4. Beatty, "Legacy to the People," 23; AAM, *Excellence and Equity*, 6.

5. Reach Advisors, Museums R+D, "2015 Demographic Update," *Monthly Memo* 2, no. 2 (December 2015).

6. "People of color" has become the accepted term to refer to people of non-white racial or ethnic descent.

7. We did not address issues of sexual diversity until after I left the museum in 2007. The institution has since taken a very active role in collecting and documenting the public memory of the June 12, 2016, Pulse nightclub shooting in Orlando.

8. John Cotton Dana, *The New Museum* (Woodstock, VT: Elm Tree Press, 1917), 38.

9. Chris Taylor, "From Systemic Exclusion to Systemic Inclusion: A Critical Look at Museums," unpublished manuscript, 2016.

10. Ibid.

11. AASLH, about.aaslh.org/aaslh-mission-vision-statements/, accessed February 8, 2017.

12. Dichtl, "Letter from the President."

13. Hugh H. Genoways and Lynne M. Ireland, *Museum Administration 2.0*, revised by Cinnamon Catlin-Legutko (Lanham, MD: Rowman & Littlefield, 2016), 147.

14. Anne W. Ackerson and Joan H. Baldwin, *Leadership Matters* (Lanham, MD: Rowman & Littlefield, 2014), 18–19.

15. Ibid., 19.

16. Katherine Kane, "AASLH Aspirations," *Broadside*, September 29, 2017, accessed February 8, 2017, blogs.aaslh.org/aaslh-aspirations.

17. Genoways et al., 147.

18. Cynthia Robinson, email correspondence with Cinnamon Catlin-Legutko, January 10, 2016.

19. Ackerson and Baldwin, 20.

20. Chris Taylor, "Getting Our House in Order: Moving from Diversity to Inclusion," *The American Archivist* 80, no. 1 (Spring/Summer 2017): 21.

21. Ackerson and Baldwin, 20.

22. Taylor, "Getting Our House in Order," 26.

23. Dina A. Bailey, "Diversity and Inclusion," unpublished document.

24. Taylor, "Getting Our House in Order," 23.
25. Bailey, "Diversity and Inclusion."
26. Taylor, "Getting Our House in Order," 24.
27. Ibid, 25.
28. Bailey, "Diversity and Inclusion."
29. Dichtl, "Letter from the President." The quoted statement is from the History Relevance Campaign.

Chapter 20

I AM History: Embracing Inclusion in Social and Political Climates

Dina A. Bailey

History is action personified. History is relevant. History is each of us. Every second that passes becomes a part of history. And, as individuals, we participate in historical moments every day. That said, some historical moments make more of an impact on our consciences than others. We usually know these moments because they are attached to sentences like "I remember exactly where I was when President Kennedy/Martin Luther King, Jr./Malcolm X was assassinated" or "I remember exactly what I was doing when I learned the Twin Towers had been attacked." Those experiences change our lives forever; they influence how we see others, how we vote, what we value, and how we perceive the world around us. And too often, these events are marked by tragedy.

With these events often come choices. Both "sides" can choose to become bitter and filled with frustration and hatred, or we can choose to find the courage to see past the immediate fears and hurts and discomforts in order to embrace the values of compassion, empathy, and understanding. That is not to say that frustration and anger cannot or should not be a part of the process; they often are, but we can't allow ourselves to get stuck there. The values of compassion, empathy, and understanding are essential to embracing inclusion in today's social and political climates. And inclusion is essential in ensuring a country (and a world) where the U.S. Constitution, the Universal Declaration of Human Rights, and the United Nations' Sustainable Development Goals guide us to be engaged and informed global citizens. I use "global citizen" because now, more than ever, we live in a global community and what one individual does, what one group of people does, and what one nation does affects everyone in the world to some degree. We are tied to each other's successes, challenges, and failures. We can't afford to be isolationists, and, really, it's just not possible anymore (if it ever truly was).

History is reflected in the (global) connections that link together people's daily participation in historical moments. On January 21, 2017, the Women's March on Washington became a global movement. Estimates say that up to 4.5 million people participated in marches around the world. Women and men, boys and girls walked together on all seven continents. They marched because they could. They marched because a lot of women couldn't. They marched because they believe, as I do, that what affects one of us affects all of us. Part of what made the marches so significant was the fact that people around the globe could unite together even as being able to join a march meant something very personal and unique to each individual. It wasn't as simple as one political group marching. It was about people with many different viewpoints. Women's March signs immediately headed to museums across the globe. Museums and historic sites have scrambled to respond through gathering collections, developing programs, and building advocacy statements to support funding for programs and agencies that have been influential in ensuring that we can continue to be stewards of history and culture. Fifty years from now, those who see these collections may say, "I remember where I was when the Women's March happened."

I and more than forty fellow history professionals were in Austin, Texas, at the 2017 program committee meeting choosing the sessions for the program of the 2017 AASLH Annual Meeting. We discussed the many interpretations of the meeting theme, *I AM History*. We introduced ourselves by sharing an example of how we each are an important part of history. Examples ranged from advancements in communications—growing up with a party line and/ or rotary phones—to witnessing Vietnam War–era protest marches, to an acknowledgement of the joy of CDs versus streaming music. Through these examples, we shared the big and small ways that we have each been active participants in history; we recognized these moments as simultaneously unifying and uniquely personal.

To fully embrace the inclusive nature of history is to embrace the idea that each of us has "our" moment and each of us is entitled to an acknowledgement of that moment. *I AM History* embraces and celebrates the continuing journey of the United States toward an increase in diversity and inclusion. It asks us to consider how we take obstacles and turn them into opportunities. It challenges us to tell the extraordinary stories of *all* people in *all* places. It compels us to review our missions, visions, and strategic plans to ensure our organizations will remain relevant as our communities and their needs grow ever more diverse. And it prompts us to be more flexible, more responsive, and more adamant in supporting the transformative power of truth, transparency, and integrity.

The theme, *I AM History,* can be transformative for our field. In order to do so, we need to embrace the theme's depth and breadth and use it for the good of our organizations, our communities, our field, and our nation. It is a

Images 20.1 and 20.2.   History is reflected in the connections made through participation in historical moments such as the January 21, 2017 Women's March on Washington. *Source*: Tobi Voigt

tall order, but not an impossible one. First, we must ask ourselves who history belongs to and how it connects each individual to a larger story. Within our field, we have both the platform and the responsibility to usher in new perspectives and critical examinations of America's ever-changing identity. By reorienting history to be more inclusive, more authentic, and more about exploring the boundaries and intersections of how we understand ourselves and our stories within the larger American narrative, we may internalize the very nature of inclusion.

AASLH has embraced four aspirations that align with the principles that undergird *I AM History*. These ambitions reflect the organization's values and those of the field it supports. AASLH seeks to:

1. Promote the relevance of history
2. Build diversity and inclusiveness
3. Cultivate an experimental and creative spirit
4. Increase organizational sustainability and transparency[1]

These four aspirations support what the association and its members work toward on a daily basis. Through efforts to increase stability and transparency, AASLH desires to encourage greater engagement and trust within its own membership while also acting as a "role model for other nonprofits in the areas of financial decisions, processes, and reporting." In acting transparently and consistently, our diverse communities will more clearly see our members' motives and will increasingly rely on our organizations as stable anchors for community endeavors.

In addition to modeling behaviors in stability and transparency, AASLH also seeks to model "an adaptive and nimble, yet reflective, culture to address change and quickly take advantage of opportunities." The experimental and creative spirit cultivated through this modeling will further open the door to previously unheard voices. It encourages members to search out new ideas and new constituents within their communities. It will also support efforts under way by a number of history organizations to decolonize their operations: from collections to exhibitions to thought processes. By supporting informed risk-taking, knowledge sharing, and imaginative problem solving, AASLH members will be living through action the idea that *I AM History* embraces an openness for all people to experiment in what it means to be active participants in historical moments.[2]

The aspiration focused on diversity and inclusiveness further supports the openness the 2017 annual meeting theme fosters. This aspiration "encourages telling the stories that have not been told," promotes partnerships with other organizations that have "successfully developed inclusive policies and programming," and supports building relationships that are based on "mutual trust, balance of power, and recognition of expertise within diverse communities to democratize the historical narrative and sustain the relevance of history to a rapidly changing demographic." As we continue to coax a greater understanding of the relevance of history in contemporary local, regional, and national decisions, it is imperative that we unite together as a field and as active organizations that embrace the further diversity of our communities and acts of inclusion within our communities.[3]

Further, as an AASLH aspiration, the promotion of history relevance recognizes the complexity of history and encourages being transparent about the fact that history is often contested. *I AM History* aligns with history relevance in fostering healthy and constructive provocation. And, many of the sessions during the annual meeting will provide examples of "history and

Image 20.3.   Dina A. Bailey was program chair for the 2017 AASLH Annual Meeting in Austin, Texas. Her theme, *I AM History,* **embraces how a genuine commitment to diversity and inclusion results in positive movement forward and prompts our communities to value museums and history.** *Source:* **Dina A. Bailey**

material culture as the essential shaper of the present and as a context for each individual."[4]

History is relevant because we are continuously impacted by the legacies of past actions and reactions of people. The five Cs of historical thinking—change over time, causality, context, complexity, and contingency—constitute one of several methodologies that provide a foundation for recognizing how the past and present are strongly tied to each other. In recognizing how those ties are attached to us in both professional and, perhaps more importantly, personal ways, we have the potential to build individual and collective empathy. The ties may lead to increased community inclusion; they may also showcase the relevance of history.[5]

We saw these principles in action at the 2017 Annual Meeting. AASLH received for the meeting the largest number of session proposals in its history. This amazing depth and breadth of proposals provide strong examples to support both the theme *I AM History* and the AASLH aspirations. Following are examples of sessions that directly correlated to these objectives.

PROMOTE THE RELEVANCE OF HISTORY

> History isn't about dates and places and wars. It's about the people who fill the spaces between them.
>
> Jodi Picoult

Public historians can (and should) demonstrate relevance in new and creative ways through popular culture that is already tied to history. In "History Has Its Eyes on You," Stacey Mann and co-presenters highlighted how the hit Broadway musical *Hamilton* uses the intersection of historical and contemporary themes, deliberate inclusivity, collaboration, and a commitment to the highest artistic and intellectual standards to inform and inspire its audiences. While the musical depicts a familiar history, it does so in unfamiliar ways that invite audiences to shift their perspectives. Mann and her colleagues built off these aspects of *Hamilton* to discuss how museums and historic sites can leverage a more inclusive future by striving to diversify their stories and their audiences.

"History Has Its Eyes on You" concentrated on how storytelling can and should engage visitors on emotional and intellectual levels and therefore highlights the power of people, places, and events and the intersection of media and civic literacy today. Presenters Becky Schlomann of the Indiana Historical Society and Kate Quinn of the University of Pennsylvania Museum of Archaeology and Anthropology brought to bear their experiences translating between the languages of education, history, museums, and the arts and using the power of experimentation, collaboration, and innovation to support history relevance. And Steve Light of Monticello explored how history institutions are expected to demonstrate relevance to new audiences by connecting the institution's history to modern day issues and legacies.

Together, Mann, Schlomann, Quinn, and Light emphasized that entertainment and historical rigor are not mutually exclusive and can be leveraged together to engage audiences in compelling ways. They considered what "hooks" audiences into the narratives within our organizations and examined how and when to respond nimbly (yet responsibly) to pop culture. Ultimately, they instilled confidence in demonstrating history's relevance in response to contemporary pop culture phenomena.

BUILD DIVERSITY AND INCLUSIVENESS

I know there is strength in the differences between us. I know there is comfort where we overlap.

Ani DiFranco

With a focus on diversity and inclusion, Dr. Suzanne Seriff, senior lecturer, University of Texas at Austin, and colleagues illuminated the need to push boundaries, to engage in issues of oppression and injustice in traditional and nontraditional museum spaces. "Designing for Outrage" examined the systemic and often unconscious practice of ignoring issues of exclusion of diversity, equity, and inclusion in our field and how we should "legitimate, celebrate, and engage the voices of histories, art, and actions of people who have so often gone unheard and unseen."[6]

Prior to the Austin conference Seriff, Jennifer Scott, and Barbara Lau issued a strong call for designing for outrage in *Exhibition* magazine. "The common cause and vision for twenty-first-century museums," they declared, "involves a more confrontational, immediate, and disruptive exhibition discourse about issues that matter in our lives."[7] Productive dialogues, they maintain, converge on the intersection of outrage and hope in order to responsibly confront contemporary injustices; as a matter of fact they insist that outrage *is* hope and that strategies should begin with this premise.

Seriff and co-presenters Scott, Lau, and Yolanda Leyva demonstrated how to extend invitations to co-create exhibition experiences for individuals who do not officially "count" in our American democracy: those who are incarcerated, undocumented, underage, and/or unemployed. They highlighted the many ways institutions can create activist spaces of engagement around issues of oppression and injustice. Leyva also shared her approach to using history and culture as tools for social change in the program. She imparted her experience in projects related to women's advocacy, community organizing, creating safe spaces for women, and providing programming for disenfranchised youth and their families. Ultimately, the session did not just reflect diversity, equity, and inclusion but also critically explored the outrage that can come with the systemic exclusion of some voices from American institutions.[8]

"Designing for Outrage" offered less traditional, but important, strategies to build diversity and inclusion in communicating practical tools and strategies to engage visitors, employ disruption and controversy as tools of engagement, and prepare staff and administration to authentically host a place of disruption without becoming coopted, sanitized, or shut down.

CULTIVATE AN EXPERIMENTAL AND CREATIVE SPIRIT

You can't use up creativity. The more you use, the more you have.

Maya Angelou

Often, looking outside of the public history field brings to the fore experimental and creative ideas (and research) that benefit our field immeasurably. But this should be an active, not passive, activity. As institutions of cultural trust, we have the responsibility to engage and amplify new perspectives and critical examinations of historical narratives and events. To do so, organizations must find ways to expand connections with audiences and should design experiences to be more inclusive, more authentic, and more willing to challenge boundaries. Identifying and implementing powerful ideas from outside of our field strengthens our ability to engage our visitors. Facilitators utilized examples from humanitarian organizations, public radio, journalism, and others to focus on techniques and methods that effectively connect story, content, and experiences with audiences in innovative ways.

In "Innovative Audience Engagement from Outside the Museum Bubble," Andrea Jones of Peak Experience Lab; Stacia Kuceyeski of the Ohio History Connection; and Beth Maloney at Baltimore Museum of Industry explored the concept of engagement in twenty-first-century history organizations. They noted complexity in the increased recognition that visitors often arrive with intersecting identities (e.g., gay and Puerto Rican/African American) and that our institutions are also often intersectional (a museum, community center, school, or event space). As the field becomes more comfortable with intersectionality, they posit, it can and should expand the definition of what museums and historic sites can (and should) be.

As history organizations continue to compete for people's leisure time, searching for innovative strategies is imperative. And, in the spirit of change, there must also come a spirit of risk-taking and letting go of the fear of failure. This session revealed techniques to improve informal, transformational learning experiences and encouraged engagement strategies that lead to feelings of empowerment and permission to experiment.

SUSTAINABILITY AND TRANSPARENCY

Honesty and transparency make you vulnerable. Be honest and transparent anyway.

Mother Teresa

Sometimes looking outside the field just means looking to our "sister" organizations in the cultural heritage world: in this case, libraries and archives. Gathering together to intentionally pursue learning collectively is an extremely effective tool. Such was the case with a group of library, archive, and museum professionals who joined together in the Collective Wisdom Project.

In this session, Stephanie Allen of the Sixth Floor Museum at Dealey Plaza and her peers from the Collective Wisdom Project related their experience with the program and shared how a dedicated cohort of library, archives, and museum professionals generated solutions for cultural heritage that focus on productive collaborations, cross-sector professional development, and continuing education needs for practitioners. They addressed issues of structural barriers, diversity and inclusion, sustainability, education, and other topics that emerged as important to our organizations and professionals.

Allen, Darla Wegener of the Tulare County (CA) Library, and Sofia Becerra-Licha of the Berklee College of Music revealed conclusions from conversations between library, archive, and museum professions, building off the Collective Wisdom Project and experiences in a way that encouraged further understanding and action across the sectors. In learning about current structural barriers and cross-sector collaborations, session participants brainstormed additional ideas for future collaborations and projects between libraries, archives, and museums. And, through investigating the overall organizational cultures of these institutions, they critically explored how we currently work across sectors and how we might better do so in the future. This exploration ultimately factors into how we can become more aware, engaged, and collaborative in seeking funding for a wide variety of professional development and continuing education opportunities. As Genna Duplisea, a fellow cohort member, said, "We all believe in celebrating and preserving a wide array of cultures and knowledges; we all believe in safeguarding the

things and spaces we steward; we all believe in reaching users/communities/
patrons—people." Acknowledging and using this collective wisdom unites
us, bringing more stability and transparency across a number of fields.

These examples all highlight AASLH's guiding principles and the meeting
theme, *I AM History*. Countless others do as well. I encourage you to consider history relevance, diversity and inclusion, creativity, and sustainability
in your own work.

And more than anything, do not forget that history is about the actions
people take. The 2017 Annual Meeting theme, *I AM History*, acknowledges
that it is the awesomeness of personal participation in the big and small
moments that makes the history profession such an amazing field to be a part
of. The way we see the world is what makes us good at what we do. And,
the more we see history as always complex and often contested, the better
stewards we will be.

Adversity can bring people together just as often as it tears people apart.
Where there is adversity, there is also hope, determination, and activism.
So, as we live each day in these precious historical moments, let us see with
renewed clarity. Let us not be afraid to take action, coming together in the
spirit of inclusion and always remembering that what makes America great
is the complexity of our history, the passion of our people, and the diversity
in our culture.

NOTES

1. Katherine Kane, "AASLH Aspirations," *Broadside*, September 29, 2017, accessed
February 8, 2017, blogs.aaslh.org/aaslh-aspirations.

2. Ibid.

3. Ibid.

4. Ibid.

5. Thomas Andrews and Flannery Burke, "What Does It Mean to Think Historically?" *Perspectives on History*, January 2007, accessed February 17, 2017, go.aaslh.
org/5C's.

6. Suzanne Seriff, "Designing for Outrage: How to Create Activist Architectures
for Disruption, Engagement, and Action around Issues of Oppression and Injustice in
Our Time," 2017 AASLH Annual Meeting session proposal.

7. Barbara Law, Jennifer Scott, and Suzanne Seriff, "Designing for Outrage:
Inviting Disruption and Contested Truth into Museum Exhibitions," *Exhibition* 36,
no. 1 (Spring 2017).

8. Ibid.

Chapter 21

Epilogue

Moving History from Nice to Essential

John R. Dichtl

It is most appropriate to close with some words from AASLH president and CEO John R. Dichtl. John has worked in the history field for more than twenty-five years, having begun his career at the Organization of American Historians. He came to AASLH in 2015 after serving for nine years as executive director of the National Council on Public History.

Here, John offers his thoughts and ideas for where he sees the field, and AASLH, headed in the immediate (and long-term) future. You'll note that many of his themes resonate with those in this book. He highlights two specifically: diversity and inclusion and history relevance. The former is reflected in the chapter that precedes this. The latter undergirds much of the book's discussion.

As historians, we understand well that we cannot predict the future. We can only use the historical record and our interpretations of it to guide our decisions today. A focus on history relevance and on diversity and inclusion seems to best portend a bright future for public history. If we heed the facts that clearly point us in this direction and if we act accordingly, only time will tell if they have the effect we intend them to. Call me Pollyanna, but I believe they will.

—Bob Beatty

AASLH is the reflection of a multitude of people working together in mostly the same directions. There are staff and volunteers, participants and sponsors, individuals and institutions, members and nonmembers, at all different life stages working directly in our association's programs or participating in the conversations on which our professional lives are built. AASLH is the historical community, a fluctuating crowd over the decades in which people assist each other in advancing the field. Now in its eighth decade serving the field, the organization continues to evolve. Each time there have been challenges, AASLH and the history community responds.

Now, I think another major shift is occurring. How many of us ten or twenty years ago held out hope that mainstream America would be so engaged with the meaning of symbols of the American past? In 2015 alone we saw impassioned discussion about displaying Confederate statues, monuments, and flags. Yet even a few years ago, at the start of the Civil War Sesquicentennial, weren't we a bit disappointed, deep down, with the country's general lack of attentiveness to the commemoration?

What I want to do is point out the obvious. Something big shifted in our country in summer 2015. We now may be at a high-water mark for history organizations. Confronted by violent tragedy and simmering race relations, communities, politicians, and the media are engaged in vigorous debates about history's hold on the present. On a state-by-state, community-by-community basis, people are figuring out what history means in the context of today.

What kind of fresh openings do history organizations have today that we didn't see several years ago? Let's look at the landscape. We know that there are a lot of history organizations out there. Last year, the Institute of Museum

Image 21.1.   Honor guard presenting the last Confederate flag removed from the Confederate Soldiers Monument to the director of the Confederate Relic Room, July 10, 2015 (Official Governor's Office, photo by Zach Pippin). *Source*: **South Carolina Department of Archives and History**

and Library Services (IMLS) announced that it had found 35,144 museums in the U.S.—more than double the 17,500 that the agency had estimated there were in the 1990s. And nearly 56 percent (19,505) are categorized as "History Museums," "Historical Societies," "Historic Preservation [entities]," or "Historical Houses and Sites." This happens to echo the findings of the Indiana Humanities Council's *Humanities at the Crossroads* report last year, which was a lead case study for a national initiative "to better understand the status and future of the humanities." More than 80 percent of all humanities organizations across Indiana surveyed offer one or more history programs, including state and local, family, national, and world history.[1]

What else do we know? We know that trust in museums, especially history museums, remains high like we all learned it was in Rosenzweig and Thelen's influential 1998 book, *Presence of the Past: Popular Uses of History in American Life*. According to these two historians, 80 percent of their nearly 1,500 survey respondents ranked history museums as being trustworthy, far above the 69 percent for personal accounts by family members, 64 percent for eye-witnesses, 54 percent for college professors, and 11 percent for movies and television. Reach Advisors' Museum R+D reported some similar findings this summer after surveying 7,000 people about trustworthiness. Museums ranked the highest, at 6.4 on a scale of 1 to 10—above Wikipedia at 5.7, for example, NPR at 5.0., Fox News at 4.7, government researchers at 4.0, and corporate researchers at 3.6. History museums/historic sites actually ranked highest of all at 6.7. History organizations are everywhere and they are trusted.[2]

Third, we are compiling evidence that history organizations have a positive impact on people. Not only is the History Relevance Campaign digging into the question of impact, looking for measurable, real examples of institutions changing their communities, but the United Kingdom's *Heritage Counts 2014* survey determined that history institutions have a measurable effect on social wellbeing. "The amount of money which provides the same impact on wellbeing as visiting heritage sites overall," according to the study, "is calculated as £1,646," or about $2,800, in 2014. That's astounding. *Heritage Counts 2014* and for the previous five years determined that "adults who live in areas of higher concentrations of historic environment are also likely to have a stronger sense of place," and "participation in heritage can have a beneficial impact on personal development," meaning that history volunteers reported higher levels of mental health and wellbeing than the general population.[3]

Maybe we can be optimistic for our field.

It is worth pointing out in contrast—for all the celebration of STEM (science, technology, engineering, and math) and the enviable funding and popularity STEM institutions and research enjoy—that our colleagues in the sciences actually are not feeling very optimistic. Scientists are undergoing their own culture wars over the politicization of human evolution and global climate change, and generally feel divorced from the American public.[4]

If 2015 was a highpoint for history organizations and the public being somewhat in agreement about the importance of history and even the general interpretive direction—say, of the meaning of the Civil War, its causes and its consequences—the same is not true for science.

A couple of surveys by the Pew Research Center showed that while the public holds scientists in high regard, there is a "deep divide between scientists and the public over many topics." Back in 2009 three-quarters of scientists thought "now" was "a good time" for science. But five years later, in 2014, only half of all scientists had a similar view. In 2009, 67 percent of scientists said it was a good time to begin a career in the field, and by 2014 the figure had dropped to 59 percent. Scientists say they are troubled by scientific ignorance in the general population and by strong differences in perception between scientists and the public on key issues. According to this

Image 21.2.   John Dichtl, AASLH president and CEO, notes, "We are sharing and sharpening our standards, expertise, and creative solutions. Our discourse rejuvenates us for our work. And individually, but united, we speak the value of history." *Source*: American Association for State and Local History

Pew Research Center report, scientists are also gloomy about how journalists cover their work: almost eight in ten said news reports "don't distinguish well-founded findings," meaning that the news media give equal weight to opposing views on topics, which feeds controversy even when the vast majority of scientists are in agreement.[5]

We in the historical profession are familiar with broad public controversies, differing perspectives, and opposing views, and yet somehow, on some topics, we appear to be in closer agreement with the mainstream public than in decades.

My point is that the horizon is bright. As we collect, preserve, and interpret the past, our audiences may be listening, and we definitely are trying to listen to them and include and learn from them. Wendell Berry, the plenary speaker at the Louisville Annual Meeting, once said, "If people have forgotten or never learned each other's stories . . . how can they know whether or not to trust each other?"[6] As historians, we understand the power of possibility of stories and the past resonating in the present, opening new ways of seeing and solving contemporary problems. From places such as Ferguson and Baltimore confronting senseless deaths to hundreds of other communities with less visceral (but very real) challenges, people begin to trust each other when they know each other's stories and they see similarities and respect differences in their pasts.

History is relevant; I'm sure all of you believe that. It is constantly at play upon the present. But, do we intentionally articulate how crucially essential it is? How good are we and our institutions at stepping back from the specific history we are telling to connect it to issues and problems and opportunities today? Are we able to step back yet further and simply champion history itself as a discipline or historical thinking as vital and very special way of seeing the world? The History Relevance Campaign's message is that we history professionals and volunteers must say how vital understanding of the past is. History nurtures identity in an intercultural world and teaches critical skills and independent thinking. It can strengthen communities and be a catalyst for economic growth. An understanding of the past can inspire leadership and it certainly can help those who listen to craft better solutions to today's problems.

Maybe this is the best moment in the past twenty or thirty years to make sure we each are ready, wherever and whenever, to make the case for historical understanding, and the institutions, collections, landscapes, communities, and other resources that keep the past alive.

I'd like to challenge all of us to have an elevator speech for history—just a brief, twenty-second explanation of why history is essential to the well-being of your community. We each need to be ready to spell it out.

What is at stake? Historical understanding helps us flourish in a culturally diverse world. When we learn each other's stories, as Wendell Berry said, we begin to trust each other and can figure out how to face challenges together. The economist Scott E. Page has outlined how diversity helps in modern society. Those who see the world in the same way, in a homogenous group, often agree and can move forward together—but then they also all tend to get stuck in the same places. When this happens, when things are truly gridlocked, no one in a homogenous group can see what the next step should be. In a diverse group, where one perspective hits a dead end, there are other perspectives that can find a way forward.[7]

The AASLH Council and our Aspirations Task Force have taken up history relevance and the issue of diversity and inclusion and put them at the forefront of the organization. We are also going to be more transparent, creative, and open to experimentation.

To guide and support this effort, there are a whole host of changes in AASLH underway. A few of our priorities are these:

- In general, we will be working to amplify AASLH's ability to serve as the central place, a sort of town square, in which lots of different kinds of history practitioners and history organizations come together. We will be an ever-more diverse and inclusive association that develops relationships with diverse communities and organizations.
- I see thousands of volunteers at history organizations, many of whom AASLH currently serves and counts on as members. But we can do more. I would like, for example, to sharpen and expand the online courses and webinars, and the onsite workshops, we offer, both for the volunteers and for those employed in history organizations.
- Glancing in another direction, I think AASLH has much to offer academic historians and graduate students. Our institutions are primary employers of those earning history and related degrees. AASLH can help to establish mutually beneficial project and consultative relationships with scholars, where expertise flows in both directions. History practitioners should be influencing what is taught in public history and museum studies programs, as well as more traditional history programs.
- Another exciting opportunity is for AASLH to reach passionate, avocational historians. By these I mean genealogists, reenactors, the kinds of people who would participate in historical crowdsourcing projects, and the retiring baby boomers who are active lifelong learners. Many AASLH members already are working with these history makers. We should too as a national association—and if we want our policy makers and funders to really grasp the relevance of history, we could use the allies.

- AASLH can also seek international connections and foster efforts to place state and local history in global contexts. We need to see more of it as our communities welcome new arrivals and recognize diversities already present, and as we all see our local histories as part of global movements of people, resources, and ideas. All history is local, but it doesn't occur in a vacuum.
- Lastly, another of my hopes for AASLH is that we will help to "Pull back the curtain" on the interpretive process, encouraging historians and history practitioners to be more open about how we choose the stories we tell, and make decisions behind the scenes. This is an idea I am borrowing from Robert Weyeneth in his presidential address to the National Council on Public History last year. He described it as being more open with our visitors. "Let's explain why the old exhibits are being removed to add new exhibits on different topics. Why was the decision made to preserve, rather than to restore, that building over there—and what the heck is the difference between preservation and restoration, anyway?"[8] We should be demonstrating the complexities of what we do, and why there are high standards and refined methods. Doing so draws people into the interpretative process. Pulling back the curtain can turn questions and doubts into collaboration, tolerance, inquiry, and connection.

AASLH is uniquely positioned among historical and museum associations to be the home for history where all this happens. As your professional association, AASLH occupies a middle space, helping to connect, supply, and support thousands of history practitioners in their daily work.

They say history is about the past and remembering tradition—but it is even more about how things change. There's always change, right? Even this organization is changing. They say that historical thinking is casual, just easy reminiscing and escapism—but we know, as Sam Wineburg wrote in 2001, "Historical thinking is an unnatural act."[9]

It must be learned, it requires access to historical resources, and ultimately it can lead the way forward. They say heritage, nostalgia, and the Lost Cause would never fade away—folks just have to have their heritage. But sometimes historical rigor can make a dent.

My point is that we came together this year, built a conference on all the intellectual and professional conversations across the profession, and produced countless projects, programs, publications, and communication networks—just as AASLH has done each year for three-quarters of a century. We are sharing and sharpening our standards, expertise, and creative solutions. Our discourse rejuvenates us for our work. And individually, but united, we speak the value of history.

NOTES

1. Institute of Museum and Library Services, "Government Doubles Official Estimate: There Are 35,000 Active Museums in the U.S.," May 19, 2014, accessed July 25, 2016, www.imls.gov/news-events/news-releases/government-doubles-official-estimate-there-are-35000-active-museums-us; Felicia M. Sullivan, Nancy N. Conner, Kei Kawashima-Ginsberg, Peter Levine, and Elizabeth Lynn. *Humanities at the Crossroads: The Indiana Case Study Survey Report* (Medford, MA: CIRCLE at the Jonathan M. Tisch College of Citizenship and Public Service, Tufts University, 2014).

2. Reach Advisors, Museums R+D, "Museums and Trust," *Monthly Memo* 1, no. 8, June 2015.

3. Historic England, *Heritage Counts 2014* (London: English Heritage, 2014).

4. This also seems to be true for science museums and science centers. See Reach Advisors, Museums R+D, "Museums and Trust."

5. Guy Gugliotta, "A Deep Divide," *Trust* 17, no. 2 (Summer 2015): 19–23.

6. Wendell Berry, *What Are People For?* (Berkeley, CA: Counterpoint Press, 2010), 157.

7. Page's work is described in Gary Gutting and Jerry Gaus, "The Virtues of Political Disagreement," *New York Times Opinionator*, June 11, 2015, accessed February 18, 2017, opinionator.blogs.nytimes.com/2015/06/11/the-virtues-of-political-disagreement/.

8. Robert R. Weyeneth, "What I've Learned along the Way: A Public Historian's Intellectual Odyssey," *The Public Historian* 36, no. 2 (May 2014): 23.

9. Sam Wineburg was the keynote speaker for the 2015 AASLH Annual Meeting (audio here go.aaslh.org/Wineburg2015) and is author of *Historical Thinking and Other Unnatural Acts*: *Charting the Future of Teaching the Past* (Philadelphia, PA: Temple University Press, 2001).

Index

Note: Page references for images are italicized.

About the Editor

Bob Beatty is founder and president of The Lyndhurst Group, LLC, a history, museum, and nonprofit consulting firm providing community-focused engagement strategies for institutional planning, organizational assessments, and interpretive direction.

From 2007 to 2017 Bob served at the American Association for State & Local History, the only comprehensive national organization dedicated to state and local history. Most recently as AASLH's chief of engagement, he was also interim president and CEO, chief operating officer, and vice president for programs. He led AASLH's professional development program including workshops, an annual meeting, affinity groups and other initiatives, and publications as editor of *History News* and managing editor of the AASLH Editorial Board. From 1999 to 2007 he directed the Education Department at the Orange County (FL) Regional History Center.

Bob graduated with a BA in liberal studies and an MA in history from the University of Central Florida and has been an adjunct instructor of American History at the university and community college levels. He is currently a candidate for PhD in public history at Middle Tennessee State University. His dissertation topic is on the influence of Duane Allman and the Allman Brothers Band on American music.

State and local history is his particular interest, as he believes that the discovery of local heritage helps in the building of a strong community. This theory was reinforced by his work at AASLH and the History Center and research for his master's thesis, "Legacy to the People: Community and the Orange County Regional History Center," which examined the ideal of community service and in the context of the history of the American museum movement.

In 2001 he was Phi Delta Kappa Community Leader of the Year and was selected Outstanding New Professional in 2002 by the Florida Association of Museums. In addition to *An AASLH Guide to Making Public History*, he is author of *Florida's Highwaymen: Legendary Landscapes* and co-editor of *Zen and the Art of Local History*.

About the Contributors

Scott Alvey is deputy director of the Kentucky Historical Society. During his more than two-decades-long career in museums, he continues to hone his passion for creating informal learning opportunities within the overall visitor experience.

Dina A. Bailey is the CEO of Mountain Top Vision, LLC, a consulting company that focuses on supporting change management within organizations in the areas of diversity, inclusion, and strategic planning in order to further audience engagement. Prior to becoming the CEO of this company, she was employed at the National Center for Civil and Human Rights and the National Underground Railroad Freedom Center.

John R. Dichtl became AASLH president and CEO in 2015. Prior to that he was the executive director of the National Council on Public History for nine years, and worked for the Organization of American Historians for fourteen years as deputy director and in several other roles.

David A. Donath is president of the Woodstock Foundation, which owns and operates the Billings Farm & Museum and is an operating partner of Marsh–Billings–Rockefeller National Historical Park. He served as chair of the AASLH Council from 2008 to 2010.

John W. Durel is a partner of Durel Consulting Partners, affiliated with the Qm² community of consultants. As a leadership coach, he works with executives, boards, and staffs to design, facilitate, and implement processes for effective decision making, problem solving, teamwork and planning.

Barbara Franco has had a long career in American history museums and served as a past chair of the Council of the American Association for State and Local History. She currently works as an independent scholar and museum consultant.

David A. Janssen has nearly thirty years' experience in museum and historic site leadership, with a MA in history and an MBA. He is the executive director of Brucemore, in Cedar Rapids, Iowa, a museum property of the National Trust for Historic Preservation.

Edward T. Linenthal is a professor of history and former editor of the *Journal of American History*. He is most recently co-editor of *The Landscapes of 9/11: A Photographer's Journey*.

Erin Carlson Mast is the CEO and executive director of President Lincoln's Cottage in Washington, DC, where she has led the organization through a phase of steady growth, groundbreaking initiatives, transition to an independent 501(c)(3) organization, and significant awards and recognition, including a Presidential Medal in 2016 and being named one of the 50 Best Places to Work in the Washington, DC, area. She holds degrees from the George Washington University and Ohio University.

Candace Tangorra Matelic is a leading expert in community engagement and organizational development. For two decades, she has been teaching and speaking about the critical transformation that museums and cultural organizations must make to go beyond audience development and move toward civic engagement and social entrepreneurship. Her consulting helps organizations engage their communities as partners, and then transform their vision, assumptions, organizational culture, and work patterns.

Laura B. Roberts is principal of Roberts Consulting, helping cultural nonprofit organizations with strategic planning, organizational development, and assessment. She is a member of The Museum Group, a consortium of senior museum professionals in independent practice.

Max A. van Balgooy is president of Engaging Places LLC, a design and strategy firm that connects people to historic places, and director of the Seminar for Historical Administration. He regularly shares news, ideas, and opinions about the opportunities and challenges facing historic sites and house museums at EngagingPlaces.net.

Kent Whitworth has served as executive director of the Kentucky Historical Society since 2004. Before, he was director of the East Tennessee Historical Society.